Ali Shakoori is Assistant Professor in the Faculty of Social Sciences, University of Tehran.

The State and Rural Development in Post-Revolutionary Iran

The State and Rural Development in Post-Revolutionary Iran

Ali Shakoori
Assistant Professor
The Faculty of Social Sciences
University of Tehran
Iran

© Ali Shakoori 2001

All rights reserved. No reproduction, copy or transmission of this publication may be made without written permission.

No paragraph of this publication may be reproduced, copied or transmitted save with written permission or in accordance with the provisions of the Copyright, Designs and Patents Act 1988, or under the terms of any licence permitting limited copying issued by the Copyright Licensing Agency, 90 Tottenham Court Road, London W1P 0LP.

Any person who does any unauthorised act in relation to this publication may be liable to criminal prosecution and civil claims for damages.

The author has asserted his right to be identified as the author of this work in accordance with the Copyright, Designs and Patents Act 1988.

First published 2001 by
PALGRAVE
Houndmills, Basingstoke, Hampshire RG21 6XS and
175 Fifth Avenue, New York, N.Y. 10010
Companies and representatives throughout the world

PALGRAVE is the new global academic imprint of
St. Martin's Press LLC Scholarly and Reference Division and
Palgrave Publishers Ltd (formerly Macmillan Press Ltd).

ISBN 0-333-77613-5

This book is printed on paper suitable for recycling and made from fully managed and sustained forest sources.

A catalogue record for this book is available from the British Library.

Library of Congress Cataloging-in-Publication Data
Shakoori, Ali, 1962–
    The state and rural development in post-revolutionary Iran / Ali Shakoori.
    p. cm.
Includes bibliographical references and index.
ISBN 0-333-77613-5
    1. Rural development—Iran. 2. Agriculture and state—Iran. 3. Land reform—Iran. 4. Iran—Rural conditions. 5. Iran--Politics and government. I. Title.
HN670.2.Z9 C67 2000
307.1'412'0955—dc21

00-052418

10 9 8 7 6 5 4 3 2 1
10 09 08 07 06 05 04 03 02 01

Printed and bound in Great Britain by
Antony Rowe Ltd, Chippenham, Wiltshire

To

Professor Haleh Afshar
and
Professor Ali Rahnema

Contents

List of Tables	ix
Acknowledgements	xi
Glossary	xii
Introduction	1

1 Theoretical Debates on Rural Change   9
  Introduction   9
  Modernisation   9
  Agricultural modernisation and modernisation
    of the peasantry   14
  Development   17
  Rural development   21
  Rural development and inequality   30
  The problem of access: the relationship between the
    bureaucracy and the peasantry   35
  Conclusion   37

2 Historical Background   40
  Introduction   40
  Sociopolitical and economic developments from the
    mid nineteenth century to 1962   40
  Rural society and the agrarian structure   45
  Rural society after the land reform (1962)   50

3 The Revolution and Rural Society   60
  Introduction   60
  The revolution of 1979   60
  Post-revolutionary rural policies   64
  Reorganisation of the agricultural administration   70
  Conclusion   95

4 Agricultural Policies and Agricultural Growth   99
  Introduction   99
  An overview of agriculture prior to the revolution   99

viii Contents

    Agricultural development policies after the revolution   104
    Support policies   117
    Conclusion   122

5 Rural Development at the Micro Level   **126**
    Introduction   126
    The socioeconomic and geographical characteristics
      of the province, district and villages under study   128
    Participation   134
    Social mobility   144
    Income   151
    Wealth   154
    Well-being   156
    The direction of rural change   158

6 Conclusion   **164**

Appendix 1: Socioeconomic Characteristics of Eastern
    Azerbaijan, Marand and Sample Households   172
Appendix 2: Correlation Coefficients for Participation and
    Mobility   178
Appendix 3: Statistical Results (Analysis of Variance,
    Muliregression and Correlation) for Variables of Income,
    Wealth, Expenditure and Housing Status   181

Bibliography   186

Index   211

List of Tables

4.1	Per capita GNP, 1962 and 1977	100
4.2	The share of various sectors in GNP, 1963–78	100
4.3	Distribution of the urban and rural populations, 1921–78	101
4.4	Average annual population growth rate, 1956–86	101
4.5	The share of non-oil sectors in production and employment, 1977	102
4.6	Structure of investment in the development of agriculture and natural resources, 1977–83	105
4.7	The predicted share of domestic growth components, 1980–2003	106
4.8	Planned investment growth, 1983–98	107
4.9	Government fixed investment by economic sectors, 1977–96	109
4.10	Comparison of the agricultural investment rate with the inflation rate, 1989–96	110
4.11	Domestic gross fixed capital formation, 1982–94	111
4.12	Agricultural bank loans to peasants and farmers, 1977–96	114
4.13	Arable land area, 1986–88	115
4.14	Number of tractors and combines purchased, 1981–86	117
4.15	Comparison of the price of major agricultural machinery in profiles of subsidisation (1988) and liberalisation (1992)	118
4.16	Government investment in Agricultural Research, 1983–86	119
4.17	Yields of selected crops	120
4.18	Crop production, 1977–96	123
4.19	Annual rise/fall in food consumption, 1961–86	124
5.1	Characteristics of the selected villages in terms of programme provision, developmental potential and sample size	127
5.2	Degree of participation in rural development programmes in the six villages	136
5.3	Comparison of the occupation of the respondents with that of their fathers (intergenerational mobility)	147

x List of Tables

5.4	Comparison of the occupational status of the respondents with their status before the revolution (intra-generational mobility)	149
5.5	The main indices of intra- and intergenerational mobility	150
5.6	Distribution of respondents in terms of housing status	157
5.7	Gini coefficients for income, wealth and expenditure	158
5.8	Decile distribution of income	159
5.9	Decile distribution of household wealth	161
5.10	Decile distribution of expenditure	162
A1.1	Number of students enrolled in Azerbaijan, 1987	172
A1.2	Fall in the rural population of Azerbaijan by township, 1976–86	172
A1.3	Number of towns and communities, Marand, 1995	173
A1.4	Sex ratio in rural areas of the province and in the sample population, 1976–84	174
A1.5	Age distribution in rural areas of the province and in the sample population, 1976–86	175
A1.6	Age distribution	175
A1.7	Distribution by size of family	176
A1.8	Educational levels	177
A1.9	Occupational distribution	177
A2.1	Correlation coefficients (Spearman) for participation characteristics	178
A2.2	Correlation coefficients (Spearman) for intragenerational mobility	179
A2.3	Correlation coefficients (Spearman) for intergenerational mobility	180
A3.1	Comparison of income	181
A3.2	Multiregression analysis: income by measures of socioeconomic background	182
A3.3	Comparison of wealth	183
A3.4	Multiregression analysis: wealth by socioeconomic background	183
A3.5	Comparison of expenditure	184
A3.6	Multiregression analysis: expenditure by socioeconomic background	184
A3.7	Correlation between housing status and socioeconomic background	185

Acknowledgements

Many people were involved in the process that led to the publication of this book. I am grateful for their advice and support. Professor Haleh Afshar and Professor Ali Rahnema read the entire manuscript several times and made extensive and extremely useful comments. I appreciate all the comments received, which helped me to make substantial improvements to the volume.

Thanks are also due to Dr Mostafa Azkia and Dr Mahmood Ghazi Tabatabaei, who read and made useful comments on parts of the manuscript, particularly in respect of the empirical study. I owe a great deal to Dr Adrian Leftwich, who provided useful advice, and his guidance on the outline of the original research programme was of great value. Dr Mohammad Taghavi, Dr Bagher Naseri, Mrs Yukiko Yashitomi, Mr Majid Zourofi and Mr Mehdi Ekrami merit special mention for their help in the field. Their cooperation was instrumental in the gathering of a mass of information. However I take full responsibility for the deficiencies that remain. I am also grateful for the moral support I received from my friends, including Dr Hossein Raghfar, Dr Mahmood Shahabi, Dr Hossein Serajzadeh, Mr Seyed Ghavamoddin Mahdavi and Mr Mehdi Ganjian.

I express my gratitude to the Department of Planning and Design at the Undersecretariat for Rural Development, Ministry of Reconstruction (Jihad), for its help in collecting data from the field as well as permitting me to use its data, computer services and other facilities.

Last but not least I thank Mr T. M. Farmiloe and Mr Peter Dent of Palgrave for their efforts and their faith in the promotion and publication of the book.

ALI SHAKOORI

Glossary

فارسی

Behsazi (physical upgrading projects)
پروژه های بهسازی: این پروژه ها با هدف بهبود کالبدی و فضایی روستاها توسط وزارت جهاد سازندگی به مرحله اجرا در آمدند.

Boneh
بنه: به واحد های سنتی زراعی که قبل از اصلاحات ارضی در برخی از نقاط ایران وجود داشته است، اطلاق می شود.

Caliph
خلیفه: حاکم مذهبی و سیاسی جامعه مسلمین که بعنوان جانشین پیامبر محسوب می شود.

Dehyar (village animator)
دهیار: فردی که مسئول هدایت فعالیت های عمران در روستا است.

Kadkhoda (village headman)
کدخدا

Khaleseh (public land)
اراضی خالصه: به زمین های دولتی اطلاق می شود.

Khordeh-Maleki (village ownership by two or more individuals)
خرده مالکی: در این کتاب به مالکیت های ارضی در مقیاس کوچک گفته می شود.

Khushnisbhin (villagers without traditional cultivation right)
خوشنشینان: به روستائیان فاقد نسق گفته می شود.

Mosha (cooperatives)
مشاع: به تعاون های مشاع (زراعی) که بعد از انقلاب اسلامی تاسیس شدند گفته می شود.

Moshaver (adviser of mosha)
مشاور: در این کتاب به فرد مشاور و راهنما در مشاعها اطلاق می گردد.

Omdeh-Maleki (land and villages owned by major landlords)
عمده مالکی: در این کتاب به مالکیت های ارضی در مقیاس بزرگ گفته می شود.

Qanat (traditional irrigation system)
قنات: به سیستم سنتی استحصال آبهای زیرزمینی اطلاق می شود.

Sarmosha (director of mosha)
سرمشاع: به مدیر تعاون های مشاع گفته می شود.

shia
شیعه

Shoura (council)
شورا

sunni
سنی

Tuyul (benefice)
تیول: نوعی نظام ملکیت ارضی مرسوم قبل از انقلاب مشروطیت است که سلاطین به نظامیان و یا به کارکنان عالیرتبه دولتی در قبال خدمات آنها برای مدتی مشخص واگذار میکردند.

Ulama (clergy)
علما یا روحانیون مذهبی

Vaqf (religious endowments)
اوقاف: به اراضی تحت مالکیت موسسات مذهبی اطلاق می شود.

Velayat-e motlagheh-faghih (absolute rule of religious leader)
ولایت مطلقه فقیه: به رهبر مذهبی جامعه اسلامی اطلاق می گردد که در غیاب پیامبر و ائمه معصومین هدایت و رهبری جامعه را بر عهده دارد.

Introduction

Rural development, in terms of policy and practice, has been a matter of increasing concern in the Third World. Governments, international agencies and local organisations have attempted to raise the status of rural people through improvement and transformation strategies (Long, 1979). This concern arose because the development efforts pursued over several decades were failing to eradicate rural poverty and make meaningful improvements to the living conditions of the rural poor (Haque *et al.*, 1975; Griffin, 1979; Lea and Chaudhri, 1983; Ferguson, 1990).

Today rural people have, more than ever before, access to education, health facilities and occupational opportunities. But close examination of their living conditions indicates that although the aggregate level of production and consumption has increased, the distribution of benefits continues to show persistent inequalities (Hayami and Ruttan, 1971; Morrison *et al.*, 1979). Malnutrition, poverty, illiteracy and unemployment remain common problems. Their persistence and the deterioration of the social conditions in rural communities are a major concern for many developing countries (ILO, 1977; World Bank, 1991a).

Since the Second World War the mainstream approach in the development literature has been based on the experiences of industrialised countries and inspired by the ideas of such scholars as Rostow, Lewis and Nurkse. The main argument is that urban modernisation, industrialisation and rapid economic growth can help alleviate rural poverty through the trickle-down effect, and that the promotion of agricultural production will accelerate the process of poverty reduction (FAO, 1990a, 1990b). However, the impact of agricultural growth on rural people depends on the balance between agricultural growth and rural development strategies. Strategies that are aimed at radical institutional

2 The State and Rural Development

change and levelling out private ownership of the means of production and other forms of wealth might have different results. The Third World's rural reforms have rarely proved successful.

The modernisation debates that dominated development policies and practices from the middle of the twentieth century included a degree of emphasis on agriculture. Influenced by the modernisation paradigm, which considers technological advancement and output growth as the key ingredients of development, many Third World countries adopted strategies that emphasised economic growth and industrialisation in the context of increasingly centralised planning and control of the distribution of resources. It was hoped that this policy would result in economic take off and the eventual spread of benefits throughout the system (Rostow, 1990). Under the modernisation approach, from the 1950s the policies adopted for rural areas increasingly focused on the industrialisation of agriculture. In consequence there was an emphasis on economies of scale, which resulted in the emergence of large-scale, mechanised farms in many developing countries.

The modernisation of agriculture was a major plank in Iran's development policies in the twentieth century. As part and parcel of the modernisation era (from the 1920s onwards) the Pahlavi dynasty first broke the back of tribal communal holdings by privatising or confiscating much of this land for the crown. In the 1950s a modernisation programme for large holdings was initiated, first in some of the crown lands and then, in the 1960s, through a series of land reforms. These were accompanied by the industrialisation of agriculture and the creation of large agribusiness units, and in the 1970s by the introduction of rural development zones. By adhering to technocratic growth strategies, the goal of economic policy in general and agricultural policy in particular was to achieve maximum growth in aggregate output. Yet despite continued effort the modernisation policies failed to deliver rural prosperity or eradicate rural poverty. This was partly because the regime's modernisation policy had few backward and forward linkages between different sectors of the economy (traditional and modern), particularly in the case of agriculture, and partly because of the low priority given to the scattered population in rural areas and the traditional agricultural sector (Afshar, 1981; Pesaran, 1982). As a consequence, after the revolution rural reform became an important part of government policy.

Unlike the substantial research on the rural sector before the revolution, the post-revolutionary rural development policies and their impact on rural life have received comparatively little attention. Indeed they have yet to be studied in a systematic way. The existing studies of post-revolutionary rural policies can be divided into four broad groups. The first group focuses on the impact of the state's agrarian policy on agrarian change at the macro level without considering the impact of these policies on rural life. Significant studies in this category include Mojtahed and Esfahani (1989), Yeganeh (1986), Ashraf (1982, 1991), Schirazi (1993) and Lahsaeizadeh (1993).

Ashraf's early work (1981) focuses on the land question and the peasant struggles after the revolution. He outlines the peasants' uprisings and the moderate political solutions offered by parliament to deal with their grievances. He briefly discusses the effect of the revolution on the relation between the land redistribution and land use systems and shows that, on the one hand, the confiscation of large land holdings by the state resulted in the expansion of the public sector, and on the other hand, the elimination of large land holdings and the weakening of medium-sized land holdings reinforced the position of better-off peasants.

His analysis is based on a three-year period after the revolution, and his prediction that post-revolutionary reforms would eliminate private capitalism and alter state capitalism has not proved correct. Ashraf's second work (1991) compares agrarian policies before the revolution with those after the revolution. He concludes that in both cases land reforms were initiated from above and benefited the non-revolutionary sector of the rural population. In both cases the sanctions protecting private property remained in place, initially protected by landed interests and after the revolution by religious institutions, which defended it in terms of Islamic teachings (ibid., p. 305). While the prerevolutionary land reform effort was instigated from above to forestall a revolution from below, the post-revolutionary land reform was initiated by the middle stratum, primarily young urban intelligentsia aiming to radicalise the revolutionary movement. While the prerevolutionary programmes led to the fall of the old land-owning class and the emergence of a large agricultural bourgeoisie, the post-revolutionary reform led to the fall of this bourgeoisie and the survival of medium-sized commercial farmers.

Yeganeh's (1986) work is similar to that of Ashraf. An analysis of the land question after the revolution constitutes the main part of his work. He concentrates on the revolution in agrarian structures. According to him:

> the revolution brought with it new social and structural forces that further transformed the agrarian structure. The fall of the big agricultural bourgeoisie coincided with the maintenance of the middle

sector and the expansion of small holdings and peasant farming. In the public sector, the large state-owned farms were preserved, the large private farms were incorporated into the public sector, and the semi-public farm corporations and production cooperatives were dissolved (ibid., p. 79).

Like Ashraf, Yeganeh is only concerned with the few years after the revolution.

The additional points put forward by Lahsaeizadeh (1993) are, first, that in the absence of comprehensive land redistribution, rural poverty remained unresolved, and, second, that the redistribution of smaller plots of land, mostly of poor quality, meant that poverty was redistributed among the rural population.

Mojtahed and Esfahani (1989) examine the impact of government policies on the agricultural sector in comparison with other economic sectors. They state that the agricultural sector remained inefficient in the post-revolutionary era, despite remarkable increases in the use of inputs and the post-revolutionary government's proclaimed emphasis on agricultural development and self-sufficiency in food. The main causes of this weak performance were the government's lopsided control of agricultural prices and low investment in agricultural research and development due to the war with Iraq and the decline in oil revenues. Nevertheless they conclude that the agricultural sector fared better than the rest of the economy owing to agriculture's lesser dependence on capital and skills, which became scarce after the revolution, and the government's increased attention to this sector. Their analysis is based on data up to 1986, and does not include the post-war agricultural performance.

Schirazi (1993) is one of the most recent and comprehensive accounts of the agricultural policies of the Islamic Republic. The book investigates agricultural policy in order to 'examine how Islamists in power have tackled development, the problems that have arisen, the effectiveness of Islamist solutions, and the country's state of development after having been subjected to the Islamist experiment for so long' (ibid., p. 1). The analysis focuses on the perspectives of the different sociopolitical factions in respect of agricultural development until November 1979, the period in which they were responsible for policy, and those of the legalist faction thereafter. Although Schirazi discusses the diverse issues and policies put forward after the revolution, he pays little attention to the impact of agricultural policies on rural Iran. His conclusion that the state's agricultural policies failed to meet rural needs is based on a few studies of rural development projects that were carried out immediately after the implementation of these policies, without taking into account the many longer-term services and initiatives that were also introduced.

The second group of post-revolutionary rural development studies includes a few field studies that focus on specific rural development projects. Socioeconomic studies of the Centres of Services for Rural People and Nomads, the evaluation of *mosha* cooperatives (collective farming units) carried out by the Institute for Social Studies at the University of Tehran in 1982 and the Organisation of Planning and Budget in 1983, and socioeconomic studies of physical upgrading projects by the Ministry of Jihad in 1988 are notable examples. Some recent studies, conducted in 1989–90, look at the service centres. All of the latter focus on implementation problems or the organisational and interorganisational problems of the projects rather than their impact on rural life.

A major field study on *mosha* cooperatives was carried out by the University of Tehran in 1983. The bulk of the work is concerned with technical problems, and two problems in particular are highlighted. First, many peasants are not prepared to be forced into collectives, from which they do not expect to receive any concrete benefits. Second, the government has proved incapable of providing the *mosha*s with adequate resources, without which they cannot function.

A major field study on physical upgrading projects was conducted by the Housing and Improvement (*Behsazi*) Bureau of the Ministry of Jihad at a few village project sites in the eastern part of Eastern Azerbaijan (now Ardabil province) two years after the implementation of the projects in 1986. The main focus was on the attitude of the villagers towards the projects rather than on measuring the socioeconomic impact of the projects. It was concluded that the villagers had a positive attitude towards the projects and welcomed their implementation.

Most of these studies were conducted two or three years after the implementation of the programmes. As well as failing to consider the socioeconomic effects of the projects on rural life, they do not discuss the effect on the countryside of the changes in development strategy and agricultural policy and the institutionalisation of the revolutionary rural organisations.

The third category comprises reports that are mainly based on official sources, such as those by World Bank (1993, 1994) and general descriptions by researchers at rural areas, such as Farazmand (1989) and Loeffler (1983). These works lack a critical analytical approach.

6 *The State and Rural Development*

The fourth category consists of authors who are concerned with the institutional and organisational structure of rural development, such as Ferdows (1983) and Farazmand (1989). Ferdows discusses the formation of the Jihad-e Sazandegi (the Reconstruction Crusade). His main argument is that the Jihad was the product of a politico-ideological struggle between the two main post-revolutionary political and ideological factions: the liberal-nationalist faction and the Islamic Republic Party. The former was backed by the traditional bureaucratic organisations, while the latter had no status in these organisations and sought to reinforce the Jihad in order to make the bureaucratic organisations follow its policy. According to Ferdows, these ideological conflicts meant that the Jihad did little to resolve the rural problems.

Farazmand (1989) is mainly concerned with the formation of the Ministry of Agriculture and agricultural policies before the revolution, although there is a small section on state–peasant relations in the post-revolutionary era. He briefly describes the different rural institutions formed after the revolution, but in the absence of comprehensive empirical research and sufficient source material – merely a few 'tourist' observations in villages in the Caspian Sea provinces – he inevitably evaluates the post-revolutionary rural policies in a positive light.

The only study of the peasantry themselves is that by Rafipour (1986, 1989). The main aim of his 1986 work was to identify the objective and subjective needs of villagers, the ranking of these needs and the factors that gave rise to their emergence. The study was conducted in 32 selected villages in the province of Yazd. It was found that the actual needs of villagers should be determined before any attempt is made to design and implement a rural programme. The best way to identify these needs is to ask the villagers themselves. With the use of 'needs theory' he concludes that the needs of those who are more highly aware and economically better off are qualitatively and quantitatively greater than those who are less aware and economically worse off. Similarly, the needs in villages with good developmental facilities are quantitatively and qualitatively greater than in villages with poorer developmental facilities. His second work (Rafipour, 1989), which is one of the few studies to consider rural people's attitude towards the Jihad, focuses on 30 villages in the provinces of Esfahan, Fars and Khorasan. As in his earlier work, he uses 'needs theory' criteria and other qualitative indicators to conclude that the rural population is satisfied with the work of the Jihad.

Thus it is evident that on the whole rural research has focused on the macroeconomic or institutional framework of the development process in post-revolutionary Iran. Furthermore the few studies that do consider the peasantry were conducted over a decade ago and little work has been done on this sector at the micro level in the post-revolutionary era.

The focus of this book is on the long-term socioeconomic impact of post-revolutionary rural reforms in general and their effect on a number of selected villages. Its objective is to ascertain the extent to which the rural development strategies have changed the living conditions of rural people. It is the contention of this book that despite the very best endeavours of the state and obvious improvements in the rural economy and its infrastructure, the revolutionary aim of increasing peasant participation in the processes of decision making at the local level has yet to be realised.

Structure of the book

The book is organised into six chapters. Chapter 1 provides a theoretical framework to explain the process of rural development and the nature of change in rural society. The chapter is divided into three sections. The first discusses concepts and definitions, the processes and dimensions of modernisation theory, and agricultural modernisation. The second section outlines the existing debates on the meaning of development and rural development in a historical context. It also looks at dominant rural development approaches and strategies in developing countries from the 1950s to the early 1990s. The final section traces the direction of rural transformation in developing countries. The main argument is that macro development does not necessarily lead to micro development.

Chapter 2 provides a historical background of agricultural modernisation and rural development in the prerevolutionary era. It starts with a brief outline of agrarian change before the 1962 land reform, with emphasis on the impact of world capitalist development and state policy on agrarian relations. The discussion then moves on the land reform programme and other state rural development policies, and their consequences for Iranian society in general and rural society in particular.

Chapter 3 focuses on the post-revolutionary agricultural and rural development policies. It explains the major changes in rural and agricultural organisations, such as the reorganisation of the prerevolutionary agricultural administration, the establishment of a revolutionary organisation for rural development (the Jihad), the implementation of

8 *The State and Rural Development*

a land reform programme, the creation of *mosha* cooperatives and the establishment of rural councils.

Chapter 4 discusses the effects of the government's agricultural policies and other factors on agricultural output. The discussion is divided into two sections. The first briefly reviews the state of agriculture before the revolution. The second provides a detailed examination of the post-revolutionary agricultural policies, focusing on fiscal policies and their role in capital formation, land and water use policies and their role in the expansion of cultivated areas, and support policies such as provision and pricing policy to support agricultural growth.

Chapter 5 deals with post-revolutionary rural reform policy at the micro level and is based on empirical research. First, the socioeconomic and geographical characteristics of the province, district and villages under study are briefly presented. Next the impact of rural development programmes on the process of change in rural life – including the variables of income, wealth, social mobility, participation and the wellbeing of the sample households – is discussed. Then the direction of rural change as a consequence of the rural programmes is analysed. The main aim is to discover the extent to which rural development programmes can change the pattern of resource distribution among different rural groups.

Finally, Chapter 6 sums up the issues discussed in the preceding chapters.

1
Theoretical Debates on Rural Change

Introduction

This chapter reviews the main debates on development in general and rural development in particular, and provides a theoretical framework to explain the process of rural development and the changes that occur in rural society as a consequence of rural development programmes. The discussion is organised into three sections. The first deals with modernisation theory and agricultural modernisation. It examines how changes occur and the strategies that can be used to lead the process in the desired direction. The second section traces the history of development and rural development theories and approaches from the 1950s to the early 1990s, and examines the nature of rural change with reference to developmental experiences over the decades. The final section considers the direction of rural transformation through an analysis of topics such as poverty and inequality in rural communities.

Modernisation

According to modernisation theory, all societies are either traditional or modern, and the former will change into the latter (Moore, 1963). Modernisation has been defined as the transformation from traditional stability to 'certain desired sorts of technology and associated social structure, value-organisation, motivations, and norms' (Dube, 1992, p. 112). During the process of transformation, societies abandon their traditional features and take on the characteristics of modern advanced societies, usually those typified by the industrialised West (Lerner, 1958; Eisenstadt, 1966; Harrison, 1988; Dube, 1992). This dichotomy of social types is also used to explain differences and changes within a particular social sector (Boeke, 1953). The characteristics of traditional societies are seen as hindering the process of modernisation, and therefore need to be changed to allow the growth and predominance of universal achievement norms, a high degree of social mobility, a well-developed employment system, an egalitarian class structure based on generalised patterns of occupational achievement, and the prevalence of 'associations' or 'functionally specific', 'non-ascriptive structures' (Sutton, 1966; see also Lerner, 1958; Eisenstadt, 1966).

Modernisation theory has largely focused on the 'new' nation states, and tends to assume that what occurred in the West can be repeated elsewhere, with a little help in the way of capital, technology, expertise and rationality (Rostow, 1960). This assumes that developed countries have reached perfection in terms of social structures and cultural processes, whereas developing countries have yet to realise their potential in terms of adopting the 'developed' forms and states of being of the modernised countries (Luke, 1990). Third World societies will eventually become mirror images of the West, and consequently societies will tend to become homogeneous. As Levy (1967, p. 207) states, 'as time goes on, they and we will increasingly resemble one another ... because the patterns of modernisation are such that the more highly modernised societies become, the more they resemble one another'. This will result from the metrocentric characteristic of modernisation, which is based on technological innovations first developed in the West. The technological factor will generate common cultural, economic and sociopolitical functions and structures that will join the 'metropolitan' (the industrialised and developed) with the 'peripheral' (the underdeveloped) nations.

The modernisation process was experienced by Western countries 'organically' (Sugar, 1964) as a consequence of the long-term evolutions of different aspects of these societies, such as the disintegration of feudalism, the growth of trade, the scientific revolution, religious reform, the commercialisation of agriculture and the growth of manufacturing.

Modernisation of the developing nations, which have not experienced this organic historical process, can take place through coercion (Luke, 1990), 'induced development' (Sugar, 1964) or 'planned development' (Long, 1979) by external forces such as international agencies by means of economic and technological aid or by national elites through policy initiatives that stimulate and create the necessary changes to achieve modernisation. As Luke (1990) argues, the entire thrust of the language used in the modernisation debate is that modernised countries know better how to make changes to traditional – underdeveloped – societies and how to develop them along the lines of modernised countries:

> The modernised metropolitan countries and their social forces subject the pre-modern and the modernising nation to political actions and social processes in order to quicken their transition to modernity. Such core social forces, and local modernisers in the periphery, labouriously work to make the peripheral society into 'modern' social complexes, to make these people like 'modern' man, to put the Third and Fourth Worlds into conformity with the metropolitan world, and to render the pre-modern culture into a 'modern' state of existence (ibid., p. 225).

In many underdeveloped nations the first stage of modernisation has involved the transformation of the political structure. The existence of a strong centralised state was recognised as a precondition for or a facilitating factor in the levelling out of diversities and the removal of vertical and horizontal disparities in society. It was seen as a necessary condition for the formation of a nation-state and the consequent changes in numerous areas, particularly in the economic field (Sugar, 1964). A strong nation-state requires effective communication between the elite and the masses, a high literacy rate with an adequate proportion of the population having higher education, the secularisation of politics and so on (Dube, 1992). All of these require a social framework that provides incentives and opportunities for development. This involves interrelated changes at various levels: social, political–administrative, psychological, economic and cultural.

Modernisation refers to multiple and interdependent factors in the social system that fall under two headings: structural characteristics and the adaptiveness of the sociocultural system. Differentiation and specialisation are basic elements of the social structure. The most significant of these are structural differentiation, specialisation of roles and organisational complexity. The key factor in the modernisation process is the proliferation of the basic elements of all social systems, so that their roles and institutions are rapidly increased. Proliferation is a process of differentiation whereby roles and institutions undergo continual specialisation and engage in more limited areas of activity. For example, during the transition of a society from domestic to factory production, the division of labour broadens, new roles emerge and the economic activities previously undertaken by the household are transferred to the firm. As a formal education system emerges, the training functions previously fulfilled by the family or a religious institution are taken over by a new, specialised organisation – the school. With the emergence of specialised institutions, relationships become increasingly complex (Friedland, 1969). The new collection of specialised structures fulfils the same functions as the original structure, but more efficiently (Smelser, 1964).

Structural differentiation brings with it the problem of coordinating the management and activities of the new institutions. When differentiation begins, individuals are separated from their traditional units, such as religious groups, family networks and so on. In such a situation, as Smelser (1964, p. 110) states, modernisation involves a 'contrapuntal interplay' between differentiation, 'which is divisive of established society and integration which unites differentiated structures on a new basis'. From a structuralist-functionalist perspective, it can be argued that the period of transition necessarily involves such features as a disjunction between the required new roles and the existing patterns of behaviour, conflicts between the values appropriate to different states of equilibrium, and the need for new, more specialised roles to be fully integrated into the system. It follows that integrationary mechanisms need to be created to equilibrate the system at its new level and to handle any conflicts that appear during the transition period. This requires either the transformation of existing organisations or the establishment of new institutions to regulate the new forms of conflict. At the new level, greater differentiation means that more specialised tasks can be performed than was previously the case.

Therefore society is confronted with increasingly formal institutional arrangements related to the growing structural complexity. The new institutions collectively perform better than did the old structure. The underlying element in the process of specialisation and differentiation is an advancement of rationalisation. It is inevitably made necessary by differentiation, and is seen as a precondition for and a main characteristic of modernity (Smith, 1970). It should be added that the functionalist approach to modernisation theory, which emphasises such functions as adaptation, integration and homeostatic equilibrium (Soja, 1980) in the process of transformation, has a more optimistic view of the future of non-modernised society and failed to predict the serious disturbances in and failure of the process of modernisation in many underdeveloped countries. These failures, as will be discussed in the following sections, have resulted in reactionist approaches to policy making at the political, ideological and scientific (development) levels.

A modern society is one that is highly differentiated in numerous spheres, such as the economy, the family, religious institutions, the political system and the psychology of individuals.

At the economic level, modernisation first of all refers to an increase in per capita output. Economic development is characterised by the development of industrial systems based on high levels of technology, growing specialisation, differentiated units of economic activity – production, consumption and marketing – and growth in the scope and complexity of the major markets for goods, labour and money. This is in turn associated with interrelated changes in other institutions that sustain the process of modernisation. Smelser (1966, pp. 28–9) outlines these changes as follows: in technology, the change from simple techniques to the application of scientific knowledge; in agriculture, the evolution from subsistence farming to commercial agricultural production, which means specialisation in cash crops, the purchase of non-agricultural products in the market and often agricultural wage labour; and in industry, the transformation from human and animal power to power-driven machinery. With industrialisation there is growing migration from rural areas to the city and the economic enterprises located within it.

At the political level, modernisation refers to differentiation of the political structure and the secularisation of political culture, which in turn result in the enhancement of the capacity of the political system to cope with problems, to adapt to continuous change, and to strive creatively for the achievement of new societal objectives (Coleman, 1986).

Political differentiation refers to the progressive separation and specialisation of roles and institutional spheres in the political system. For instance the separation of universal legal norms from religion, the separation of religion and ideology, and the separation of administrative structures and public political competition (ibid., 1968).

At the cultural level, a modern society is characterised by differentiation of the major elements of the cultural and value systems, such as religion, philosophy and science; improved literacy rates and secular education; and a more complex institutional system for the advancement of specialised roles based on intellectual disciplines (Eisenstadt, 1966, pp. 4–5).

At the psychological level, modernisation denotes a change in individuals' personality and their patterns of behaviour: attitudes, values, and their means of receiving information, expressing their ideas and valuing the outside world (McClelland, 1961; Hagen, 1962; Inkeles and Smith, 1974). A modern person is someone who is informed, open to new experiences and willing to try new activities or develop new ways of doing things; is independent of authority and not under the control of such figures as parents, tribal heads or rulers, especially when he or she is making basic decisions about the conduct of his or her personal affairs; who believes that human beings can conquer nature; who understands events and situations in terms of cause and effect and determines strategies of action by careful consideration of ends and means; is ambitious and eager to climb the occupational ladder; and as an informed citizen identifies him- or herself with the newer, larger entities of region, state or the world, and takes an interest in public affairs, national and international as well as local. Unlike traditional individuals, the modern person rejects passivity, resignation and fatalism in respect of the course of life's events. A modern person is active in civil politics and participates in voluntary associations and local community affairs. These characteristics make the modern individual more responsive to and supportive of modern institutions, and thus able to facilitate general modernisation in society (Inkeles and Smith, 1974, pp. 19–25, 312–13; Dube, 1988, p. 18).

Rapid economic growth and sustained development cannot take place without the widespread diffusion of these qualities across the population. Likewise the features of a 'modernised' personality are promoted and sustained by structural, institutional, attitudinal and value changes at the personal, social, economic and cultural levels. Adoption and diffusion are the main means by which development occurs in the underdeveloped world. The primary mechanisms to promote adaptiveness are the proliferation and differentiation of roles, institutions and norms, which are in turn generated by innovation and/or diffusion (Friedland, 1969, pp. 35–42).

Agricultural modernisation and modernisation of the peasantry

In general, agricultural modernisation refers to (1) technical progress in relation to the growth of output and productivity, and (2) the process of commoditisation in relation to the expansion of commodity production, markets and divisions of labour (Bernstein, 1990, p. 6).

Modernisation in this context articulates ideas about the development of technical aspects of production and certain social aspects of production, namely markets (Bernstein, 1990, p. 6). In the field of agricultural production, technical efficiency is manifested in high input and output. The process of commoditisation involves specialisation, which is manifested in the development of a more complex division of labour, more specialised branches of production, more specialised markets and the emergence of new groups of producers (for example research scientists and seed-production industries) who are not directly involved in agricultural production (ibid.).

One aspect of commoditisation is the commercialisation of agricultural output. With the modernisation of agriculture, the number of market processes increases and an efficient marketing system becomes a prerequisite for an efficient production system. The expansion of commercial production in agriculture is an important aspect of agricultural modernisation, resulting in structural transformation and increasing sector interdependence. It is achieved through the growth of a marketable surplus of farm products, an expansion of foreign exchange and increased availability of resources for capital formation, which are all necessary conditions for the development of a diversified modern economy (Schultz, 1964; Harriss, 1982).

A particular characteristic of commoditisation and specialisation in agricultural modernisation is standardisation of the technical conditions of production in the face of environmental uncertainties. The objective of standardisation is to minimise the adverse effects of the natural environment and maximise the utilisation of existing resources. This means that increased inputs are necessary in order to increase both the quantity of output and its predictability in terms of yield and quality.

Therefore agricultural modernisation refers to a process in which there is a strong tendency to cultivate a particular crop (or crops) with the aid of capital-intensive techniques, technical innovations, market expansion and commercial production, specialisation and standardisation, and reliance on economies of scale to reduce unit costs and maximise profits. In this process, the modern entrepreneurial farmer is considered the central and ideal person to make use of modern technology and the new institutions (Lerner, 1958; Levy, 1975).

The link between communities and the outside world is considered to be a source of great change, and thus it is necessary to have access to modern technology, which in turn helps economic growth by creating a pluralistic social structure that releases people from poverty and tradition (Rogers, 1969; Long, 1979). This is based on the fundamental assumption that the village is a distinct social entity, 'isolated' from the rest of the wider system, and on the premise that there is one 'stock of knowledge' which is located in centres of innovation, namely the industrialised societies or cities where technologies are developed, and where decisions are made about their merits and the strategies to be used for their diffusion (Hulme and Turner, 1990; Luke, 1990). If farmers are provided with necessary technological and institutional requirements, they will adopt modern methods. In situations where the distribution of resources is equal, all the people should benefit equally from agricultural modernisation programmes. Even if there are inequalities, and if the lower stratum is deprived of resources, meaningful areas of employment can still be provided within the modernisation framework. Increased commercialisation is accompanied by increased employment opportunities. In an ideal situation, and with a competitive market structure, everyone should enjoy a high level of social well-being.

Regarding the significance of external sources of change in the traditional community (or its agriculture), the intervention of non-local agencies is considered necessary to bring about this transition and develop the characteristics of modernity (Preston, 1980). Any problem in agriculture or in human well-being can be resolved by intervention. Baily's (1969) argument of political encapsulation is a radical explanation and provides a clear illustration of a modernisation theory of social and political change in peasant societies. He distinguishes between encapsulating (the state) and encapsulated (the village) political structures in terms of role differentiation. The model maintains that the encapsulating structure is larger and significantly differentiated, whereas the encapsulated structure is smaller and has not undergone differentiation (ibid., p. 147).

There is a tension between these two structures. In order to resolve this problem, the integration of the encapsulated structure into the encapsulating structure is necessary. It is expected that this process will result in a higher degree of structural differentiation that is consistent with the political and economic systems of an integrated nation-state. Baily offers several strategies to put an end to undifferentiated structures and create a united nation. One of the most common strategies adopted by developing countries is to integrate the encapsulated structure into the encapsulating structure, which means a radical change to the existing structure (Preston, 1980, pp. 149–51).

This intervention is not only important for political ends but it is also seen as a crucial means of promoting change in rural communities and their connection with the outside world. In explaining this idea, Warren (1978) distinguishes between horizontal linkage and vertical linkage. In most countries the government initiates and implements rural and agricultural development strategies to improve the living standards of the people, but such strategies are inevitably influenced by the political ideology of the government and the overall thinking that dominates social change theories. The following section will provide an extensive review of rural development strategies and policy orientations in developing countries, across different periods of development thinking.

Development

In spite of a general consensus on the significance of development, there still exists notable disagreement among scholars about what the concept actually means, mainly due to the conflicting paradigms in the literature, which have led scholars to conceptualise development issues from their own ideological perspectives.

The term 'development' is a multidisciplinary concept that involves social, cultural, political and economic factors. It has been described as a generic term meaning growth, evolution, stages of inducement or progress (Mehta, 1984, p. 1). Adam Smith's *Wealth of Nations*, published in 1776, marked the beginning of the idea of development, particularly in economic terms. Growth was the main emphasis in the economic writings of the classical period. Adam Smith's most important idea in respect of growth was the specialisation of labour. He formulated the principle of economies of scale and stated that the size of the market governs the degree of its specialisation.

The first dynamic theory of economic growth was formulated by Ricardo. According to him, economic progress depends on capital formation through labour productivity. All the neoclassical economists saw *laissez-faire* policies as the only avenue to growth. By the end of the nineteenth century, scholars' interest shifted from economic development to problems such as economic fluctuations and the distribution of resources among social groups in industrialised countries. This shift may be attributed to the fact that some industrialised countries, such as Britain and the USA, had already achieved sufficient development to sustain growth, and the European countries were rapidly catching them up.

The great recession of the 1930s and the Second World War led Western scholars to formulate theories and strategies for Third World development. In recent decades development theory has taken several sharp turns, but has been dominated by the growth-based paradigm.

Inspired by the experience of developed countries and influenced by the neoclassical economists, in the 1950s and 1960s development was defined mostly by economists, in the operational sense, as a rise in gross national product and an increase in investment and consumption. Therefore the development policies focused on 'growth maximisation'. The basic assumption was that 'once the growth process gained momentum, an invisible hand would take care of the distributional dimension' (Dube, 1992, p. 72). The idea behind this perspective came from modernisation theory.

There are several interpretations of modernisation theory. One well-known interpretation emphasises that the primary cause of mass poverty and economic stagnation in underdeveloped countries is the backward nature of their economies in the field of subsistence production, the use of primitive technology, conservative attitudes, low levels of aspiration, an inability to save, a selfish preoccupation with family welfare and parochialism (Long, 1977). The situation described by Myrdal (1970) as 'vicious circles of poverty' can be reversed by industrialisation, and then economic progress should be achieved. The most influential theory was formulated by Rostow. He conceptualised stages of economic growth as a route by which to move from a traditional to an industrialised society. This is basically an economic theory of development in which development is considered as or is equated with rapid economic growth, and in which a large quantity and mixture of savings, investment and foreign aid is all that is necessary for underdeveloped countries to proceed along the route of economic growth followed earlier by the more developed countries. In the 1960s it was assumed that economic growth would result in the transformation of both traditional societies and the 'static and retarded economy', and that poverty would be eradicated as a result of the trickle-down effect (Rostow, 1960). Development would promote autonomy at the national level and increase the capacity of the people to influence the pace of growth and the ways in which its fruits were distributed (Wolf, 1971).

Influenced by this school of thinking and policy formulations, many Third World countries adopted development strategies based on urban or industrial policies. Heavy capital investment in infrastructural projects and industry was viewed as the main means to achieve high growth rates and increased per capita income. There was also a universal assumption that countries which depended mainly on agricultural production and agricultural employment were 'backward', and that the way to progress lay in industrialisation. This assumption was based on the historical fact that world's most powerful nations had long been industrialised. Policy makers in Third World countries saw industrialisation as the only way to reduce their dependence on the West. There was a belief that industrialisation would provide jobs for a large number of unemployed or underemployed people from the rural sector. It was thought that it would provide new inputs such as machinery and fertilizers to increase productivity in the agricultural sector, while the industrial labour force in the towns and cities would provide a large market for food and industrial goods. But a lot of aid-based and national industrialisation programmes were unable to achieve their targets or eliminate poverty.

In the late 1960s it was realised that the benefits of rapid growth were not only taking too long to reach the poor, but also would probably never reach most of them. Industrial and urban-based programmes had resulted in expanding bureaucracies, and projects directed at the poor had reached only a small target population and had often created a dependency relationship with metropolitan centres (ILO, 1977; Griffin, 1981; Lea and Chaudhri, 1983). It was broadly accepted that application of the development theories of the 1950s and 1960s could not lead to a positive outcome, because as GNP increased, so too did poverty, inequality and underdevelopment. The process was called paradoxical by Chenery et al. (1974, p. xiii), who argued that 'while growth policies have succeeded beyond the expectations of the first development decades the very idea of aggregate growth as a social objective has increasingly been called into question'. After studying a great number of developing countries over the period 1965–80, Jazairy et al. (1992) came to a similar conclusion. It was largely recognised that economic growth filters upwards from the lower-ranking urban centres in response to agricultural development in the surrounding areas, rather than filtering down the urban hierarchy and outwards to the surrounding rural areas (Friedmann, 1981). By the early 1970s an increasing number of academicians and policy makers were questioning the validity of the 'economic growth' approach. They concluded that insufficient attention had been given to social and political factors in planning. The following decade was a time of soul-searching, rethinking, redefining, new proposals and new strategies. One of the dominant issues during this period was growth versus equity. The debate centred on the question of whether the observed tendency for the benefits of growth to be distributed inequally during the early stages of development would necessarily continue in the later stages, and if so, whether corrective intervention would prevent further growth.

Research proliferated on income distribution and poverty in the development process. In 1974 the Institute of Development Studies at the University of Sussex and the World Bank Development Centre argued for a revision in the way that development policy was formulated, based on: (1) a statement of objectives for continued growth and distribution in a single measure of social welfare; (2) identification of the linkages between the growth of different economic sectors so that incremental benefits could be distributed according to the social objective defined above; and (3) following on from the above, definition of the scope for policy intervention – that is, maximal growth of GNP, a redirection of investment to raise the incomes of the poor, and adoption of policies of income redistribution (Chenery et al., 1974). In a complementary proposal the ILO called for the promotion of employment and an improvement of incomes through national and international strategies to meet the basic needs of deprived people, suggesting that this was the best way of inducing equitable growth.

The new strategy of 'growth with equity' represented a modification of previous strategies. Alongside redistribution, emphasis was put on poverty-oriented policies. For example the World Bank (1982, p. 20) maintained that: 'GNP does not measure items that are important to welfare in most societies, such as the distribution of income and wealth, employment status, job securities and opportunities for advancement, and the availability of health and education services'. Similarly Todaro (1981, p. 30) characterised development as 'a major change in social structure, popular attitudes, and national institutions as well as the acceleration of economic growth, the reduction of inequality, and the eradication of absolute poverty'.

It was necessary to redefine the concept not only because of the ineffectiveness of the development approach in practice, but also because the paradigm shifts over the previous decades had hindered the elaboration of universally acceptable definition of development. This is best illustrated by Seers (1979). According to him, development is a process that involves not only economic growth, but also adequate food and job provision and the reduction of income inequality. 'If one or two of these central problems have been growing worse, especially if all three have, it would be strange to call the result development, even if per capita income had soared' (ibid., p. 12). Similar conclusions were arrived at by other scholars. Haq (1976) asserted that 'what was produced and how it was distributed' was more important than 'how much was produced and how fast'. Later (Haq, 1978) he went further and argued that a drastic restructuring of political and economic power relations was also required if the benefits of development were to spread to the vast majority of the population. Brookfield (1975) and Goldsworthy (1988) emphasised the same points. Another definition, particularly from the mid 1970s, emphasised on the 'equality of life'. A strong argument was put forward by Sen. He defined development as the process of enhancing the entitlements and capabilities of people.

During the same period there was a tendency among some Third World countries to adopt what was called an 'agropolitan' approach to development. The idea was that the economic growth approach did not pay sufficient attention to the potential for internally generated growth, while agropolitan development was based on a country's own resources, skills, discourses and learning, and did not depend on the input of donor countries. China could be mentioned as a perfect example of this sort of development, and partial features of it can be found in Vietnam, Pakistan, Sri Lanka, Tanzania and Bangladesh. The aim of this approach was to benefit the whole population.

Rural development

The concept of rural development, like development in general, has been variously interpreted. Modernisation theory tends to equate rural development with agricultural growth. This was influenced by the dominant paradigm after the Second World War, which emphasised industrialisation and was a copy of the Western experience of economic development. In the rural development literature this was known as a 'technocratic rural development strategy' (Griffin, 1974) or an 'improvement approach' (Long, 1979) and was pursued by most developing countries, particularly in the 1960s. It assumed that 'rural development can be achieved by adopting the technologies of the developed countries without simultaneously and profoundly reforming social structure. Existing power relationships, traditional land tenure system and class structures are accepted as the starting point' (Aron, 1981, p. 485). The main economic aim of this strategy was to increase agricultural output. The emphasis was on a liberal capitalist ideology, competition, the free market and private property. Land ownership was highly concentrated in plantations, large-scale farms and large corporate farms. It was assumed that the concentration of income and wealth would lead to capital formation, which would eventually be devoted to investment and growth, thereby achieving increased output. The bureaucracy was considered an effective instrument to achieve development objectives. Reliance on large landowners and domestic and foreign investors was seen as a quick way to increase capital accumulation (Griffin, 1979; Aron, 1981). The conventional wisdom behind these strategies was that they would allow for the accumulation of the necessary capital and that ultimately the benefits accruing to advantaged areas, town or growth poles would trickle down to the mass of the population. As a consequence of the dominance of this approach the development of rural areas focused on: (1) settlement and land colonisation schemes that necessarily served political purposes and benefited a small or privileged population; (2) agricultural programmes that emphasised high technology, high-yielding crop varieties, extension services, especially for cash crops for export, credit schemes and marketing facilities for export crops; and (3) large capital-intensive projects with a technological emphasis (Lea and Chaudhri, 1985, pp. 15–16).

However, despite some successes this strategy was often socially inappropriate (ibid.). Many studies during this period (for example Ahluwalia, 1974, 1976; Hirashima, 1974; UNRISD, 1974; ILO, 1977; Jazairy *et al.*, 1992) documented the increasingly inequitable distribution of income and the declining relative income of the rural poor. The strategy of the first decade had failed to alleviate unemployment and poverty or to pass on the benefits of growth to the most backward areas.

Indeed in the 1950s and early 1960s the idea that rural development was distinct from overall economic growth had not yet arisen, and for the most part the rural sector was ignored during this period. Although modernisation and the expansion of the export sector was promoted in some areas, development of the traditional, staple-producing sectors was by and large left to chance. Therefore the current interest in rural development is a relatively new phenomenon. It was not until the late 1960s, and particularly the 1970s, that the main focus of individual, national and international development thinking shifted in that direction. Increasingly, rural development came to be defined as a comprehensive approach that incorporated but was not restricted to questions of agricultural change and development. For example Mosher (1969) recognises the interdependence between agricultural growth and rural welfare and states that increased welfare depends on agricultural growth. Some writers point out that growth is not necessarily unconducive to egalitarian income distribution (Chenery *et al.*, 1974). The new policy direction, based on an analysis of past experience – discontent with the 'technocratic strategy' and the narrow definition of rural development (Lele, 1975) – has been well summarised by the World Bank (SAREC, 1979, p. 20):

> the central concept of rural development presented here is of a process through which rural poverty is alleviated by sustained increases in the productivity and incomes of low-income rural workers and households. The emphasis is on raising output and incomes rather than simply redistributing current income and existing assets, although the latter may be desirable or even essential in an overall rural development strategy which links production with distributive or equity objectives.

There was general agreement that the objective of rural development was to improve the living standard of the rural population as a whole, not only through increased agricultural production and the resulting rise in income, but also through an improved quality of life. Furthermore, 'Rural development recognises however that improved food supplies and nutrition, together with basic services such as health and education, cannot only directly improve the physical well being and quality of the life of the rural poor, but can also indirectly enhance their productivity and their ability to contribute to the national economy' (World Bank, 1975b, p. 1).

From the above discussion it might be concluded that rural development and agricultural development are overlapping concepts. However, rural development refers to broader issues and is more specific than agricultural development, in that the former entails much more than the development of agricultural production. Rural development, therefore, is an interdisciplinary approach in which social and political factors interact with economic ones (Harriss, 1982, p. 15). Chambers (1983, p. 148) argues that increased production which leads to net impoverishment is not development. Production is a means, not an end, to enable the poorest to demand and control more of what they want and need.

Towards the end of the 1970s the World Bank, together with other international organisations such as the FAO and ILO, began to raise awareness of rural poverty and formulate policies for its alleviation, and sought to provide a wider and clearer definition of rural development:

> the Bank policy on agricultural development reflects both social and economic factors. It reflects the fact that the mass of the rural

poor in developing countries depend on agriculture for living. It also reflects the belief that unless projects have, as an explicit goal, the alleviation of poverty, little can be done to improve living conditions among the rural poor. Through rural development, the productivity and output of small farms can be raised and increased; rural development projects also provide added employment and earnings opportunities through their reliance on labour-intensive farming practices. Bank policies on agricultural development also reflect the belief that balanced development of urban and rural areas depends, in large measure, on the benefits of rural development reaching the rural poor (World Bank, 1978, p. 11).

From the late 1960s, along with the criticism of the technocratic development strategy, two major rural development strategies emerged: the reformist strategy and the radical strategy. A brief discussion of the characteristics of each of these may help to clarify the debate on rural development issues over two decades of development.

The reformist strategy was basically a compromise between the technocratic and radical strategies. The proponents of this strategy acknowledged that the benefit of distribution had proved inequitable, but stressed that the mistake did not lie in growth or in the unequal distribution of the means of production. Growth was still regarded as essential, and it was thought that an equal distribution of benefits could be achieved, not necessarily by restructuring the existing production relations, but by changing the agrarian institutions. However, the changes made to the rural power structure were marginal and the reform of agrarian institutions was generally partial and fragmented (Griffin, 1974; Heck, 1979; Aron, 1981). Therefore the green revolution, for example, was not fully rejected, but redesigned into an equity-oriented system (for instance, by providing subsidies, credit facilities and so on). The right to private land ownership was not abolished, only restricted; and equal income distribution, through organisations such as cooperatives, became the major objective. The gradual combining of cooperative, collective and state farming was considered the best way to achieve egalitarian growth.

The dominant ideology embodied in the reformist strategy was mostly nationalist, or occasionally populist. 'Though the bureaucracy is the main instrument of action, in certain cases attempts were made to ensure popular involvement in rural development, through political parties, local governments and cooperatives' (Aron, 1981, p. 485).

However, the main beneficiaries of this policy were the large and medium-sized landowners (Griffin, 1974; Heck, 1979). The policy resulted in the creation of a dualistic structure – the emergence of an enclave of large, modernised commercial farms within a national agrarian structure that was near-subsistence in character (Long, 1979; Aron, 1981).

During the shift from the technocratic approach to the reformist approach, considerable attention was paid to the success of the Chinese commune system in eliminating unequal distribution and unemployment (Aziz, 1978; World Bank, 1979). This attention, coupled with severe criticism of the technocratic growth strategy during the late 1960s and the 1970s, led to the elaboration of the 'radical strategy' for rural change.

The radical or egalitarian strategy was based on communist ideology and its main objective was to achieve rapid social change and a redistribution of political power. Social objectives were awarded greater priority than economic or technological considerations. Concerning agriculture, the main features of the radical strategy were the establishment of large collective or 'state' farms and the mobilisation of labour to increase agricultural production. Approximate equality was achieved by abolishing private land ownership and establishing large production units – collectives, communes and state farms. The major beneficiaries of the radical strategy were small peasants and landless labourers, but because of the low priority given to modern technology, overall growth was very low.

The poverty-eradication and distribution-oriented aspects of the reformist and radical strategies became absorbed into a more vigorous and comprehensive rural development strategy, or what is known in the literature as integrated rural development – that is, agricultural development plus distributive justice:

> Rural development is a strategy designed to improve the economic and social life of a specific group of people – the rural poor. It involves extending the benefits of development to the poorest among those who seek a livelihood in rural areas. The group includes small-scale farmers, tenants and the landless (World Bank, 1975b, p. 3).

The term rural development also refers 'to processes of change in rural societies' (Harriss, 1982, p. 16). The important question raised by this definition is what does 'processes of change' actually mean? The phenomenon of change has a number of dimensions (Lele, 1975; Silva, 1978; Harriss, 1982; Poostchi, 1986) that can be categorised as follows:

- An increase in agricultural productivity.
- A change in rural employment, unemployment and underemployment.
- A change in the distribution of wealth and income, as identified by changes in the income of different income groups and changes in the ownership of land.
- A change in the distribution of power and influence and participation in the process of rural change.
- A change in the mobility of the rural population.
- A change in welfare indicators.
- A change in the values, beliefs and attitudes of the members of state agencies and the rural population.

Another question provoked by the above definition is who instigates these changes? The processes of change involve government action, but 'state intervention is considered simply as one of the forces concerned – although it is one which has become of increasing importance' (Harriss, 1982, p. 16). However, any development strategy has to work through the national power structures: 'In most developing countries, it is only government which has the power and the means to create the conditions favourable to rural development' (Aron, 1982, p. 485). Even when rural development activities are carried out by international organisations they have to work through government channels. At the very least, they have to obtain the approval of governments before any intervention (Williams, 1982). However, the state's role differs according to the political philosophy or ideology that dominates its policies and actions. This in turn affects the degree of change, and may or may not lead to a significant change in society (Aron, 1982).

The dominant idea in all policy suggestions and approaches, as mentioned earlier, is that rural development is brought about by external agencies. The verb 'to develop' is often used transitively in development strategies, whether reformist or radical. In this sense development is induced or imposed. It is 'they' who 'extend' the benefits of development to the poorest sectors of society (Chambers, 1983, p. 147). This is a top-down approach. National governments and international agencies 'represent development as an impossibility without their intervention'; 'if external intervention did not take place there would be no development at all' (Heyer *et al.*, 1981, p. 1). The peasants are assumed to be unable to develop: they must be developed (Williams, 1982, p. 381); they are 'targets' or 'objects' rather than 'subjects' (Pearse, 1980; Wood, 1984; Wignaraja, 1991).

There is also a strong argument in favour of a bottom-up approach that is typified by 'development from within' and characterised by the concept of popular participation evolving from below. The major reason for the emergence of this approach was the growing awareness that no single strategy or model of rural development was applicable to all socioeconomic and cultural environments, so each society had to seek out strategies and approaches that were suitable to its own historical background, the current circumstances, available resources and, most importantly, local knowledge (Stravenhagen, 1975; Galli, 1981; Blomstrom and Hettne, 1984; Goulet, 1989; Taylor, 1992; Burkey, 1993).

Participation is sought as means of using the community as a vehicle for social change: 'to get the community to help itself'. In this sense participation is a return to tradition. Hence while modern institutions are designed to deal with rural problems, the traditional strategies of collective action and survival are being encouraged in an environment where traditionalism is considered a hindrance to social progress. In this sense the participation of the people is regarded not only as an end in itself, but also as a fundamental precondition for any successful development strategy. It is essential to bring the rural poor on to the centre stage of development.

'Participatory development' has become an established umbrella term for the new types of development in recent years (Griffin, 1979; Oakley and Marsden, 1984). Participation is regarded by its advocates as a means to reach the rural poor, by providing employment, using local resources and indigenous knowledge and limiting dependence on external sources of relief. In short, the process of participation is regarded as an indispensable and reliable means of making the largest possible number of people in the community the masters of their own development (Galtung *et al.*, 1980; Gran, 1983; Mathur, 1983; Lea and Chaudhri, 1985; Jazairy *et al.*, 1992). The aim is to empower people, as summarised in the ancient saying: 'Give people fish, and they can eat that day. Teach people to fish, and they can eat for the rest of their lives' (Korten and Alfonso, 1983, p. 60).

Support for the participatory approach arose from the negative impact of a quarter century of development on large numbers of poor people, and the impact of the first generation of positive experiments at the grass roots level. For example a study by the Agency for International Development (1975) of 36 rural development projects in 11 African and Latin American countries revealed a clear connection between project success and small farmers' involvement in decision making and resource commitment to the project. Hickey and Flamming's (1977) study in the Philippines, Korten's (1982) in Mexico, Uphoff's (1982) in Sri Lanka and Mlay's (1985) in Tanzania all came to similar conclusions about participation. In the wake of these successes, the need to incorporate popular participation into rural development policies gained worldwide attention. For example the World Bank (1978) outlined four requirements for an effective rural development strategy, of which one was the participation of the rural poor in the planning and implementation process through local government, project advisory committee cooperatives and other forms of group organisation.

The theoretical basis was brought about by the general shift from positivist paradigms in the social sciences to new alternatives in which practical engagement with people and local communities, openness to complexity and diversity is regarded as the prime turning point in research. It supports methodological pluralism and democratic local diversity. Post-modernism and populism can be seen as a new theoretical shift from traditional ideas on social change and development (Wignaraja, 1991; Corbridge, 1994; Long and Douwe, 1994; Pretty, 1995). Populism emphasises the poor, especially the rural poor in the Third World. Post-modernism is concerned to challenge the possibility of any single site of representation. Rather it advocates a plurality of voices and representations, including those who were long defined as marginal to the march of progress but are now encouraged to put forward accounts of their own circumstances and aspirations. Instead of a monolithic political modernisation or socialist struggle, such approaches stress a multiplicity of methods of action that consider the needs and experiences of very different social groups: women, the landless, migrant workers, ethnic minorities and so on. The central point was put forward by Foucault. According to him, the acquisition of power over mass population through powers of human sciences and the state marked the advent of modernity. Having traced genealogies of modernity, he recognises that 'the procedures of power', or the myriad techniques of social controlling that he labels 'disciplines', reduce the body and mind of individuals through scientific classification and objectification to things, enabling their powers to be spatialised and mobilised more rationally (Luke, 1990, pp. 242–3).

The above shifts reflect the reversal from top-down to bottom-up policy making, from centralised standardisation to local diversity, from blueprints to a learning process. Related to these ideas, changes have begun to be made to the modes of learning. An attempt has been made by some scholars, for example Chambers (1987, 1993, 1994a) and Wignaraja (1991), to theorise participation as a new discipline. In this regard 'the crisis of the modern knowledge system confirms the need for devising new methods of scientific inquiry' (Wignaraja, 1991, p. 207). 'The move here is away from extractive survey questionnaires and toward new approaches and methods for participatory appraisal and analysis in which more of activities previously appropriated by outsiders are instead carried out by local rural or urban people themselves' (Chambers, 1994b, p. 953). The basic assumptions behind these approaches are that:

- poor people are creative and capable, and can and should do much of their own investigation;
- in analysis and planning, the weak and marginalised can and should be empowered;
- outsiders have roles as conveners, catalysts and facilitators;
- all actors – local people, planners, researchers, agencies and so on – constitute a 'knowledge system' in which: (1) local people share knowledge among themselves, especially through analysis in groups and visual presentations; (2) local people share that knowledge with outsiders; and (3) outsiders share what they learn with each other and with local people (Chambers, 1995a; Thomson, 1995).

From the above we can conclude that participatory development is the process of involving people in the various stages of development programmes such as decision making, implementation, evaluation and sharing the benefits (Oakley and Marsden, 1984). The ultimate aim of participation is to empower people by providing them with the opportunity to build up their capacities – 'to move from the status of objects, and passivity (that is the status in which people are manipulated by external forces) to the status of subjects (guided by self-conciousness)' (Wignaraja, 1994, p. 226).

The main problem is the difficulty of bringing about an authentically indigenous, people-initiated form of development. Despite the emphasis of the participatory approach and the recommendations of international organisations and development scholars, in the Third World most participatory development programmes have been formulated and monitored by what could still be termed outside agencies. Such outside agencies include the state, bureaucrats, administrators, foreign advisers and foreign development agencies (Wassertrom, 1985). Thus changes often do not emerge from people at the grass roots level, but from those who hold political power and who, for a variety of reasons, are likely to make a different assessment of development needs from that made by the local inhabitants themselves.

The important questions that have emerged from the debate are: whether decision makers actually intend to affect change in favour of the underclasses, and whether changes have actually improved the living conditions of the rural poor. These are the main themes of this book.

Rural development and inequality

Improving the status of rural people has long been the goal of governments, local organisations and international agencies when introducing institutional transformation programmes, technocratic strategies, social programmes, economic incentive systems such as guaranteed price schemes, and massive doses of capital investment in modern infrastructure. Some improvements can be credited to these strategies, including increased food production and the availability of goods and services over large areas. More rural people now have access to education, health services, information and material benefits, leading to improvements in the aggregate indicators of socioeconomic well-being. Today, rural communities also have relatively greater access to modern industrial products and better services. There are increased opportunities to improve the quality of life in rural areas because the industrial sector, through technological progress, is able to supply a broad array of resources to people that enable them to meet their needs. The modernisation of agriculture and the implementation of rural programmes – particularly technocratic ones such as the 'green revolution' – have resulted in improved production by farming families and made it possible for them to produce a surplus, the profits from which can be used to obtain the services and products of the service and industrial sectors.

All of this has contributed to an improvement in rural life at the aggregate level, but a closer look at rural life reveals a somewhat different picture. Although the aggregate level of production and consumption has increased, the distribution of benefits has remained inequal (Griffin, 1974; Ladejinsky, 1977; Morrison *et al.*, 1979; Gibbons *et al.*, 1980; Preston, 1980; Griffin and Khan, 1982; Sarma, 1982; Lea and

Chaudhri, 1983; Howe and Richard, 1984; Grindle, 1986; Nabi *et al.*, 1986; Nazir, 1991; Jazairy *et al.*, 1992). The expected 'trickle down effects' – such as the elimination of poverty and inequality, and sustained growth that would ensure the fulfilment of human needs – have never materialised. Haymai and Ruttan (1971) state that economic growth in developing countries has largely been accompanied by near stagnation, growing inequality and absolute poverty in rural areas. A study of the movement of key social indicators for the highest and lowest 20 countries, as measured by the annual GNP per capita growth rate in the period 1965–88, found 'some improvements . . . among both groups of countries. However, it is clear that in both groups many rural populations continue to be deprived of some basic amenities' (Jazairy *et al.*, 1992, p. 8). The change in rural development strategies and approaches over the past decades and their orientation towards the alleviation of rural poverty and improvement of the quality of life is a good indication of the failure of several decades of development efforts to improve the socioeconomic well-being of people in rural areas.

Even structural changes such as land redistribution have not resulted in the eradication of unemployment, poverty, malnutrition and the unequal distribution of the means of production. Decades of rural development efforts appear to have resulted in the coexistence of extreme poverty and the greater affluence enjoyed in some rural areas.

Although radical rural reform policies such as land reform, community development, Ujama villages, etc., have been based on egalitarian ideology and have emphasised structural change in rural areas, in practice they have seldom approached to these ideals. Rich peasants have been the major beneficiaries of such policies. As a distinct class, they have been capable to reinforce their own class interests and their own political power.

Reviewing the literature on Sierra Leone, Mexico, India and Egypt, Migdal (1988) found that rural development efforts had reinforced the position of implementors, regional politicians and rural strong men – landlords, rich peasants and moneylenders. From a more optimistic perspective, rural development programmes in general and the modernisation of traditional agriculture in particular, via external agencies, have improved conditions in rural areas, although only in certain respects, such as improved aggregate well-being and increased equality in terms of material inputs and resources within communities. However, the adverse effects have been many (Griffin, 1974; Pearse,

1980. Some researchers (Wood, 1984; Migdal, 1988) state that even government programmes that have addressed the welfare of rural people, as well as rural infrastructure, mass communication and education, have most benefited those who were already better off. In addition, areas where greater development efforts have been concentrated have, as a result of concerted government action, achieved higher levels of aggregate well-being, but have continued to experience both regional inequality and intracommunity inequality. This is particularly apparent in areas where technocratic strategies have been implemented (Griffin, 1974, 1982; Ladejinsky, 1977; Gibbons *et al.*, 1980; Preston, 1980; Byres, 1982; Howe and Richard, 1984; Grindle, 1986; Nabi *et al.*, 1986; Nazir, 1991).

A question that might be raised here is why government policies for rural and agricultural development that combine a number of objectives – the most explicit being increased productivity, a marketable surplus, equality, redistribution, rural employment, political participation, basic need provision and a reduction in emigration from rural areas (Wood, 1984) – provide neither equal treatment nor egalitarian allocation of resources? Why does actual practice diverge from the stated objectives?

The literature on this point is sharply divided along ideological lines into two main camps: modernisation theory versus critical theory. Each tradition provides a different explanation of the problem.

Modernisation theory provides a functional analysis of issues relating to rural change. According to this perspective, during the process of change, social differentiation, stratification and inequalities are normal, necessary and inevitable occurrences, but the process of modernisation gradually begins to benefit the lower strata of society. Likewise regional and other spatial disparities are unfortunate, but inevitable and transitory (Berry, 1984). According to Perroux (1955), growth does not appear everywhere at the same time, but rather manifests itself in certain places, or poles of growth, in varying degrees, and spreads through different channels and with variable effects for the economy as a whole. According to Friedmann (1981 pp. 28–9), economic growth tends to occur in the location where potential conditions for economic development exist: 'The location decisions of most firms, including those in agriculture, are made with reference to cities or urban regions.' Cities and city regions have been identified as the catalysts for development, which eventually spreads throughout the country to even the smallest villages.

Hence the agonies of modernisation are many, but in the long run modernisation is not only inevitable but also desirable. It is a lengthy process. It is an evolutionary change, not a revolutionary change. It takes generations to complete, and its ultimate impact – an affluent and egalitarian society – will only be felt in time (Huntington, 1976). From the point of view of modernisation theory, any attempt to accelerate this process is beneficial. Accordingly, the development apparatus and development agencies are part of a great collective effort to fight poverty and raise living standards, and so are a potential force for progress (Myrdal, 1970). Development planning should be understood as 'mankind's most ambitious collective enterprise', and the activities of nation-states as attempts to create an 'ideal world' (Robertson, 1984, cited in Ferguson, 1990, p. 10).

The critical perspective adopts a holistic approach to the study of social change and the relationship between different social phenomena. It sees rural communities, urban centres, developing nations and developed nations as forming an interrelated world system, each segment of which has an influence on the other. Thus each component must be studied in relation to the others, characterised by relationships that are often asymmetrical in respect of their historical background (Wallerstein, 1964, 1987).

The uneven development of regions within a country is viewed as the result of 'internal colonialism'. The development of certain regions is possible due to the transfer of resources to these areas from others, which remain underdeveloped. According to this perspective, inequality and uneven development within a nation are intrinsic to capitalist development. This asymmetry results in inequality and the impoverishment of the majority of people in rural areas (Frank, 1969, 1978; Amin, 1976).

Regional inequalities are viewed by some critical theorists as necessary or inevitable within capitalist development because they are a consequence of the logic of capitalist production (Amin, 1974b; Hechter, 1975; Hartwing, 1978; Browett, 1984). Rural development efforts, at most, attempt to prevent social tension in the countryside by making limited improvements to the means of production (de Janvry, 1981). Rural development projects are thus seen as instruments of social control.

According to this approach, capitalism and any attempt to modernise within its framework 'is not the cause of development but the obstacle to it, not the cure for poverty but the cause of it' (Ferguson, 1990, p. 11). Any development project within a capitalist system involves the promotion of capitalist relations, reinforcing the system and working against radical social change. Thus it cannot be an instrument for development, or at least not real development.

It is of utmost importance to move the discussion on development and rural change from macroanalysis – beyond the question of whether it is a 'good thing' or a 'bad' thing', whether it generates equality or inequality – to microanalysis and consideration of the mechanisms that give rise to the deviation of rural development programmes from their original objectives. The point to be emphasised here is that both the development perspective and the critical perspective accept that rural development programmes do in fact bring about some degree of development and economic transformation.

Inspired by the political economy tradition, the second point to be emphasised is that rural development involves a complex set of institutions and initiatives that encompass 'multiple, and often contradictory, interests' (Heyer *et al.*, 1981). The interested agents are many and they may be classes, national governments, individuals or bureaucracies. For the purpose of this study, two main agents are examined: the peasantry or rural people and the rural development administration. The interaction of these two is also considered. These agents affect the distribution of the benefits of rural development programmes.

Before discussing these points it is necessary briefly to consider two basic factors in the divergence of rural programmes from their objectives: the nature of the economic and political structures, and administrative deficiencies. The political structure consists of a range of substructures from the top level (government) to the local level (villages). At the same time, unified interest groups influence rural programmes from formulation to implementation.

The focus here is on the dominance of rural and urban elites at different institutional and organisational levels. As the experience of many developed countries has shown, these elites have played a considerable part in bringing agrarian policies to the fore for specific groups or, conversely, undermining the implementation of redistribution policies (Alavi, 1976; Frankel, 1978; Wood, 1984; Sims, 1988; Sarker, 1990). Distortion of reformist programmes at the decision-making and particularly at the implementation level does not take place without the cognizance of state decision makers. For example India's Panchayat Raj cooperative programme was aimed at establishing a direct link between the state and the peasantry without the involvement of intermediaries. However, rich peasants with direct representation in the Congress Party were afraid of this reform, resulting in a divergence of the formal contens from the actual achievements (Alavi, 1976; Bertocci, 10970, 1976; Khan, 1989; Migdal, 1988; Von Freyhold, 1977; Westergaard, 1985.) Similarly, failure to implement the radical land reform programme after the revolution in Iran, in spite of pressure from various political factions and the peasantry, was due partly to Islamic legal constraints but mainly to the dominance of landed interests in the state apparatus.

Thus even the implementation of redistribution programmes faces obstacles. Under the prevailing socioeconomic and political structures of rural society, an honest, efficient and ideologically committed bureaucracy is required for the effective implementation of egalitarian programmes (Sandbrook, 1982; Sarker, 1990). In the majority of Third World countries such a bureaucracy has been rare or absent, and if present it has not been sustainable. The past performance of the rural development bureaucracy has engendered doubts about the possibility of achieving the objectives of redistribution programmes.

The problem of access: the relationship between the bureaucracy and the peasantry

Access is defined as 'the relation between the administrative allocation of goods and services and the people who need them or for whom they are intended' (Schaffer and Lamb, 1974, p. 73). The main philosophy behind state intervention in the distribution of resources originates from the fact that markets in rural economies are very seldom perfect, and rural economies often suffer from an unfair market system. Accordingly other systems of distribution make access problematic, essentially because the target groups are in a weak market position (Schaffer, 1980, Harriss, 1982; Wood, 1984). 'Access becomes important where the state intervenes to affect the supply and demand of resources so that their allocation depends less, or not at all, on market or traditional allocation mechanisms' (Wood, 1984, p. 343). Access, therefore, is a mediatory instrument that characterises the relationship between people and services distributed by outside institutions.

Access has at least four components: (1) access to information; (2) access to inputs; (3) access to markets; and (4) access to social services (Huda, 1983, pp. 44–5). All these components are interrelated, and access to one could affect access to the others. Another important feature of access is that it has a preventive aspect, in the sense that small-farmer development programmes are difficult to administer because it is not possible to secure access in perpetuity.

The key determinants of access are education, ownership of the means of production and so on. These provide people with a secure and continuous income, which helps them to buy goods and services that add to their ability to generate further income. Furthermore the economic diversification that results from the process of rural development helps the rich to forge links with urban elites. These factors combine to enable the richer sections to gain access to all the components listed above, but small farmers, because of their precarious position in the social structure, do not have access to all these components. For instance small farmers may be informed about improved agricultural practices, but they are denied access to crucial inputs; the unequal social structure prevents them from securing a proper share of the resources. It is neither lack of innovation nor lack of motivation but rather inadequate opportunities that crucially affect small farmers (Griffin, 1979).

Another facet of access is related to institutional arrangements. The non-market allocation of resources requires institutional provision and bureaucratic procedures. This engenders several problems such as the problem of allocating resources and the difficulty of establishing organisational connections and links between clients and institutions (Schaffer and Lamb, 1974; Schaffer, 1980). The central problems are, first, that public institutions are not neutral arenas, and second, that bureaucratic systems of allocation are not themselves perfect.

For all institutions a three-dimensional process typifies the links between clients and the bureaucracy:

- Entrance: the claimant or client must demonstrate eligibility.
- Queue: an order of priority is established in cases where resources are scarce.
- Contact: face-to-face contact between official and client, where the former may have wide discretion in determining the client's level of need, and therefore entitlement to benefit (Smith, 1988, p. 82).

One problem with non-market or bureaucracy-based systems of distribution is the set of rules by which the eligibility of individual clients to receive the services of the institutions is determined. In the beginning the provision of services hinges on inclusion or exclusion. Some people are able to negotiate the entrance, queue and contact process to secure scarce resources, but some people are not, owing to their inferior position in the social hierarchy (Schaffer and Lamb, 1974). The problem is exacerbated when there are a multitude of entrances and queues to negotiate. Lower-class claimants do not have the necessary resources to do so, but the problem can be bypassed by the rich through such means as political pressure, bribery, exploitation of class position and nepotism (Smith, 1988, p. 186).

Even when the total package for agricultural improvement is provided by the government to small farmers, administrative allocation is not a matter of general goodwill but is controlled by factors such as ownership of the means of production, market access, power, knowledge, status and influence (Huda, 1983, p. 72), as well as physiological stamina, the geographical position of the community in which the farmer lives (proximity to roads and so on), and the quantity and quality of land.

All of these factors are interlinked and constitute a complex system that may be termed the 'access constellation' or 'potential developmental conditions'. They may affect the distribution of benefits of development policies. Evidence from many developing countries indicates that distribution of the above factors is highly unequal and people do not have equal access to developmental resources (Byres, 1982; Griffin and Khan, 1982; Clayton, 1983). Many authors have come to the conclusion that under the existing social structure, even with greater governmental and non-governmental effort, intracommunity inequality may rise (Griffin, 1979; Gibbons *et al.*, 1980; Galli, 1981; Huda, 1983; Krinks, 1983; Grindle, 1986; Nazir, 1991).

Conclusion

This brief sketch of the concept and dimensions of modernisation – extracted from the experience of Western industrialised societies – has provided us with a definition of modernisation: the transition from economic, political and social structures that are traditional or underdeveloped to those that are modern or developed. Hence a modernised society can be identified by increased production, innovation, efficiency and a high capacity for problem solving, all of which serve substantially to improve the material well-being of the people. Modernisation in developing countries can be promoted through ties with external forces – that is, developed societies.

The discussion on the modernisation of agriculture indicates that the process involves a gradual transition from subsistence farming to differentiated structures and specialised production. The type of agricultural development that is undertaken in most cases is one that encourages market participation in order to increase production, thus raising personal income for the purpose of purchasing inputs and technology. This can be seen as an attempt to replace subsistence farming with capitalist farming. Adoption and diffusion are the main mechanisms for connecting the rural economy to the outside world. Intervention, usually by governments within the framework of rural or agricultural development strategies, is an important factor in the acceleration of this process and depends on the political ideology of the government and overall thinking on social development.

In general, a review of the literature reveals that the following trends in both general development and rural development approaches and strategies during the past decades have been dominant:

- Reorientation from an economic to an interdisciplinary framework.
- Reorientation from a Eurocentric perspective to a perspective that incorporates factors particular to the Third World.
- Growing recognition of the structural determinants of societal conditions and the way they influence change.
- A shift in focus from the macro level to the micro, from the top-down approach to the bottom-up approach.

The main question to arise from the review of the literature was whether the rural development efforts have improved the circumstances of rural people, including the poor. Several decades of rural development efforts have had positive consequences, but in many cases they have resulted in poverty and inequality. The explanation for this differs according to the level of analysis and the theoretical perspective. The best known explanations can be separated into two main camps: modernisation theory and critical theory. The former applies a functionalist analysis to the problem, seeing differentiation and inequality as necessary and inevitable but temporary phenomena that are eliminable in the long term. The latter adopts more a holistic approach and provides a historical explanation for the underdevelopment of developing countries in general and rural areas in particular. According to this perspective, inequality and poverty are intrinsic to capitalist development, which is based on asymmetrical relationships. However, both perspectives agree that development efforts at least bring about some sort of change.

Beyond these two main perspectives, another explanation has been developed, based on an examination of the role and interaction of agents in the distribution of the benefits of rural programmes. The main emphasis is on the theory of access and the relationship between the bureaucracy and the peasantry. Access appears significant when the allocation of resources is affected by state intervention through bureaucratic channels. Such intervention is due mainly to the imperfection of the market in rural economies. Two factors are significant in the process of intervention. One is concerned with the fact that bureaucratic systems of allocation are themselves imperfect in the sense that the provision of services begins with a process of inclusion or exclusion. Some people are able to negotiate or bypass the barriers to scarce resources and some are not, thereby falling into an inferior position in the social hierarchy. The second factor is called the access constellation (or potential development conditions), which is based on the preexisting social structures or is created in the process of resource allocation. The access constellation involves a range of additional factors, such as land ownership access to power and knowledge, geographical position and the physiological state of the individual, all of which govern the individual's ability to aquire services. Given that there are marked differences in social and economic relations and the ability of individuals to gain access to and make effective use of resources, all too often development efforts benefit those who can gain access to resources to the detriment to those who cannot, resulting in increased intra- and intercommunity inequality.

In this book rural development refers to the process of change. Two dimensions of change are considered: the degree to which rural communities are changed by the implementation of rural development programmes; and the degree of inequality the change causes among the members of the community (villagers).

Areas that receive more rural development assistance experience more change, and usually an increase in social stratifications. But due to the benefits that elites and the better off derive from rural programmes and modern technology, the aggregate level of production and incomes increases.

2
Historical Background

Introduction

This chapter provides a historical review of agrarian relations and rural change in prerevolutionary Iran. The discussion covers two distinct periods. During the first period – from the middle of the nineteenth century to the Shah's White Revolution (1962) – changes took place as a result either of the influence of the West and the demands of world capitalism, or of overall state policy within the modernisation framework. During the second period – from 1962 to the Islamic Revolution – rural development programmes took place alongside land reforms.

In order to understand the nature of agrarian change and rural development policies, the chapter first provides a brief description of the structure of the political economy and the transformation of the state.

Sociopolitical and economic developments from the mid nineteenth century to 1962

The nineteenth century and the first half of the twentieth century are viewed as a transitional period (Issawi, 1971; Keddie, 1981; Abrahamian, 1982) which important transformations took place in the socioeconomic structure of Iran under the impact of Western capitalism. This gave rise to the emergence of new institutions and interest groups that interacted with the old structures, which in turn set the stage for changes in agrarian relations and rural development.

During the nineteenth century the fundamental impetus behind these changes was the gradual integration of Iran into the world economy. This was accompanied by a slow but steady growth in output, market expansion and an exchange economy (Issawi, 1971;

Katouzian, 1981; Keddie, 1981). With the 1928 treaty with Russia, and similar treaties with other trading partners, the state lost its autonomy in respect of tariffs. Under the terms of these treaties all imports and exports were subject to a single 5 per cent customs duty, and foreign merchants were exempt from all inland and transit duties (Issawi, 1971, p. 73). From the early nineteenth century until the start of the First World War there was rapid growth in foreign trade, and this high growth resumed from the 1950s onwards.

The structure of foreign trade reveals the part played by Iran in the world division of labour. By the turn of the twentieth century imports were totally dominated by manufactured products – mainly textiles, which along with tea and sugar constituted over 80 per cent of imports. Exports, with the exception of carpets, consisted of raw agricultural products (Issawi, 1971; Karshenas, 1990; Shakoori, 1991).

As far as this study is concerned, two interrelated effects can be identified as consequences of the adoption of the capitalist exchange system by Iran.

Structural convergence between Iran and the West

The essence of structural convergence was the adoption of a Western-style constitutional government. The weakness of the state was the result of internal factors, but this was exacerbated by Iran's defeat by two imperial powers (Britain and Russia), involving heavy territorial losses, increasing interference by and rivalry between these two powers, and Iran's subordination to the position of a quasi-colony. European penetration was accompanied by the granting of a series of concessionary rights to foreign powers by the ruler, who enjoyed theoretical ownership of all resources. These concessions were unpopular in Iran and resulted in a rise in nationalism and anti-imperialism.

During the nineteenth century, two attempts were made to reform the traditional state apparatus. The first attempt involved the establishment of a modern professional army, which was an immediate response to the military and technological superiority of the West. The second involved the restructuring of the entire state apparatus on the Western model. These reforms were designed and carried out by a small group of bureaucratic elites. There was no socioeconomic reform apart from the restructuring of the state machinery. The state administration remained as it was, mainly because of strong resistance from traditional officials whose interests were endangered by the reforms, which led to the total breakdown of the state's authority and legitimacy. The gradual dissolution of government, which had begun in the mid nineteenth century, finally resulted in the constitutional revolution (1906–11). This revolution can be seen as marking the start of the formation of the modern nation-state of Iran. The process continued under the reign of Reza Shah (1925–41).

It is worth mentioning that the main reason why various social groups with different interests united to campaign for a constitution was the perceived need for a change in the existing political structure, which was seen as a major obstacle to the progress of society. A constitution, it was thought, would remedy the deep economic crisis and provide a cornerstone for future economic development (Adamiyat, 1976; Katouzian, 1981; Abrahamian, 1982). However the initial attempts by revolutionaries to introduce constitutional institutions, such as a centralised state apparatus and a national assembly, were unsuccessful due to strong resistance by internal forces – counterrevolutionaries led by Mohammed Ali Shah – and the intervention of external forces: the occupation of the country by Russia and later by Britain. So instead the country experienced economic crisis and political chaos. This situation and the emergence of the oil sector as a major source of foreign exchange and state revenue helped strengthen the centralised authoritarian regime of Reza Shah. The political and economic chaos prompted a temporary coalition of conservative forces – the clergy–landlord–merchant oligarchy, together with traditional government elites and many intellectuals – and allowed the formation of a strong centralised state. The oil revenues enabled the state to implement some infrastructural programmes and finance the modern military and bureaucratic machinery, which served to make the centralisation of power more effective. As Katouzian (1973, p. 223) argues, 'the [constitutional] revolution might have finally broken up the absolute and arbitrary power of the state, had it not been for discovery of oil almost at the same time'.

The existence of this centralised and unified bureaucratic machinery in a predominantly precapitalist economy with a diversity of sociopolitical structures, and most importantly the new income from oil, allowed the separation of the state from the land-based economy and the relative autonomy of the state from the economically powerful classes (Katouzian, 1981; Karshenas, 1990). However the most important factor in the rise of state autonomy and its authoritarian character was that the traditional classes had been unable to resolve the country's socioeconomic crisis or play a decisive political role during the previous decades (Bashiriyeh, 1986; Karshenas, 1990). This led to the state taking a direct role in restructuring society.

In spite of its extensive bureaucratic-military organisation, the regime suffered from a lack of urban civilian support. This could be one important reason for the weakness of the regime against the large landlords. The consequence was a sort of political compromise and a division of rule in the sense that the landlords gave the Shah total control over the state machinery, and in return the state did not intervene in agrarian relations (Karshenas, 1990). This seems to be one of the main reasons why the land reform programme was never implemented in the Reza Shah period.

During this period Iran experienced economic growth and infrastructural modernisation, but the failure to establish a democratic government and the implementation of some 'pseudo-modernist' programmes gave rise to potent internal tensions.

The regime's pursuit of close political and economic relations with Germany to counterbalance British and Russian pressures, and the subsequent outbreak of the Second World War, led to the abdication of Reza Shah in 1941. This was followed by a temporary change in the balance of power that led to the Anglo-Iranian dispute in the early 1950s. In 1953 Mossadiq's national-democratic government was overthrown by a CIA-backed coup. Gradually power returned 'to where it has traditionally belonged' (Katouzian, 1973).

One important aspect of the structural convergence was the commercialisation of agriculture and a change in agrarian relations, which due to its significance for this study will be discussed separately.

Partial divergence

Discontent with the incorporation of Iranian society into Western capitalism and the process of structural convergence led to the emergence of Iranian nationalism among three groups. First, in the bazaars the petty commodity mode of production was being undermined by Western penetration. As a result the traditional petit bourgeoisie emerged as the bastion of nationalism and resistance against Western influence. Second, most of the intelligentsia were influenced by Western ideas of political liberation and wished to find a way to change the despotic political system and preserve the sovereignty of the country. Third, the expansion of Western capitalism and its political and cultural consequences alarmed the *ulama* (clergy) (Keddie, 1981; Bashiriyeh, 1984; Parsa, 1989; Moaddle, 1992). The *ulama*'s opposition to Western influence, along with other socioeconomic forces, gave Iranian nationalism its Islamic character (Bashiriyeh, 1984). In the constitutional revolution the authority of the *ulama* and the supremacy of the laws of Islam were reorganised, but the *ulama*'s opposition to the state led to a doctrinal rethinking. Withdrawing their legitimisation of the absolutist shahs due to the granting of concessions to foreigners, the majority of the *ulama* favoured limited monarchy and emerged as the leaders of the indigenous nationalist movement. To clarify the role of the *ulama* in the development of society it is important to analyse briefly their nature and their relationship with the state and society.

Traditionally, there was always a close alliance between the merchants and the *ulama*. The former were the main source of religious taxes, which enabled the religious establishment to be financially independent of the state. The *ulama* also played a significant part in the moral, intellectual and political lives of the merchants. Merchants lacked the power to oppose the state, so did so under the umbrella of the *ulama*, who sanctified their protests and protected them against the state.

The *ulama*'s independence from the state theoretically posed a threat to state authority, according to the terms of the Shiite doctrine of imamate (Enayat, 1982; Momen, 1983). However in the main the *ulama* cooperated with successive rulers because the latter enjoyed greater power. The Safavids (1501–1737) were the first Shiite rulers of Iran and declared themselves as descendants of imams, and therefore the *ulama* could not claim sole right to divine legitimacy.

Unlike the Safavids, who combined political and religious authority, the Qajars (1796–1925) had no claim to direct religious authority and under their rule, owing to a functional differentiation of the structure of authority, religious and political powers became separated (Enayat, 1982; Momen, 1983). During the Qajar period the *ulama* were supported by the shahs and extended their sphere of influence into the courts, *vaqf* (private and religious endowments) lands, tax collection and so on. These activities resulted in the *ulama* building up their own retinue and two kinds of leadership began to emerge in Iranian society: leadership by the government, with the monarch in charge; and leadership by the *ulama* on behalf of local populations. Any *ulama* opposition to the state was nationalist in character rather than based on doctrinal disputes (Fisher, 1980; Bashiriyeh, 1984).

In the 1920s Reza Shah's modernisation policies reduced the *ulama*'s influence and resulted in their political and social marginalisation. They became increasingly subordinate to the new bureaucracy, prompting them to form alliances with other social groups and eventually leading to their active engagement in the 1962 protest and the revolution of 1979.

In summary, then, the constitutional revolution did not lead to a stable, liberal-democratic regime; instead the country was subjected to authoritarian rule and recurrent economic and political crises. The inability of successive governments to deal with these crises strengthened the cultural–religious alliance, which functioned as the ideological base for protest against the state's Western-oriented approach.

Rural society and the agrarian structure

Before discussing rural society and agrarian relations in the late nineteenth century it may be helpful to look at the basic structure of rural society before the land reform.

Iranian villages were typically small, independent units of production. In most parts of the country, villages consisted of households with traditional cultivation rights (the *nasagh*-holders), households without such rights (the *khushnishins*) and a number of tradesmen and moneylenders. Most villages were almost self-sufficient and the use of new technology in agriculture was rare. Villages in most parts of the country included a few traditional group organisations (*boneh*) because water was a scarce resource and the irrigation system required teamwork (for details see Safinazhad, 1971). The basis of village organisation was *nasagh*, the traditional right to exploit the village's arable land and water resources.

The most important feature of land ownership before the land reform was large-scale proprietorship. According to one estimate, just 37 families owned 19 000 villages (around 38 per cent of the total), whilst another group of medium-sized landowners owned between one and five villages each, adding up to 7000 villages or 14 per cent of the total (Halliday, 1979, pp. 106–7). Large-scale land ownership was predominantly a mixture of public and private. The major types of land ownership were *Khaleseh* or public land (state-owned), crown land, *vaqf* or religious endowments, *Omdeh-Maleki* (land and villages owned by major landlords), *Khordeh-Maleki* (village ownership by two or more individuals), and collective ownership of tribal pastures (usually by nomadic people) (Lambton, 1953). In 1960 state land accounted for 10 per cent of the total, crown land 4 per cent, *vaqf* land 10 per cent and private land 76 per cent (Danesh, 1992, p. 161).

The landlord's business dealings with the village community (the landlord might be a land assignee, the state or the trustees of a charitable trust) were conducted by his local agents. Given that most landlords were absentees, they were considered to be outsiders.

The traditional method of product distribution was based on sharecropping, but the share taken by the peasant was subject to state tax, religious dues and the settlement of debt obligations, which meant there was little marketable surplus (Nomani, 1977; Hooglund, 1982). Likewise the dominance of sharecropping over other forms of farming hindered the development of large-scale agricultural production. For instance before the land reforms about 60 per cent of the total 11.4 million hectares of cultivated land in Iran was used for various forms of sharecropping, and close to 40 per cent of the 1.9 million farming units were organised into a sharecropping tenure system (Danesh, 1992, p. 154).

Generally speaking the internal socioeconomic structure and external circumstances (geographical, politico-economic, historical) meant that Iranian villagers had few links with the outside world (neither other villages nor the state) and very little contact with urban-based state functionaries (Farazmand, 1989). (For details of the inward looking nature of the Iranian peasantry and its consequences see Kazemi and Abrahamian 1978. For further information on the effect of the political structure on the underdevelopment of society see Ashraf, 1978 and Katouzian, 1980.) Nevertheless the state was dependent on the villages for taxes, food and military recruits, with landlords acting as intermediaries (Ashraf, 1978; Kazemi and Abrahamian, 1978; Farazmand, 1989). Katouzian (1981, p. 299) views this as 'the likely origin of the despotic state'. He argues that the peasantry served 'two major (social and historical) functions: it was exploited by the cities through the despotic state and its dependents; and it helped preserve the basic cultural continuity of the land, in spite of periodic internal upheavals (which are a part of the "logic" of despotism) as well as external invasions and raids' (ibid., pp. 299–330).

Before the land reforms the principal changes in rural society and agrarian relations were part of the overall process of adapting to world capitalism and the integration of the Iranian economy into the world capitalist system through trade. One aspect of this was the appearance of certain features of capitalist agriculture, namely the commercialisation of agriculture and the commodification of land in response to foreign demand for certain crops, which turned parts of the country into specialised production areas (for example opium was cultivated in the south and cotton was cultivated in the north: see Keddie, 1960).

The commercialisation of agriculture in the late nineteenth century had the following effects on the agrarian structure and the countryside.

First, it introduced large-scale landholding institutions and landlordism. As Keddie (1960, p. 367) points out, 'Western influence brought a gradual development of modern private property in the place of the various forms of feudal tenure that had previously existed'. This situation favoured feudal landlords and nomadic leaders, who took advantage of the economic changes brought by Western capitalism to enhance their position. They also managed to turn traditional and conditional land assignments (*tuyul*) into unconditional private property (Lambton, 1953; Keddie, 1960). This happened alongside the dissolution of the traditional state as a result of the influence of the West and the financial crisis of the period, caused by the defeat of Iran in its wars with Russia and Britain. The struggle between the latter for influence in Iran weakened state control over tribal areas and some of the fief lands, resulting in a loss of tax revenue from these areas. Furthermore the central government was in constant and acute need of money to buy Western goods, including arms to defend itself. All of these factors led to the large-scale sale of state land and the systematic sale of offices.

The growing profitability of cash crops (such as cotton, tobacco and opium) for export made the ownership of land and *tuyul* attractive to government officials and local landholders (Lambton, 1953). In addition the ability to buy state land and the potential profits from it attracted many outsiders, for example members of the merchant class and other rich city dwellers (Keddie, 1960; Khamsi, 1969; Issawi, 1971). The entry of these people to the landholding class led to the unification of their interests with those of the traditional landowning class. (For details on class formation see Lambton, 1953; Keddie, 1960, 1968; Karshenas, 1990.) This, it can be argued, was a significant reason for the lack of fundamental reform of the agrarian structure until the land reform. Even during the constitutional revolution, which could be seen as a major force for reform due to this unification of interests and the significant role of these social groups in the leadership of the revolution, reform of the land tenure system was not put on the government agenda (Katouzian, 1973).

The second effect of the commercialisation of agriculture was a change in peasant–landlord relations and a worsening of the peasantry's living conditions. This was mainly because of the emergence of landlordism and its direct consequence: the subordination of the peasants to their overexploitation by the landlord. It is worth noting that the monarch was historically seen as the owner of all land and he assigned it to his subjects as a grant. The subjects had legal possession but not ownership of the property. The main reason for perpetuating this kind of land tenure was the fluidity of political power and its cyclical change. It is worth noting that Iranian society, particularly between the thirteenth and nineteenth centuries, experienced a system of tribal-based dynastic cyclical change. The prevalence of pastoral nomadism formed a distinguishing feature of the society during this period, and the military potentials of nomads shaped the backbone of the rise of various tribal dynasties. The perpetual rise and fall of various tribal dynasties led to an unstable political configuration. Given the direct involvement of the state in the structure of the relations of production in the economy of the society, this unstable characteristic of the political configuration had a certain effect on the structure of the economy. This was particularly reflected in the structure of the land tenure system. That is, each dynasty viewed land and its revenue as the object of its power acquisition. Each new dynasty carried out a policy of massive confiscation and redistribution of the land and other forms of wealth in favour of its functionaries (Karshenas, 1990; Moghadam, 1988). However, under an established dynasty the functionaries tended to convert the land into their private property. This never created any absolute right to the land, in practice the right was determined by the ruler's will, so it was possible and usual that the already assigned land to the subjects be revoked and transfered to someone else at any moment (Lambton, 1969). This situation prevented the formation of a stable landed aristocracy.

The gradual development of private property ownership was accompanied by the expropriation of peasants' land by landlords, who 'used their superior power to assert absolute property rights on the Western model . . . and although individual peasants could not be sold as serfs, whole villages were freely sold, with implied rights to the labour of their inhabitants' (Keddie, 1960, p. 5).

The consolidation of semi-feudal production relations in the agricultural sector acted as a major obstacle to productivity improvement in that sector. Although the period 1860–1914 was most dynamic from the point of view of new export cash crops, there were no notable improvements to traditional techniques or production relations, and few attempts were made to introduce new seed varieties or other new agricultural inputs (Keddie, 1960; Khamsi, 1968; Issawi, 1971; Karshenas, 1990).

The second major change took place between the early twentieth century and the land reform. The expansion of capital-intensive agriculture based on wage labour, private ownership, the abolition of benefice landholding and the consequent development of a new landowning class were the principal features of this period. The Constitutional Law of 1907 abolished benefice (*tuyuldari*), thus officially departing from the use of land for revenue administration. It established private land ownership and helped consolidate the economic and political position of the landowning classes at the expense of other classes.

There were two interrelated outcomes of the abolition of *tuyuldari*. First, the *tuyul* system had constituted an intermediate source of power between the state and the peasant. From a functionalist point of view it can be argued that, since *tuyuldari* was not compatible with the modern state, it was doomed to disappear (Yeganeh, 1986). In effect *tuyuldari* had amounted to a decentralisation of political power since it assigned economic power (land) to tribal chiefs and high-ranking state officials, whereas the modern nation-state was based on centralised power. Second, the holders of *tuyul* land became independent owners instead of managing the land for the state (Lambton, 1953; Keddie, 1960). The final outcome was extensive private land ownership, which was conductive to the growth of the modern state and capitalism.

During the Reza Shah period (1925–41) the private ownership of agricultural land was consolidated through legislation and the sale of state and crown land – mainly the less profitable holdings. The December 1935 law concerning the village headman (*kadkhoda*, the official representative of the landowner and responsible for the execution of state laws and government regulations) was designed to rationalise landlord–peasant relations. According to this law, village headmen, who were already considered as the executive representatives of the government in the villages, were to be appointed and paid by the landlords (Lambton, 1953). This law officially recognised the landlord's political authority in the countryside.

All of these measures strengthened the position of the landowning class and made no provisions for the peasants. Neither did they give the peasants a fair share of the crops: 'the section of the code dealing with crop-sharing agreements was weighted in favour of the landlords' (Keddie, 1960, p. 372).

One of the notable policies of the state towards the agricultural sector was to encourage a capitalist farming system with cash crops, which was seen as adding another element to the land tenure system during Reza Shah's reign but had in fact been part of the overall process of modernisation begun by the Qajars in the nineteenth century. Promotion of the capitalist farming system continued after the Reza Shah period, particularly from 1949 onward. The state exempted agricultural machinery from customs duties and cash crops from taxes. Large-scale mechanised agriculture was developed by merchants, landlords and the ruling elements. These enterprises became an important aspect of economic development in the second seven-year plan (1955–62) (Richard, 1975). The capitalist farming system was largely concentrated in certain regions – the northern provinces of Mazandaran and Gilan, particularly in the Gorgan area, and the western province of Khuzistan. The construction of the Sefid Rud dam in the north and the Dez dam in Khuzistan to assist agribusiness activities was a determining factor in the development of these enterprises. Thus the development of private ownership and encouragement of large-scale land holdings, along with the expensive irrigation projects of the 1950s, to a large extent contributed to the intensification of the capitalist farming system.

During Mossadiq's premiership two partial attempts at land reform were made. One of these was the Shah's decision to distribute the land of villages seized by his father. One third of this land was royal land and was sold to various wealthy favourites of the Shah (Keddie, 1972, p. 309). The second attempt took the form of two decrees to change the land tenure system. According to these decrees, landlords would be compelled to pay 10 per cent of their share of the output to the peasants, and another 10 per cent into a fund for rural development and cooperation. Between 1953 and 1962 another attempt to alter the land tenure system was made, and despite the opposition of landlords and some religious groups the law was passed by parliament (Shaji'i, 1965, p. 210). The law limited the size of individual holdings to 400 hectares of irrigated land or 800 hectares of unirrigated land. However, none of these decrees and laws was implemented (Katouzian, 1973).

In spite of these developments sharecropping remained the main form of production and the predominant method of surplus extraction. Indeed it is the nature of capitalism to exploit non-capitalist modes of production (in the case of merchants' capital or that of commodity exports). It reinforces or utilises the existing production relations to establish its dominance over non-capitalist production.

Rural society after the land reform (1962)

By the second half of the twentieth century, various national and international trends resulted in a number of social, political and economic transformations and gave rise to the major social unrest that eventually made reform of the agrarian structure possible. This section provides a brief description of the agrarian reforms and the subsequent changes in Iranian society.

At the national level the transformation of the state was the first point of departure. As already mentioned, the transition of Iran to a modern nation-state began in 1906 with the constitutional revolution and proceeded under the reign of Reza Shah (1925–41). The emergence of oil as a major source of state revenue, the establishment of a centralised military–bureaucratic machine and the implementation of secular and modernist programmes were the most prominent developments during Reza Shah's reign.

The sociopolitical background and the character of the Shah's regime were to some extent similar to that of Reza Shah in the 1925–41 period; however, essential changes were made to the nature of the state and the form and function of its economic institutions. The most central of these was the capacity of the state to intervene in the economy in the face of new economic circumstances. The most significant aspects of this were the substantial rise in oil revenues and easy access to foreign capital in the post-1953 period. This altered the role of the state in the process of accumulation (Pesaran, 1982; Bashiriyeh, 1984; Karshenas, 1990). While in the interwar period the main task of the state had been to mobilise the agrarian economic surplus through the control of trade, it now turned its attention to the distribution and allocation of oil revenues. Generally speaking, two broad policies characterised the Shah's regime: a systematic attempt to exclude all the lower classes from major political positions and the process of economic decision making; and an economic strategy that promoted capitalist development (Katouzian, 1980; Karshenas, 1990). These political and economic policies, under the direction of advanced capitalist countries, had a significant effect on the country's class structure and class politics. In the years following the Shah's White Revolution this effect intensified, and the consequent societal discontent, with the state set against the various social classes, finally led to the revolution of 1979.

Rising oil revenues, especially after 1973, intensified the rentier character of the state (Katouzian 1980; Zubaida, 1988). Oil became a determining feature of the Iranian political economy, structuring the relationship between the state and civil society. Oil, a geographically limited resource, employed only a small percentage of the labour force (0.4 per cent prior to 1973, 1 per cent after 1973: Katouzian, 1980) but accounted for a huge proportion of the national income and gave the state considerable financial (if not political) autonomy as it had a monopoly on the oil sector. Other domestic revenues – that is, taxes and returns from public enterprises – made up only a small proportion of public receipts.

Social stratification became a function of economic dependence on the state, which provided various incentives (high wages, low interest rates and so on) to encourage private investment and accumulation. The negative effect of this was that speculation and consumption increased significantly and the inflationary, open-import license conditions made long-term investment even more risky. The service sector expanded rapidly, as did urbanisation and the demand for food and consumer items (Katouzian, 1980; Skocpol, 1982).

Oil had a contradictory role in the Iranian political economy. On the one hand the state became highly independent from the people and was able to pursue social reforms and development projects in total disregard of social opposition. Land reform was just one of the measures the state introduced without the participation of the parliament or senate, both of which had been dissolved by the shah in April 1962, and without regard for the clerics' views. On the other hand, since the oil sector expanded primarily in response to the world's energy requirements rather than to domestic demands, the state and the entire economy became dependent on international economic forces. Moreover oil gave extraordinary power to the state in terms of capital allocation and accumulation. It converted the state into the most influential actor in the country's development, totally dominating society and the economy (Parsa, 1989). This high level of state intervention undermined the role of other forces, such as the markets, and eventually politicised the country's social and economic conflicts. Consequently all conflicts came to be directed towards the state, culminating in the revolution of 1979.

Another long-term structural change was the decreasing importance of agriculture in relation to government revenues from other sectors, such as industry, services and especially oil. This resulted in a weakening of the economic power of the monarchy and the landowning classes, which were founded on agricultural enterprise. For example, at the time of Reza Shah's abdication in 1941 the crown owned over 2000 prosperous villages, valued at about $4.3 to $5 million. Government revenues from oil at that time were about $40 million per annum, illustrating the relative lack of importance of agriculture as a source of revenue. Agriculture accounted for one third of GNP in 1960 as opposed to about three quarters at the turn of twentieth century. Its contribution continued to decrease, reaching about one fifth at the end of the 1960s (Bharier, 1971, p. 132). Agriculture, as compared with oil, was also becoming a smaller source of the royal family's income (Lahsaeizadeh, 1990).

In addition to long-term developments in Iranian society, a number of short-term factors contributed to and finally made land reform possible in 1962. After the coup of 1953 the elimination or weakening of the opposition seemed certain. However, a number of unanticipated developments undermined the stability of the regime, propelling the Shah to introduce a series of reforms that fundamentally changed the Iranian social structure. The first of these developments was an economic crisis in the late 1950s, which caused social and political tensions in the country (Moghadam, 1996). The second was the political pressure exerted in late 1959 by the US State Department on the Shah to liberalise his politics. US concern had been heightened by the July 1958 revolution in neighbouring Iraq. These developments were coupled in early 1960 with the Kennedy administration's advice to Third World countries to introduce land reforms in order to reduce the likelihood of peasant uprisings and communist revolutions such as those that had taken place in China and Cuba. In the case of Iran, greater economic development and financial aid were recommended. The response of the Shah to these pressures was the White Revolution, the centrepiece of which was land reform. (The other measures were the nationalisation of forests and pastures, the sale of state-owned factories to finance the land reform, profit sharing in industry, reform of the electoral laws to enfranchise women and the establishment of a literacy corps.)

The land reform was carried out in three stages. Broadly speaking, the stated objectives were to increase agricultural production, eliminate traditional peasant–landlord relations, create political support for the regime, create an independent peasant proprietorship system, increase the purchasing capacity of peasants, supply the labour power needed for industry, create a home market and remove the large landowner as an obstacle to economic development (Arsanjani, 1962, pp. 97–104; Khosravi, 1976, pp. 150–65).

The first stage involved the distribution of large holdings that belonged to absentee landlords and limiting individual land ownership to one village. Under the law, ownership of the land was collectively transferred to the peasants in proportion to the existing rights of cultivation (*nasagh*).

The aims of the second stage were to eliminate the sharecropping system without necessarily altering the land-ownership pattern, to prevent the emergence of an independent peasantry and to create a new system of large land holdings and agricultural practices. All owners of villages exempted from the first stage had the right to choose one of five methods of settlement: (1) rent the land to peasants on 30-year leases; (2) sell the land to peasants at a mutually agreed price; (3) divide the land in proportion to the prevailing distribution of the harvest; (4) set up joint-stock companies in which the landlords and peasants were shareholders; or (5) purchase the land from the peasants (Lambton, 1969, p. 194). The overwhelming majority of landlords chose the rent option – only 8 per cent decided to sell or divide their land (Hooglund, 1982, p. 67).

The third stage was aimed at transferring some of the tenancies created in stage two into peasant ownership. According to the law, at this stage the landlord could either sell the land to tenants on a 30-year lease for a price equivalent to twelve years' rent, divide the land among the peasants according to their customary share of the harvest, or buy the peasants' cultivation rights (Katouzian, 1980; Lahsaeizadeh, 1993).

Individual holdings were limited to one village or to six *dangs* (sixth part of a real estate) in separate villages. Landlords were required to sell their excess holdings to the government, but exempted were orchards, tea plantations, homesteads, groves and land that was cultivated mechanically using daily wage labour. Other measures included fixing the price of land taken from landlords and redistributed among the peasants; allocating holdings among the peasants without changing the existing field layout; compulsory membership of a rural cooperative for those peasants who were eligible to receive land; and redistributing land among those peasants who were *nasaqh*-holders (holders of the right to cultivate) (Halliday, 1979, p. 110; Lahsaeizadeh, 1993, pp. 134–5).

Some of the provisions of the land reform proved very beneficial to landlords, for example they could choose a *dang* from each of their most prosperous villages. They also found a legal loophole to enlarge their property by transferring their holdings to relatives or dependants (Danesh, 1992). Many landlords were also able to retain some of their lands by passing it off as mechanised, or bribing reform officials (Azkia, 1986; Danesh, 1992). Approximately 1.5 million *khushnishin* (villagers without cultivation rights) or 42 per cent of all Iranian peasantry were excluded from benefiting from the land reforms (Danesh, 1992, p. 162).

In 1972 the redistribution of land was officially completed. About 963 403 peasant households had received or bought land as a result of the first and second stages. The supplementary law of 1969 added about 738 119 peasant households to this group. In total these 1 701 522 households represented about 58 per cent of all rural households in Iran (Azkia, 1986, p. 117).

The slogan of the land reform was 'Land to the tiller'. While this appeared logical, in practice it caused an unequal distribution of land. Its main beneficiaries were the richer farmers, and about half of the rural population were excluded from the distribution. The reason for this was that the customary *nasagh* (cultivation right) system was used as the basis for the distribution and there was great variation among peasants in respect of cultivation rights within individual villages and from peasant to peasant, leading to marked inequalities in the allotment of land between peasants (McLachlan, 1968; Moghadam, 1996).

From the standpoint of policy makers, the main problem was the failure of the reform to increase agricultural production to a satisfactory level. In order to attain this objective and improve the living standards of the rural population, agriculture had to be mechanised. To this end, structural obstacles to the process of mechanisation had to be removed. First, the villages were small, numerous and widely scattered (about 68 000 villages and independent farms each containing no more than about 33 hectares of irrigated and 51 hectares of unirrigated land). The development of these villages needed infrastructural investment and agricultural extension services, but their scattered distribution made this uneconomical (Moghadam, 1996, pp. 66–7). Second, the majority of peasant holdings were too small and too fragmented to use machinery efficiently, which caused the national economic planners to question the economic viability of independent peasant farming (ibid.; Afshar, 1981). Inspired by the economic development literature of the 1950s and early 1960s, the government concluded that the rural sector was backward, suffered from extensive disguised unemployment and was undercapitalised. To overcome these problems the government decided to intervene directly in the structural transformation of the agricultural sector (Afshar, 1981).

The state's overall development policy had a dualistic approach with strong emphasis on the modern industrial sector. The prevailing assumption among planners was that the wealth generated by the industrial sector would trickle down to the agricultural sector (Afshar, 1981; Pesaran, 1982). In the latter the proposed plan involved the systematic destruction of small villages and their integration into 5000 centres (*shahraks*) of agricultural production, and the creation of large-scale agricultural growth poles irrigated by large dams or deep wells (Moghadam, 1996, p. 67). Stage three, in particular, was a preparation

56 The State and Rural Development

for this. Two types of farm enterprise were established: private, capital-intensive farms modelled on US agribusinesses; and farm corporations modelled on Israel's *moshavim* cooperatives (Halliday, 1979). Politically these corporations were a response to leftist criticisms of state promotion of agribusiness (ibid.). The assumption was that the difficulties the country faced after the land reform could be overcome by the creation of farm corporations (Lahsaeizadeh, 1993; Moghadam, 1996) and would

- increase the per capita income of peasants;
- increase output through the provision of facilities for farm mechanisation;
- create opportunities for the use of agricultural machinery;
- ensure the maximum utilisation of manpower in the villages;
- prevent the division of land into small and uneconomic units;
- improve the standard of living of the members of farm corporations (Ministry of Corporate and Rural Affairs, 1973, p. 20).

The farm enterprises enjoyed generous government financial support. For example by 1975 the 85 farm corporations were jointly receiving about 2000 million rials per annum, or about 23.5 million per corporation. By contrast the annual 5000 million rials of credit earmarked for over 700 000 loans to peasant proprietors corresponded to an average annual loan of about 7000 rials each. Farm corporations were entitled to long-term loans from the Agricultural Development Bank of up to 600 million rials. Peasant properties were generally entitled to short-term loans of up to 17 000 rials from the Rural Cooperative Bank, but this was not enough to pay for agricultural improvements and was often used to cover incidental expenses (Afshar, 1981, pp. 65–6).

The government's policy on smallholdings included the creation of a network of rural cooperatives to compensate for the loss of the village system and its productive functions. Indeed they were 'established as the modern equivalent of traditional patron–client systems of support . . . to fulfill their assigned role for the newly landed peasants' (Danesh, 1992, p. 167).

Generally speaking, none of these enterprises was successful (Okazaki, 1968; Azkia, 1986; Schirazi, 1993). The reasons for the failure of the large mechanised farms included the high cost of mechanisation and overcapitalisation, the huge area cultivated, high wages, the failure to use appropriate technology, lack of knowledge about local conditions on the part of management, lack of interest, and corruption. Likewise the cooperatives suffered not only from financial problems such as funding and credit resources, but also from organisational problems such as a lack of mutual understanding between the cooperative members and the state's representatives in the cooperatives. This was due to the fact that the cooperatives were mostly run by official bureaucrats with an inadequate knowledge of village life, and that most of the rural people were illiterate and therefore unable to participate properly in the quasidemocratic arrangements of these new institutions (Azkia, 1986; Danesh, 1992). In 1976 about 83 per cent of the 2.46 million agricultural workers were unable to read or write. (Danesh, 1992, p. 167).

However, the land reform and the supplementary measures had a considerable impact on Iranian society. Some of the more important effects on rural society are outlined below.

Elimination of traditional relations of production

As a result of the land reform the modes of surplus extraction changed considerably. Although the land reform did not totally eliminate large landownership, the new land tenure system was not intended to perpetuate sharecropping, which continued in only a small fraction of farms (Halliday, 1979; Lahsaeizadeh, 1993).

Along with the decline in traditional production relations, particularly after the first and second stages of the reform, capitalist practices increased. First, commodification was promoted and land became a commodity. The role of money was increased, especially with the expansion of state and private credit institutions. Second, a social class consisting of the rural bourgeoisie and the new proletariat was created. Landless peasants, the near landless and those who had only small plots of land and could no longer profitably cultivate their fields migrated to the cities in search of work or stayed in the village as wage labourers.

This process emanated from the breakdown of traditional units of production (*boneh*), which had been initiated and safeguarded by the old landowning class, and the establishment of large-scale capitalist farms in some regions. Specialisation and cooperative working had been an important feature of the *boneh*, and the redistribution of land among the individual members led to a situation in which some peasants had no experience of the specialised tasks required in agriculture. Consequently the disintegration of the *boneh* caused rapid social and economic polarisation of the village population. In addition, unequal land redistribution and the exemptions granted to some landlords were significant factors in the process of differentiation (Halliday, 1979; Ashraf, 1981; Azkia, 1986; Mohtadi, 1990; Lahsaeizadeh, 1993).

The political influence of the state in rural society

The land reform had political goals as well as the socioeconomic goal of adapting the structure of society to capitalist requirements. An effort was made to strengthen the political role of the state in rural communities, and the reordering of village life and social relations was conducted by a variety of new organisations controlled by government agencies.

The first institutional connection between the government and the villages was the traditional headman of the village (*kadkhoda*), historically the most powerful person in the community due to his function of collecting dues for the state in the precapitalist period and latterly for the landlords. He had always been relatively independent from the political state apparatus, but the land reforms reduced his power and put him under the supervision of the government (Azkia, 1986; Shashani, 1985).

A new institution to be established in rural areas was the House of Justice, whose purpose was to resolve disputes. Theoretically it was to be headed by an older man who was well respected by the villagers and whose advice would be accepted by them, but in practice its members were the same individuals who served on the village councils and cooperative societies, such as the *kadkhoda* and a few rich peasants, all approved by the government (Denman, 1978; Shashani, 1986).

Another new institution was a network of Rural Cultural Houses, whose task was to introduce universal values to rural Iran and pave the way for the integration of the rural communities with the outside world (Denman, 1978).

Finally, the Literacy Corps, the Health Corps and the Extension and Development Corps, consisting of military conscripts, were established 'to implement quickly and uniformly various social and economic programmes which the Shah had decided to carry out in the rural areas' (Hooglund, 1982, p. 134). The main function of the corps was to teach the villagers to obey the government bureaucrats. On the whole the corps failed in their duty due to the extremely poor economic conditions in the villages. Although the corps members were military conscripts they had to report to one or other of the ministries such as Education, Health or Agriculture. Thus in effect they were civil servants working in the villages (Katouzian, 1980).

If one evaluates the specificities of the state policies the following points emerge. First, although the land reform did curtail the political power of those landowners who had occupied key positions in the bureaucracy and legislature in the prereform era, absentee landlords continued to exist because many had been able to retain some of their land by fraudulent means or by using the exemption conditions built into the reform legislation (Halliday, 1979; Azkia, 1986).

Second, some of the landowners who received money in compensation for their land moved into private business, while others were encouraged to take shares in state industries as compensation for their land. Thus many landowners were converted into urban capitalists (Halliday, 1979; Azkia, 1986).

Third, the land was unequally distributed among the peasants. Indeed the land reform clearly benefited the wealthier peasants, particularly the market-oriented ones. But by favouring them the reform widened the gap between the social groups and created additional social tensions in the countryside (Najmabadi, 1987; Mohtadi, 1990).

Fourth, contrary to the stated aims of the reform, which stressed the transfer of land to the peasantry and the transfer of power from landlord to peasant, in practice land was transferred only to some peasants and power in the villages was appropriated by the state. The Iranian peasantry remained as powerless as it had been before 1962. Indeed the major beneficiary of the rural development programmes was the state, which was increasingly able to control peasants' lives.

Finally, the land reform and other rural development policies did not substantially increase the supply of food to urban centres, and neither did overall agricultural productivity rise relative to the rapidly growing population. Furthermore the programmes served to reinforce the existing social strata in rural areas, widened the socioeconomic gap between the various strata and eliminated the traditional organisations without replacing them with new and more appropriate ones. The declining living standards in rural areas and increasing poverty ultimately resulted in the massive migration of the rural poor to the cities (Afshar, 1981; Najmabadi, 1987; Mohtadi, 1990).

3
The Revolution and Rural Society

Introduction

After the Islamic Revolution new social and structural forces came into play, resulting in a certain transformation of the agrarian structure and the adoption of specific policies in the rural sector. This chapter reviews these policies and structural transformations. The discussion is organised into three main sections. The first deals with the post-revolutionary reforms. The second discusses the reorganisation of the prerevolutionary agricultural administration, the establishment of a revolutionary organisation (Jihad) for rural development, the creation of *mosha* cooperatives and the establishment of rural councils. The third section analyses the effect of the government's agricultural policies and other factors on agricultural output. The discussion focuses on fiscal policies and their effect on capital formation, land- and water-use policies and their role in the increase of cultivated areas, and support policies such as provision and pricing policies for agricultural growth.

Since socioeconomic policies in general and agricultural and rural policies in particular were influenced by the formation of the post-revolutionary state and its subsequent development, there follows a brief account of the roots, philosophy and salient characteristics of the revolution.

The revolution of 1979

The revolution of 1979 was the consequence of long-term dissatisfaction in Iranian society and its causes were similar to those of the constitutional revolution. The underlying ideology of the Islamic Revolution represented a continuation of the earlier nationalism but expressed in terms of Islam. It was anti-Western in character and reflected the bitter hostility of the petit bourgeoisie towards the modern capitalist world and its social and cultural practices. The revolution was also directed against the Iranian state and its bureaucratic machinery, whose primary function was to maintain the political and socioeconomic interests of the absolutist regime and its principal international allies. In summary, the 1979 revolution was anti-monarchy, anti-dictatorship, nationalist, anti-imperialist, democratic and Islamic (Abrahamian, 1982; Bashiriyeh, 1984; Amirahmadi, 1990).

The revolution brought with it social demands and policy expectations for a fundamental change to the economic and social system and for the adoption of policies that would enable independence from the West. An examination of all of the factors that determined the post-revolutionary policies is beyond the scope of this study, so the discussion will be limited to the factional conflict within the ruling power bloc, the changing balance of power between the various sociopolitical groups and the formation of the post-revolutionary state. The changing balance of power between sociopolitical groups in post-revolutionary Iran can be separated into four distinct phases. The first phase took place immediately after the revolution with the setting up of a provisional government (February to November 1979) – the first step towards the realisation of an Islamic Republic. The period marked the coalition of a number of social groups: the majority of the liberal intelligentsia, the moderate left, small and middle-ranking entrepreneurs, merchants, the state and private-sector employees. The state basically consisted of technocrats with a liberal-democrat perspective. They sought to establish a Western-style democracy with capitalist economic relations but guided by the moral values of Islam. Their immediate aim was to restore the former institutions, the bureaucracy and, most importantly, the normal functioning of the economy. They argued for gradual reform within the existing social structure and opposed any radical social change – Bazargan's response, as prime minister of the provisional government, to the growing demands of the people for social change was 'we asked for rain, we got a flood'. However the deteriorating economy and the radicalisation of the political atmosphere did not allow for a gradualistic approach and led to the resignation of Bazargan.

Although this phase was characterised by balance of power, there was growing conflict between liberal technocrats and populist Islamists. The majority of the latter were from the middle or lower classes and wanted more radical change. Since they preached revolutionary slogans, they were supported by revolutionary organisations as well as members of their own classes. The conflict between the populists and the liberal technocrats focused on the criteria for the selection of new members of the state bureaucracy during the presidency of Bani-Sader, when the Islamist populists succeeded in obtaining a majority in parliament and gained direct access to the executive body. The liberals considered that technical competence and specialisation in different scientific fields were the most appropriate criteria, while for populist Islamists, religiosity and familiarity with religious matters were more important. The former group were concerned about the lack of experts in the state bureaucracy, while the latter argued that morality should take precedence over science, and values over knowledge. With the dismissal of Bani-Sader the populist Islamists became more dominant in the executive and parliament, the revolutionary organisations were strengthened and opportunities arose to implement radical social changes.

The second phase took place between the resignation of Bazargan and the end of the Iran–Iraq War. It was characterised by radical discourse on internal and external affairs, a war-like atmosphere, the governance of jurisprudential Islam on the administration of the country, the gradual withdrawal of intellectuals (both religious and non-religious) from the sociopolitical arena, and a reduction in the country's economic capacity.

The third phase started with the ceasefire with Iraq in 1989. Considerable changes were made to the constitution and the structure of the state and the balance of power shifted between factions. The constitutional reform led to the birth of new concepts, such as the absolute rule of religious jurisconsul (leader) (*velayat-e motlagheh-e faghih*) and authoritarianism based on the Muslim chief civil and religious ruler (Caliph rule). A pragmatic, technocratic, reformist group gained political power and dominated the executive body. (*Velayat-e motlagheh-e faghih* is based on shia belief that Muslims or people in an Islamic society should be ruled by the descendants of the Prophet. It is a steward to the knowledge transmitted from the prophet, through the hereditary imams. The clergy claims that they have the right to become the legitimate rulers of the country. *Velayateh motlagheh* means that all tasks entrusted to the prophet must be fulfilled by the religious leaders. *The political philosophy of Caliph* refers to the Muslim chief civil and religious ruler. It is based on the idea, mainly by the Sunni sect of Islam, that religious leaders are the trustees of the prophet and all tasks entrusted to the prophet must be fulfilled by Caliph and he is the only ruler. The caliph was the absolute leader of Muslim society. He did not have the right to legislate, but he could only issue decrees within the limits of the sharia. So long as the ruler protects Islam, and does not use his rule for his personal interests, the believers were to obey.) Economic reforms were launched and had a nationalist/pragmatist stant: free-enterprise capitalism in a market-based economy, but with an Islamically acceptable trading system. Although both political and economic development were put at the top of the policy-making agenda, the priority was given to economic development.

Politically, the period witnessed a struggle between right-wing conservatives, who dominated parliament after the fourth session (1996), and left-wing reformists, who dominated the executive. While both factions were in favour of economic pluralism, the conservatives opposed politico-cultural development, believing in limited development in the political sphere and uniformity in the cultural sphere. The tension was settled by the resignation of a number of reformist ministers (Interior, Culture and Islamic Guidance, Culture and Higher Education) and their replacement by conservatives. Economic, cultural and political management was divided between the executive and the legislature: the former took charge of economic affairs and the latter became responsible for politico-cultural affairs.

Generally speaking, two broad policies characterised the third phase: a systematic effort to exclude all reformist left wing forces from positions in the state apparatus, and the adoption of a strategy to improve the country's economic capacity.

The fourth period started with the victory of Khatami in the presidential election of 23 May 1998. Khatami was supported by reformist forces in the state apparatus, the left wing and religious and secular intellectuals. The main emphases of the new government were civil liberty, the governance of law, social justice and the elimination of state interference in people's privacy. The new policy stance was a consequence of dissatisfaction with past policies in a number areas, particularly in the political and cultural spheres, but it was also a reaction to the growing economic crisis, resulting mainly from the mismanagement of the country's economy and the government's adjustment policies in the third phase.

Taking into account these transformations, economic policy in general and agrarian policy in particular varied during the four periods, but in general they shared two main aims: solving the land question by implementing a land reform programme; and meeting the basic needs of rural society by reorganising agricultural organisations and implementing rural development strategies. The following section will focus on these policies and their outcomes.

Post-revolutionary rural policies

With the weakening of government power towards the end of the revolution, a peasant struggle began to emerge. With the fall of the Shah's regime, two different trends in peasant and land questions came into existence. The first was the demand by remnants of the former landowning class for the reversal of the Shah's land reform, based on the Islamic principle of sanctity of private property. In some regions – such as Kurdestan, Baluchestan, Urumieh and Khorasan – they succeeded, at least temporarily, in regaining their former land.

The second trend was the raising of agrarian question by various social groups, such as peasants and radical forces (leftist and Islamic). In addition, peasant movements started with the expropriation of large tracts of land under the leadership of revolutionary groups. The government took over a considerable amount of land, mainly that belonging to associates of the former regime who, with the victory of the revolution, had abandoned their holdings and left the country. It should be mentioned that the radical forces (Islamist or Marxist) and the peasants were two distinct groups with different interests, and while each attempted to use the other for its own purposes, on the whole there were no concrete relations between them. The radical forces thought that land distribution would bring the peasants into the revolution and deliver a serious blow to the remaining enemies of the revolution – the landlords and the bourgeoisie. Since the peasants did not have their own organisation they felt they could use the radical organisations to obtain land (Ashraf, 1982; Yeganeh, 1986; Rahnema and Nomani, 1990). The peasant movements were widely supported and violence broke out in places such as Gorgan and Gonbad, where the Shah's land reform policy had been disadvantageous for the peasants. The consequence was that Fadayian Marxist organisations penetrated the regions. In some regions, such as Kurdistan and Tukmanshahra, the land question was inflamed by ethnic discontent. (For details of the peasants' uprising and the role of the left see Azar, 1980; Yeganeh, 1981; Ashraf, 1982; Parsa, 1989; Rahnema and Nomani, 1990.)

Depending on the individual regional circumstances the peasant movements demanded possession of the land belonging to landlords who had fled the country, requisition of the land of large agricultural enterprises where disputes had broken out between the owners and workers, possession of the nationalised forests and pastures, dissolution of farm corporations and an end to debt payments to institutions identified with the previous regime (Rahnema and Nomani, 1990; Ashraf, 1991; Lahsaeizadeh, 1993). About 800 000 hectares of agricultural land owned by larger farmers were occupied by peasants during the first two years of the revolution (Ashraf, 1982, p. 25).

Broadly speaking the peasants' uprising and land seizure elicited three responses:

- The conventional jurisprudential response by some religious scholars and teachers, based on legitimacy of ownership.
- The conventional economic response by agricultural and economic experts, who advocated the mechanisation and commercialisation of agriculture. Their main concern was to increase agricultural production and reduce direct state intervention in agricultural affairs; hence they opposed equal land distribution among peasants.
- The state legislative and executive response, which was based on propaganda campaigns against land seizure, an emphasis on law and order and the necessity of rural stability for increased agricultural production, and a land reform bill to resolve the land problem.

Eventually a moderate solution was found: restricted and legitimised land ownership. The argument was that this Islamic concept would not only prevent the accumulation of wealth but would also give rise to individual incentives for agricultural production (Lahsaeizadeh, 1993, pp. 256–7). This Islamic approach to land reform was proclaimed by the revolutionary council in March 1980.

According to the Act approved by the council, land was classified into four categories: (1) waste land and pastures; (2) land reclaimed by individuals or firms and later confiscated by the writs of Islamic tribunals; (3) the holdings of large landlords whose ownership had been legitimised by the previous regime; and (4) land under cultivation. The notes of Article 4 specified that land in categories 1–3 had precedence over category 4 land in terms of distribution. In the same Act a plot of cultivated land was defined as large (category 3) if it was three times the size of what 'local custom' saw as necessary for the subsistence of a peasant family (Azkia, 1993b).

Category 1 and 2 land was under the jurisdiction of the Islamic government and would be divided among the peasants or turned over to revolutionary foundations under state supervision. Agribusiness land and orchards, the redistribution of which would not be in the interests of society, would be run by the public sector. With regard to category 3, any land that was more than three times the size deemed necessary for subsistance farming would remain in the hands of a legitimate landlord. An absentee landlord could hold land that was twice the determined size (Yeganeh, 1986; Azkia, 1986).

The implementation of this land reform was the task of the seven-member Committees of Land Devolution, consisting of the following members:

- two representatives from the Ministry of Agriculture;
- one representative from the Interior Ministry;
- one representative from the Ministry of Construction;
- two representatives from the village council;
- one representative from the Islamic Court.

Those eligible to receive land were mostly from the poorer strata of rural society, especially the landless (the *khushneshinan*, who had received no land during the Shah's land reform), small peasants and agricultural graduates. Under the Act, land ownership would be collectively transferred to those eligible: that is, a deed would be received by each new owner, but this would not give him the absolute right to any defined piece of land, merely a share of the land being distributed among eligible persons. None of the land could subsequently be sold or transferred to others. There was an obligation for all peasants to implement the cropping plans dictated by the Committees of Land Devolution (Schirazi, 1993).

In practice the implementation of Article C (category 3 land) faced serious problems and was the subject of dispute for over a decade, not only among rural Iranians but also among different political and religious factions. Broadly speaking it divided the major socioeconomic forces into two camps: those who supported and those who opposed Article C. Its supporters included radical members of the new elite, a tiny segment of the ruling *ulama*, and the young Jihad workers serving in rural areas. Since the government initiatives on land reform disarmed the leftist groups, these groups had to support the party's position on the land question. The opponents of Article C consisted of a broad coalition of social forces, including a large group of *ulama* from within and without the ruling circle, the traditional bourgeoisie and commercial farmers (Ashraf, 1991, p. 300).

The dispute over Article C occurred at three levels: at the theological level among the *ulama*, at the level of general political campaigning, and in rural areas, where violent clashes took place.

At the theological level the focus was on the legality of the clause: the sanctity of private property as a fundamental principle of Islamic law suggested a legal escape. Ayatollah Mishkini, a prominent supporter of Article C, forwarded a proposal based on the principle of maintaining Islamic order (*zarurat*), which permits the suspension of a primary rule (Ashraf, 1991) under specific conditions that harm the unity of the society.

The *ulama* were divided on the question of the legality of Article C. A small segment of the ruling *ulama*, including Ayatollah Ali Behishti and Hossienali Montizeri, were in favour of it, while a large proportion of the prominent *ulama* of Qum, Mashad and other cities opposed it and issued edicts questioning its legality. Other opponents of the article included grand ayatollahs such as Gholpayeghani and Rohani, and powerful leaders and *ulamas* such as Rabbani Shirazi (a member of the Council of Guardians of the Constitution), Mohammad Mohammadi Gilani (a well-known judge at Tehran's Islamic Tribunal), Shaikh Mohammad Yazdi (then deputy speaker of the Majlis and later chief justice) and Nasir Makarim Shirazi (editor of the monthly journal *Maktab-e Islam*) (Rahnema and Nomani, 1990, p. 248; Ashraf, 1991, pp. 300–1).

As well as the above attempt to nullify Article C, parliament was sent an open letter signed by 20 professors of theology at the Qum Theological Centre, stating that the Land Reform Act was incompatible with Islamic principles of ownership and the edicts of prominent religious authorities, and that implementation of the Act would ruin the reclaimed lands and lead to the bankruptcy of and backwardness in the agricultural sector at a time when there was a need for self-sufficiency because of the termination of Iran's relationship with the United States (Ashraf, 1991, pp. 301–2).

General campaigning was conducted by commercial farmers and Islamic extremists. Landlords organised a campaign in the Agricultural Councils, published propaganda in the weekly *Kishavarz-e-Imrouz* and arranged a meeting with influential authorities in Tehran and Qum. In December 1979 *Kishavarz-e-Imrouz* reported that:

> thanks to Reza Esfahani, the new deputy minister of land affairs, last week was a most turbulent week for Iranian agriculture. The small landowners, who are the members of the Agricultural Councils, instigated a widespread campaign against Esfahani and demanded his dismissal from office. They were also given [an] audience by the Imam [Komeini] and submitted their protest to him (Ashraf, 1991, p. 301).

There were also floods of telegrams, letters, petitions, cables and leaflets from landlords in various cities to the grand ayatollahs and government authorities (Moaddle, 1992, pp. 242–7). In response, proponents of the article 'using radio, television, daily newspapers, and Islamic committees of the offices and institutions of higher education ... launched a fierce attack on [the] Tehran Agricultural Council and labelled its members "feudal" ' (Ashraf, 1991, p. 301).

In rural areas the article provoked violent confrontations. For example in Bujnurd the representatives of the Committee of Land Devolution were hanged, and in the provinces of Kurdistan, Khozistan and Azerbaijan a number of Jihad representatives and committee members were killed by landowners (ibid., p. 302).

Strong pressure by landowners, merchants and leading conservative *ulama* eventually succeeded in preventing the implementation of the reform, and on 21 October 1980 parliament rescinded Article C. Despite several amendments, which resulted in many exemptions, a revised version of Article C proved ineffective and the reform was restricted to land in categories 1 and 2. The main reason for this was a conflict between parliament and the Council of Guardians. The majority in parliament, unlike the Council of Guardians, was in favour of radical social change. An analysis of the background of the members of the first parliament to some extent explains their political tendency. The available data indicate that 51 per cent were *ulama* (the majority of whom were students at the religious school), 22.8 per cent were teachers, 6.5 per cent were students, 12.5 per cent were professionals, 3 per cent were merchants, 3 per cent were government employees and the rest were from other social classes (Moaddle, 1992, p. 225).

The members of the Council of Guardians were leading *ulama* with a conservative interpretation of Islam based on the sanctity of private ownership. Most of them were from the propertied class and were opposed to any radical programme that threatened their interests. The council consisted of 12 members, six of whom were *ulamas* and experts on Islamic law, and were selected either by the religious leader or by the Council of Leadership. The other six were lawyers (specialising in different areas of law) and were elected by parliament. The six *ulama* were responsible for determining the conformity of any law to the Sharia (religious law) passed by parliament, but all twelve members were responsible for interpreting and determining a law's conformity to the constitution. Hence the Council's task was to ensure the compatibility of legislation with the constitution and general Islamic principles. Indeed all parliamentary legislation was subject to the Council's approval – in other words the Council had the power to veto all acts of parliament that it found incompatible with *sharia* law and the constitution. Taking into account the significant role of the Council of Guardians in the state apparatus, and the fact that the majority were conservative and large property holders (land and factories), one can understand why they were resistant to radical social change.

In 1986, when the conflict between parliament and the Council of Guardians ended in a compromise law based on titles being awarded in the case of land already seized by the peasants, the government policy on land reform changed and became highly conservative. The new law put no limit on the size of land ownership by individuals, and restricted redistribution to land confiscated from the previous regime's dependants, or land whose owners had emigrated and would not return to claim their property. According to a senior official at the Eastern Azerbaijan Land Affairs Bureau (the former committee of Land Devolution):

> There is no longer land redistribution, now we deal with conflicts concerning the distributed land, like landowners complaints against the illegal occupation or redistribution of their lands, and returning such lands to their original owners who had acquired their property (land) licitly (personal interview).

Following Ashraf (1991), we may argue that there were two reasons for the failure of the radical land reform: eradication of the factors that had placed land at the forefront of the agenda, and a change in the political and economic circumstances of the county. The main factors behind the first reason were a decline in rural unrest, the elimination of leftist groups from the political arena, and suppression of the populist and revolutionary interpretation of Islam (in the case of land, radical redistribution). By the end of 1980 the peasants' uprising had subsided throughout the country, while the leftist groups had been disarmed by the radical posture of the ruling party and gradually eliminated in the power struggle. After the invasion by Iraq the government, the radical ruling groups and the revolutionary institutions (the Jihad and the Revolutionary Guard, who were proponents of land redistribution) agreed that all efforts had to be directed at the war, and that it was vital for the country to return to law and avoid contentious issues such as land reform. The revolutionary interpretation of Islam in respect of land reform by some ruling *ulama* was subjected to a similar argument.

Article C was eventually ratified by parliament in October 1986 by a two-thirds majority, in spite of the opposition of the Council of Guardians, allowing some 120 000 farmers to claim about 800 000 hectares of occupied land for a just price.

The second reason for the failure of the radical land reform relates to the lack of pressure to implement Article C after 1986. The main factors in this were the lack of success in the Iran–Iraq War, mounting economic problems in the post-war period, the priority awarded to the country's economic reconstruction by the ruling group, and unprecedented changes in the Soviet bloc that put the radical camp in a defensive position. The moderates therefore managed to resist the pressure of the radicals and obstructed the implementation of Article C.

The result was limited land redistribution. For instance, according to the Committee of Land Devolution, by mid 1991 approximately 602 000 hectares of uncultivatable, state and pasture land had been distributed among 100 000 households, and a further 681 000 or so hectares of temporarily cultivated land had been distributed among 130 000 households. Therefore the total number of households who benefited from the reform did not exceed 6 per cent of total rural households (Azkia, 1993b, p. 13).

Reorganisation of the agricultural administration

Reorganisation of the agricultural administration was the principal response by the government to pressure by various socioeconomic forces to deal with the country's rural problems. The government first established the Centres of Services for Rural and Nomadic People. Then, due to great pressure by political factions, it set up a revolutionary rural development organisation, the Jihad-e Sazandegi.

This section deals first with the establishment of the Centres of Services for Rural and Nomadic people and then focuses on the philosophy behind the creation of the Jihad-e Sazandegi.

The centres of services for rural and nomadic people

A significant measure in the reform of the agricultural administration was the establishment of Centres of Services for Rural and Nomadic People. These were set up in 1979 and constituted important reform at the Ministry of Agriculture and Rural Construction, carried over from the Shah's regime. The project was introduced as the major rural development strategy (Azkia, 1986, p. 286). The measure was first and foremost a response to criticism of the Ministry of Agriculture and its bureaucratic features in the prerevolutionary era, when 'the magnificent glass skyscraper in which the ministry resided at one of the finest addresses in the capital was regarded as a symbol of its alienation from its real tasks' (Schirazi, 1993, p. 136). The new move was aimed at bringing it more into the service of rural people.

The idea of establishing such service centres was proposed long before the revolution. In the early 1970s, a planning commission headed by Majid Rahnema and supervised by the then prime minister designed a development project for the Selseleh region, located in Lorestan province. The object of the project was to promote comprehensive and regionally balanced development, taking into account the full range of the region's potentials (Centre of Indigenous Studies, 1977, p. 1). The project was based on a holistic approach that included:

- a human dimension, which was concerned with such issues as education, health, social welfare and participation;
- an economic dimension, which was concerned with agriculture, animal husbandry, handicrafts, rural industries, small-scale industries and so on;
- an infrastructural dimension, which was concerned with the construction, maintenance and expansion of the communications network, power network, roads, housing, water and other infrastructural services (ibid., p. 3).

The idea behind the project was to treat 'a region as a system with inseparable development elements, each being complementary to the others' (ibid., p. 5). It was thought that the project would lead to total optimisation of the system, 'considering all the possible elements involved in the process, their relationship, their interactions, and their effects upon each other' (ibid., p. 5).

At the same time a planning commission worked out a plan for the economic development of Khorasan province that included centres that would provide various services for the villages under their supervision. In 1977 this proposal, which was very similar to the Centre of Development Services projects in India, formed the basis of an experimental programme at 11 locations.

In addition to the above projects, Centres for Agricultural Services, which were very similar to the other projects, were set up shortly after the revolution to deal with the agricultural problems of the country. The centres were intended to replace the farm corporations, many of which had been liquidated before the revolution (Azkia, 1986, pp. 276–89).

The plan to set up service centres received considerable attention in the draft agricultural policy prepared in May 1979 by the Ministry of Agriculture. The main reason for this attention was that the revolutionary atmosphere in the country demanded an indigenous and homogeneous rural development strategy that would be fully compatible with the social, political and economic conditions in rural and nomadic regions (Eftekhari, 1986).

The proposal to establish the service centres was approved by the Revolutionary Council on 4 June 1980. The centres would help with practically all aspects of rural life, including the expandsion of agriculture and the improvement of rural areas. According to Article 10 of the proposal they would provide general, technical and infrastructural services, as well as services related to credit, training, research, welfare, marketing, counselling, and planning, plus assistance with setting up Islamic Service Councils, investigating local land ownership, encouraging peasants to form agricultural collectives or set up small industrial enterprises, and so on. The purpose of these activities was to encourage self-sufficiency in agricultural development; to boost agricultural production; to bring development programmes into line with the actual needs of the rural sector; to meet the basic needs of the rural population and improve their welfare; to ensure social justice; and to reduce the socioeconomic gap between town and country (Azkia, 1992, p. 117; Schirazi, 1993, p. 137).

Due to the unfortunate consequences of state intervention in peasant affairs before the revolution, the government would not directly interfere in the affairs of the centres, but merely provide inducements for production according to farmers' needs. A service centre would be established in each district and would be an independent executive unit for planning. According to the Ministry of Agriculture its policy was 'based on the principle of noninterference . . . this is the reason the District Village Councils have been given the main power' (Schirazi, 1993, p. 137).

Initially all programmes would be administered by the centres, but local people would be trained to take over responsibility for the programmes. This would reduce the reliance of villagers on the centres and enhance their self-confidence (Azkia, 1990, p. 117), as well as alleviate the disadvantages of top-down rural development planning and allow the utilisation of local expertise and knowledge in the process of planning (Efterkhari, 1988, pp. 472–3).

In order to realise these objectives the centres were organised at four levels: national (the central administration under the supervision of the Ministry of Agriculture), provincial (the agricultural organisations and agricultural councils), county towns (the county town centre) and district (the district centre and the village councils). The service centres at the district level would be subordinate to the Centres for Rural and Agricultural Development in the county towns. The latter would include groups of resident and itinerant experts who would be sent to the districts to provide particular services as required. At the country level, Agricultural Councils would help the centres to coordinate and supervise the local projects. Plans would be worked out by these councils and decisions to be taken 'with due regard for the general objectives of agricultural policy and for the needs of the centres in the district villages had established' (Schirazi, 1993, p. 138).

The district centres would act as executive and coordinating units, which would help to avoid 'bureaucratic and technocratic confusion' (ibid). Each centre would have a panel composed of representatives from each village council and would deal with local needs and priorities, using resources available in the villages themselves. The village council would ensure that all funds were used to meet the stated needs. The aim of this arrangement was to involve villagers in decisions that affected their lives and avoid direct interference by the government in their affairs (ibid., p. 137).

The country centres would help to implement projects if the district centres could not do so independently (ibid., p. 140), and would gradually replace the branches of the revolutionary institutions and the Ministry of Agriculture at the county level (Articles 49 and 64), enabling bottom-up planning.

The agricultural organisations and agricultural councils would not have any executive duties, but would merely plan, check and determine aims at the regional level and allocate the necessary funds (Azkia, 1986, p. 295). At the highest level (the national level) would be the central machinery of the Ministry of Agriculture, whose duty would be to coordinate, allocate funds and supervise research and planning (ibid.)

The centres would function as harmonious development forces in rural areas, taking into account regional differences that required separate management. By this means the centralised administrative system for agriculture would gradually disappear. All affairs at the regional level would be handled by officials responsible for agriculture in cooperation with the agricultural councils and the service centres (Schirazi, 1993, p. 139).

In line with the principle of non-interference by the government in agricultural affairs, the participation of rural people in the entire process of rural development – planning, decision making, implementation, supervision – was seen as the main aim of the service centres. The Islamic village councils would be the main channel for people's participation in this process (Article 51). The village councils were seen as the link between the rural and nomadic populations and the service centres through representation in the district council, which would consist of people in positions of responsibility in the district service centre, including one member of staff and seven representatives from the district council plenary, which in turn comprised one representative from each village council. The district council would be the official agency at the district level for the planning of activities concerned with well-being, services and production (Article 57). Plans approved by the district council would be implemented by the service centres at the district level. This council would authorise all the centre's financial operations (Articles 67 and 83).

A review of the progress of the service centres indicates that, in spite of the state's great emphasis on the reform of the agricultural and rural organisations, its objectives are far from being achieved. For example in October 1979 the then minister of agriculture, Zali, stated that by 1983 centres would be established in 1703 districts and 190 county towns. Although there are no precise figures on the number of centres set up, according to one estimate in 1988 only 730 district centres had been opened, 58 per cent below the target set in the 1983 development plan (Schirazi, 1993, p. 142).

Evaluation of the centres' work by various researchers and experts is based on the extent to which the centres have met the stated objectives. There have been some positive achievements with respect to the provision of funds and the implementation of infrastructural measures to increase both the area of land in agricultural use and the area of irrigated land (Azkia, 1986, p. 323). However, there is no quantitative data on the efficacy of the centres' programmes. With regard to the distribution of agricultural inputs and infrastructural programmes, it is reasonable to assume that these measures have contributed to a rise in the per hectare yield (ibid.; Totonchiyan, 1986). The centres have also provided capital goods such as agricultural machinery to speed up the application of agricultural inputs (seed, fertilizer, pesticides and so on). Nevertheless the successes in this respect have not been dramatic or occurred throughout the country (Azkia, 1986, pp. 318–24).

Contrary to the spirit of the project and its regulations, in practice the service centres have made all the major decisions and acted very much like farm corporations in dictating peasant policies, rather than playing a purely consultative role (Azkia, 1990, p. 17). Most of the planning has been imposed from above, not from the village level. In many places the village councils, which were intended to help the staff at the service centres, have not been set up or are few in number compared with the service centres (Sabetghadam, 1983; Azkia, 1986; Totonchyan, 1986).

No attempt has been made to use traditional skills and local knowledge or take into account the customs and values of the rural people. There has been no attempt to encourage their participation in identifying problems, planning or decision making, or in supervising or utilising technical and economic provisions. This lack of participation means that in most areas only the influential and better-off peasants have benefited from the services and inputs provided by the centres (Azkia, 1986, pp. 315–19).

Most of the district and county service centres are located in the more prosperous areas of provinces or in areas that already enjoyed access to services, and they have proved to be not dissimilar from other governmental institutions. In many cases regional particularities have been overlooked, causing an uneven distribution of services (ibid.) Even in prosperous areas, more services have been provided to the better-off villages. This was confirmed by the head of the agricultural bureau and the centres in the district under study in the summer of 1996. In response to the question 'What criteria do you use for the provision of services to the villages?', he said:

> The criteria are capabilities and potentialities. These include the area of cultivated land and orchards and importantly the potential of the villages with regard to absorbing the service. This policy does not mean we discriminate against poor and small villages, but it is unwise [uneconomical] to pour in services and inputs where there is less possibility of obtaining results (personal interview).

Concerning the relationship between the service centres and the village councils and rural population, the staff at the centres have no real knowledge about the villages in their area. Likewise the members of the village councils have scant knowledge of the centres' aims and tasks, mainly due to the lack of regular contact between the councils and the centres. This, along with ill-qualified 'experts', could be the main reason why it is difficult for rural people and their councils to participate in decision making (Azkia, 1986, pp. 310–12, 1990, pp. 128–9). As for the different governmental organisations working in the rural sector, in most cases instead of cooperation there has been competition between the various state organisations – particularly between the Jihad-e Sazandeghi and the service centres – offering rural people the same services in the same place and at the same time. Although some areas have benefited, most villages have received few or no services at all (Sabetghadam, 1981; Azkia, 1986, pp. 310–12). Part of the reason for this competition and duplication is that officials working in the local organisations have been reluctant to dissolve them or integrate them with the centres (Azkia, 1986, p. 302). As far as the Ministry of Agriculture and the Jihad are concerned this competition is technocratic and political, indicating a struggle for survival in the sense that both of these organisations want to prove their competence and efficiency in order to defend their existence and prevent their dissolution or integration. The lack of cooperation also originates from the fact that the reform was 'not an organic part of a general administrative reform policy . . . the administrative reform of agriculture was carried out piecemeal, while the other areas of the administration have not been reformed . . . which is one of the reasons for many of its contradictions' (Schirazi, 1993, p. 135). This was confirmed in 1996 by a senior expert and long-term employee at the agricultural organisation:

> The reform [setting up the service centres] was very comprehensive but its implementation only a short period after the revolution was too hasty. The main reasons for the reform were, firstly, the revolutionary zeal inside the ministry; and secondly, political motives – that is, an immediate response to criticisms of the prerevolutionary state policy and a great demand in society for a new strategy. Effective implementation required a well-organised and well-coordinated administrative system between the centres and the various units and organisations of the Ministry of Agriculture, as well as between the centres and other government organisations. We failed to convince the organisations under our supervision of the need for cooperation. The most important first step was to secure the cooperation of the Agricultural Bank to solve the financial problems involved in the implementation of projects and the provision of credit. We could not obtain the cooperation of other organisations. The aim of the centres was to avoid red tape and accelerate the

implementation of rural programmes, but we had to involve ... the regional governor, the head of the energy bureau, the chairman of the road and transportation bureau, and so on, in order to convince them to cooperate with us. It was too hasty because the project needed well-trained and qualified staff, and even now we have a shortage of this kind of staff at the provincial bureau (personal interview).

With regard to devolving the activities of the service centres to the rural people, here too the centres have not had notable success. Most activities – ranging from simple measures such as writing a letter of request for agricultural inputs to more technical questions – are still handled by the centres (Azkia, 1992, pp. 115–16).

The Ministry of Agriculture was to have reorganised its administration in conformity with the Act setting up the centres, but it has failed to do so and there is now a sort of dual structure within the ministry (Eftekhari, 1987, p. 480). This problem was described by Minister of Agriculture Kalantari in 1989:

> Unfortunately, from the point of view of the people who have made sacrifices for the revolution, we have in the past been unable to create a successful administrative order. I have often warned the heads of department [at the ministry] to desist from obstructing the work . . . Unfortunately, the administrative system in agriculture has been transformed into an office for procuring material in which the question of expanding production represents an unknown link in the chain (quoted in Schirazi, 1993, p. 147).

The Islamic village councils: changing the political structure of villages

The setting up of village councils was part of the broad programme to create an administrative system for all organisations and regions at all levels. According to Article 100 of the constitution:

> in order to have a rapid progress in social, economic, developmental, sanitary, cultural, educational plans and other welfare affairs through the cooperation of people with respect to local circumstances, the administration of the villages, districts, towns, county towns or provinces is to be conducted under the supervision of an appropriate council whose members are chosen by the inhabitants of the same locality.

However, by 1999 this programme had still not been fully implemented due to (1) the fear of demands for regional autonomy in non-Persian-speaking provinces, which had begun to emerge immediately after the revolution in some regions; (2) the assumption of power by etatist Islamists, particularly during the war with Iraq, who strongly supported state intervention in all sociopolitical and economic arenas, as well as a centralised administration (Schirazi, 1993); and (3) the continuation of etatist rule in the post-war period, but with strong emphasis on a particular interpretation of state–society relations based on the political philosophy of the caliphate and authoritarianism by the ruling bloc.

The motive behind the establishment of Islamic village councils was first of all political. Other village councils had been set up before the revolution or later by leftists and autonomists, and the best way to disband these councils and disarm the leftists was to replace them with Islamic ones or Islamise the existing councils, ejecting the incumbents in the process. This task is reflected in Article 6 of the Islamic village councils' law on administrative regulations: 'the holy key task of the Village Councils lies in the preservation of the achievements of the Islamic Revolution and in the efforts that are to be made for enforcing the line of the Imam and in the fight against all the groups that are active against Islam and Islamic people'.

The Islamic village councils were part of the Bazargan government's programme to reorganise the Ministry of Agriculture by setting up the Centres of Services for Rural and Nomadic People. The councils were seen as a key tool in the implementation of the centres' rural and agricultural policies. In general the Islamic village council is a participatory institution in which the efforts and endeavours of rural people are coordinated in order to improve the economic, social and cultural conditions of their village. It acts as a link between the government and the rural population and is an official reference point for the village. It is a means to discern the needs and determine the priorities of the village and make it responsible for technical, economic and production management (Azkia, 1986, p. 309).

According to the regulations approved in 1981 and amended in 1985, the duties of the village council are as follows:

- To create a spirit of cooperation between the people and the authorities by informing the people about the country's affairs.
- To enlist the cooperation of the people in national affairs such as referendums and national and regional elections.

- To obtain population statistics.
- To issue village identity cards.
- To cooperate with the executive responsible for cultural affairs.
- To increase knowledge among rural people through literacy programmes (*Nehazat-e-Savad Amouzi*).

Each council consists of a proportional number of representatives of the various social strata (farmers, the landless, livestock breeders, labourers and so on). The members are elected by secret ballot by the villagers for a term of two years. The number of members ranges from five to seven (Azkia, 1986, p. 308).

As mentioned in the previous section, according to the general policy of the Centres of Services, the district centre is an independent executive planning unit but it must function with the participation of village people (via the members of the councils). This means that needs are determined by the village council and are then examined by the district council from technical, economic, social and executive points of view. Subsequently, and taking into regard general government policies and the potential capabilities, development projects are designed, costed and arranged by centres at higher levels.

With the exception of changes in such matters as the term of office of council members, the election and dismissal of the *dehyar* (the official representative of the lieutenant-governor of the district, called *khadkhoda* in the prerevolutionary era and *dehyar* in the post-revolutionary period), the number of council members and any imbalance in their social composition, the main characteristics and duties of the councils are laid down in the Law of the Islamic Councils, approved in 1996 (Articles 3, 4 and 68).

Field studies of village councils (conducted before the 1999 plan to set up the rural and urban councils) revealed that the councils are failing to carry out their duties. An investigation was conducted in three regions – Jiroft (Kerman province), Bandar Abbas (at the entrance to the Persian Gulf) and Garmsar (near Tehran) – of the relationship between the district councils and the service centres on the one hand, and the village councils and the peasants on the other, by examining the extent of peasant participation in the work of these agencies. The study found that:

> the members of the Village Councils had very little information about the work of the Service Centres with which they were supposed to cooperate through their representatives. The members of

the District Village councils were not much better informed about them and also knew very little about the villages they supposedly represented. The major problem was that the Village Councils in no way represent the villagers. The researcher reports some disproportionality between the social composition of the villagers and that of the Village Councils. The presence of teachers, students, drivers, shopkeepers and civil servants questions the principle of proportional representation .... The members do not possess adequate information about their tasks and responsibilities. In some cases they are unfamiliar with agriculture and have no social standing at the village level (Azkia, 1986, p. 309).

The members of the village councils are nominated by the service centres, and even if the former participate in the decisions of the latter, it does not mean that peasants do so too. The peasants are involved in implementing the measures decided by the government, but more in terms of construction and infrastructure.

In respect of informed participation, state organisations have taken no positive steps in the villages: 'the peasant who is a council member is one because the government wants him to be one and not because he feels the need for it' (ibid., p. 317). According to the regulations, the councils are obliged to inform people about the progress of their work and consult with them once a month. For important issues they should hold general meetings, but the study revealed that no such meetings are held (ibid., pp. 309–10).

The studies indicated that, contrary to the provisions in the service centre regulations about the identification of needs from below – through the village councils – in practice needs are not named by the village, the village council has no effective role in the verification of them, and development projects are not planned in the district centres due to the weakness of their technical personnel. Perhaps the projects that have been conducted to date cannot really be termed development projects. The reason is that the councils are ineffective and their composition is unsuitable because not all the strata of the rural population are represented (ibid., p. 309).

According to a report by the Jihad, in December 1987 there were around 40 000 village councils, whose activities reached 96 per cent of the rural population. However, my own field study and interviews with officials at various organisations concerned with the rural sector revealed that in most villages, particularly in remote ones, the village councils had been or were being dissolved, and that only two or three rural elections had been held. In those councils that continued to exist the members had long exceeded their term of office. The main reason for the dissolution of the councils and the lack of elections is that no clear status has been given to the councils in the national legal and administrative system. Hence, they have become dysfunctional.

However, the establishment of the councils has resulted in changes to the political structure of villages in the sense that the prerevolutionary village headman system has been replaced, although the prerevolutionary structures of power and influence in the villages have not been eliminated. In most villages there is a dual power structure, the first arm comprising semi-official village officials and the members of the councils, and the second the actual village leaders, elders and the prerevolutionary village headmen. The reason for this dual structure is that the village councils are mostly made up of young or middle-aged villagers who have insufficient knowledge of village life and agricultural issues. This feature has been identified as existing in the abovementioned areas and six other provinces – Khorasan, Mazandran, Khozistan, Markazi, Zanjan and Esfahan. For example in 1988, according to a survey of the latter provinces, over 55 per cent of council members were under 40, 38.5 per cent were between 41 and 60 and only 3.9 per cent were 60 or over (Ministry of the Interior, 1988).

As the council programme implemented in 1999 is still in its early stages it is too soon to evaluate its performance. The previous experiences of the rural councils might or might not be repeated in the current council programme – it all depends on political, social, economic and cultural developments nationwide. Broadly speaking, it seems that the council programme will be affected by at least two factors.

The first factor is a structural one and concerns the historically overcentralised nature of the national political and administrative system. There is likely to be great resistance by both bureaucrats and political forces to power being handed over to the people (the councils). Theoretically and politically, there is a fundamental contradiction between the principle of the sovereignty of the people and the political structure and philosophy of the Islamic state, as manifested in institutions such as the constitution, parliament and the leadership (the absolute jurisprudence). This contradiction has been justified by the claim that the Islamic system is democratic in the sense that the main actors are elected by the people. The success of the councils also depends on which of the two main political and ideological factions is in power: the conservatives do not believe in the legitimacy of people's rights, while the reformists are in favour of popular participation.

The second factor concerns the councils themselves and their relations with other organisations including the lack of experience and education on the part of council members, and the lack of clarity about the councils' duties, particularly in connecting and dealing with different governmental organisations.

Ministry of Jihad

The third measure after the revolution was to establish the Jihad (holy struggle) organisation (later the Ministry of Jihad). It was formed a few months after the revolution under the direction of the provisional government and was staffed by volunteers from all occupational groups. Its mission was to plan and carry out development projects in rural areas, to serve the most deprived segments of the population (the rural people), to bridge the gap between town and village and to find a solution to the complicated problems facing villagers. The goals of the Jihad were officially stated as:

> a) to unite the energetic volunteers, especially university and high school students, unemployed high school graduates and others without work; b) to create lines of communication between the intelligentsia and the disinherited; c) to assist rural economic development; d) to increase literacy among peasants; and e) to propagate Islamic culture and Islamic Revolution in rural areas (Ferdows, 1983, p. 15).

Compared with the service centres, which were a moderate reorganisation of the existing administration and a strategy designed by experts and bureaucrats in the Ministry of Agriculture long before the revolution, the establishment of the Jihad organisation was a revolutionary move, supported by reformers within the ruling stratum, most of whom had a radical approach to agrarian reform. If the establishment of service centres can be seen as a reaction against the prerevolutionary agricultural organisation, the creation of the Jihad may be seen as a reaction against the whole traditional (prerevolutionary) administrative machinery. The prevailing idea was that the traditional rural organisations, with their technocratic approach, could not combat rural deprivation; therefore the tackling of rural issues required a revolutionary administrative system 'based on the mobilization of the masses', unfettered by bureaucracy and run democratically to increase the participation of the population and 'put an end all sort of privations in the countryside' (Schirazi, 1993, p. 148).

The driving forces behind the establishment of the Jihad were mainly political and ideological. After the revolution, in spite of the administrative reforms announced by the Ministry of Agriculture, some radical and leftist groups who had been purged from the ministry or had left because the ministry itself and its policies were not in accordance with their approach, were dissatisfied and raised the idea of establishing a new rural organisation. To curtail the influence of these leftist groups in rural areas it was necessary 'to ensure that the opponents of the revolution – i.e., the left – did not use the opportunity to go out into countryside and conduct anti-Islamic propaganda' (ibid.) Furthermore the Jihad would provide a means of obtaining rural support for the revolution and spreading the message of the revolution amongst the villagers. The revolution was an urban phenomenon and the rural people, who traditionally were politically marginal, did not take full part in the revolution, or joined it only on the eve of victory. To have a stable political system it was necessary to gain the support of the rural people. For this and many other reasons, which will be discussed later, the Jihad was generously funded and enjoyed excellent facilities. To follow the policy of support achievement, the generous distribution of money to rural people under the guise of loans (*garz*) was also conducted mostly through the Jihad. Some revolutionary leaders recommended that the lenders should not to be strict in calling in their loans, and in many cases the villagers never paid back the money.

From the point of view of organisational structure, according to the charter published in the *Gazette of the Islamic Republic* on 24 October 1979, the Jihad was set up at four levels: the district centre, the county town, the provincial centre and the central council. The tasks at each level were similar to those at the Ministry of Agriculture's centres. For instance the district centre level was an executive site. It provided educational, communication and agricultural extension services, and identified the needs, potentials and resources (such as fertility of soil, road, etc.) of villages and referred them to higher levels.

The county town centre was in charge of management and executive coordination. Its main duties were to analyse data received from district centres; prepare initial proposals; carry out regional operational programmes; supervise and cooperate in the evaluation of district centres; administer and regulate budgets; and follow up the the funds allocated for the implementation of rural programmes. The provincial centre, which was considered to be an independent organisation with legal powers and financial independence, was responsible for Jihad activities at the provincial level. It had a coordinating role in regional planning and an authority to evaluate the feasibility of the plans recommended from the lower levels, from financial and regional points of view, and to set budgets and allocate credit. It was the central site of rural development programmes at the provincial level. Besides maintaining constant contact with the district centres, county town centres and the central council, it was responsible for collecting and analysing data and information received from the counties and towns in order to prepare comprehensive rural development programmes at the provincial level. The central office (Jihad-e Markaz) was responsible for policy making, macro programmes, and the coordination and supervision of provincial projects (Eftekhari, 1988; Schirazi, 1993). Like the Centres of Services, the aim of this arrangement was to reap the advantages of both top-down and bottom-up planning.

During the first stage of its existence the Jihad was an interministerial organisation presided over at the decision-making level by representatives from the ministries concerned, including the Ministry of Agriculture, and its main responsibility was rural improvement. The state administration preferred the Jihad to remain an assistant organisation rather than emerge as a rival bureaucracy (Ferdows, 1983; pp. 11–15; Schirazi, 1993, p. 149).

The second stage of the Jihad's development began after Bazargan's resignation in November 1979, which led to the transfer of political power to Islamist-populist forces under the leadership of the Islamic Republic Party. The obstacles to the Jihad's expansion were removed, and it started to move into areas formerly under the jurisdiction of the Ministry of Agriculture and other ministries. The second draft of the Jihad's charter, which was approved after a long debate in parliament in August 1983, removed responsibility for the construction of village schools, along with the relevant funds, from the Ministry of Education and Training and transferred it to the Jihad. A similar move was made in the case of road building, the draining of underground canals, and the procurement, production and distribution of tractors and pesticides. According to the second draft of its charter, the Jihad was authorised to cooperate in the expansion of agriculture and animal husbandry, conduct rural improvement work, spread Islamic culture, take charge of irrigation projects and issue peasants with vouchers entitling them to loans for agricultural purposes (Jihad-e Sazandegi, 1992; Schirazi, 1993).

Two factors were responsible for the expansion of the Jihad. First, the radicalisation of politics led to the removal of the liberal–moderate faction from the political arena. As already mentioned, the Jihad was originally founded as an interministerial organisation, and during the Bazargan regime and for a few months afterwards there was resistance within the government to its expansion. There was a fear that it might prove to be like the Revolutionary Guard and encroach on the work of other ministries and governmental organisations (Ferdows, 1983, p. 11). Most importantly, behind this fear and resistance there was competition between the two main polico-ideological factions: the Islamist extremist faction led by the Islamic Republic Party (IRP), and the liberal–moderate faction led mainly by the National Front and Freedom Movement and other liberal groups. The IRP 'did not have a coherent development ideology around which to organise civil corps . . . it also lacked a mass base, since none of its organisers had any lasting claim to national leadership outside their association with Khomeini' (Ferdows, 1983, p. 15). Thus the IRP attempted to hold on to the Jihad from the beginning and supported its expansion when it managed to take political power: 'It resorted to frequent purges to maintain control of it.' The idea of the 'committed Muslim', which was the criterion for belonging to the Jihad, 'in practice' became a tool for 'purges intended to rid the Jihad of its more liberal and middle or upper class members' (ibid. 1983, pp. 16–17). For example Ferdows (1983) observed that when the Jihad was looking for employees there were a lot of young unemployed people looking for jobs, but they were rejected because they did not meet the Jihad's principal employment criterion. Similarly one member of parliament stated that the Jihad 'dismissed a great many specialists or [gave] them menial tasks simply because they were not members of the Party of God, replacing them with unqualified people' (cited in Schirazi, 1993, p. 154).

Second, the war with Iraq and the part played by the Jihad in the war facilitated its expansion. This is particularly significant since the war was the most crucial national problem of the time. The Jihad's role involved engineering works, including the construction of roads, bridges, canals and lines of defence, repairing equipment and weapons, supplying the front with electricity, water and so on. It also mobilised and dispatched so-called volunteers to the front, produced equipment for the war, collected money, clothes and food, provided medical facilities and distributed propaganda material.

All of these activities consolidated the status of the Jihad and assisted its expansion, which had two major consequences. First, the *shoura* (council) system was transformed into a ministerial system. Under the *shoura* system the Jihad comprised of four levels of council; the town, district, provincial and central. It had the authority to make decisions and manage its own affairs. Nevertheless the proposal of the Jihad's administration when finally approved, restricted the *shoura* system. In order to guarantee uniformity and to ensure the coordination necessary in matters affecting the Jihad it was proposed by the Parliamentary Commission for the Institutions of the Revolution that a Central Committee carry out the tasks of the ministry in due course. The committee was to consist of reliable individuals proposed by a panel of members of the provincial councils and people in positions of responsibility in the Jihad's central organisations and associated branches (Schirazi, 1993, p. 157).

Second, the Jihad's responsibilities duplicated or overlapped those of other organisations. According to the secretary of state at the prime minister's office, 'this duplication [went] furthest in agriculture, where two rival ministries were looked in combat on the backs of the rural population' (ibid., p. 153). The competition between the two ministries deteriorated into conflict, particularly in areas where the Jihad had started to establish *Jihad-e dehstan* (district Jihad) with similar tasks to those of the Ministry of Agriculture's service centres. There was a general consensus that the two ministries should be merged, but no practical plan or proposals were put forward. It was suggested that the Ministry of Agriculture be abolished and its functions and affiliated organisations transferred to the Jihad, but this resulted in the ruling classes being divided into two main camps. On the one hand there were the populist statists, the majority of whom were in the executive body. They saw the Jihad as a revolutionary institution with revolutionary values, and therefore very close to the rural population. The perceived failings of the Ministry of Agriculture was another reason put forward in favour of the Jihad. On the other hand a large number of parliamentarians were opposed to a merger. They argued that the government had 'no real programme for organising the merger', and that 'the merger would give Jihad too much power, especially in rural areas, which it might abuse to influence the elections' (ibid., p. 152). Eventually the merger proposal was rejected.

The third stage of the Jihad's development began after the end of the Iran–Iraq War (1988) with the emergence of a moderate and pragmatic approach. The merger idea was put forward again by the dominant technocratic and pragmatic groups. However this time the suggestion was to merge the Jihad into the Ministry of Agriculture, although no practical steps were taken. Instead an attempt was made to define and divide the duties of three ministries: the Jihad would be responsible for all natural resources such as forestry, pasture land, fisheries, animal husbandry, rural construction and rural industry; the Ministry of Agriculture would administer matters pertaining to farming as well as local land and water use; and the Ministry of Water and Energy would look after electricity supplies and the construction of large dams (Jihad-e Sazandegi, 1992, pp. 82–3).

With regard to the Jihad's approach to rural development, this may be divided into three periods or stages. The first was characterised by 'revolutionary zeal' or 'enthusiastic attention to village[s]' (Frouzesh, 1987). The Jihad's aim was to eliminate deprivation in rural areas, particularly in the poorest ones. Infrastructural projects such as the provision of roads, schools, public baths, river bridges, small dams and electrification were undertaken. During this period the Jihad had no strategy for its future and no concrete programme for rural activities. Most of the measures were carried out to meet immediate needs in response to demands by villagers or suggestions by Jihad staff based on their investigation of rural problems. The Jihad's main success in this period, in addition to making improvements in rural life, was political. The political vacuum resulting from the collapse of rural management as a consequence of the revolution, and the inability of the existing administrative system to fill this vacuum, meant that rural areas were being used by opposition groups for their own political and ideological goals, but the Jihad managed to neutralise these activities.

The second period ran from 1981 to 1985, when the main focus was on agricultural production. The principal factor in the Jihad's activities was the migration question, and its 'pull' and 'push' factors in rural areas. As in the first period the Jihad had no specific strategy, but based on the experience of the first period it concluded that the implementation of single projects such as road building, electrification and so on was not enough and that attention should also be paid to social problems such as poverty, deprivation, isolation and migration. No measures existed to prevent rural–urban migration or reduce the inequalities between town and country. At this stage agricultural production became the major axis of the Jihad's activities. Consequently investment was concentrated more on villages with a higher agricultural potential. However, the Jihad did not have a coherent policy and its activities did not pave the way to rural development.

The third period began in 1985 and has been called the stage of comprehensive perspectives on rural development (Frouzesh, 1987). In this stage, within the framework of physical upgrading projects, a significant part of the Jihad's work consisted of organising services and improving the physical structure of rural areas, integrating scattered villages, creating rural industrial areas and encouraging the settlement of nomads. The aim of the physical upgrading projects was to lay the groundwork for a better system of service distribution in the villages, and to pave the way for socioeconomic development by making physical and environmental improvements in the countryside to attract commercial investment. The projects were aimed at villages with over 100 households – about 11 000 villages throughout the country – and implementation began in 1988.

There has been no comprehensive evaluation of these projects, but a few field studies have been undertaken. The first was conducted by the Housing and Improvement (*Behsazi*) Bureau two years after implementation of the projects in a few village project sites in Eastern Azerbaijan. The main emphasis was on the attitude of the villagers, and it was concluded that the villagers had a positive attitude towards the projects and welcomed their implementation. The second study was conducted in a few villages of the province of Esfahan by the Rural Research Centre of Jihad in 1996. According to the researcher:

> my prime observations and evaluations indicate that the projects were welcomed by the target villages. They were successful in changing the morphology of the villages. But the future of them, from the point of view of maintenance, remains unclear. The maintenance of the projects needs heavy investment which rural people are unable to finance. While, in many villages, these projects are being destroyed, the dwellings cannot afford to safeguard them. This in turn greatly raised the villagers' expectations for the government to do this task. In most villages, the villagers believed that it is the government's responsibility to maintain the projects (personal interview).

During its establishment the Jihad, for the reasons discussed above, enjoyed a generous supply of financial resources and enthusiastic volunteers. There are no precise statistics on the extent of its financial resources, but the available data indicate that the amount of government funds spent by the Jihad on developing and renovating villages in 1978–87 was quite sizeable. During the period 1980–90 up to 59.4 billion rials were allocated to the expansion and improvement of villages, including the construction of flood barriers and sanitary installations. In addition 31.48 billion rials were spent on the health services and 65.63 billion rials on expanding the power network. Between 1978 and 1983, 61.88 billion rials were allocated solely to the building of rural roads, and in the period 1978–87 nearly 230 billion rials were spent on health and public service facilities. To this must be added the additional credit initially earmarked for other sectors, such as agriculture and education, but given over to various rural projects. All in all an estimated 610 billion rials of national credit was allocated to the expansion of villages.

At first the Jihad's projects were funded entirely by the government, but from 1988 the villages were required to contribute 20–40 per cent of the cost, otherwise the project would not be implemented.

According to a number of accounts (for example Loeffler, 1986; World Bank, 1994) the Construction Ministry was active in providing various services to the rural sector. Nonetheless over 39 per cent of the 1100 billion rials of credit allocated to rural projects was absorbed by the Jihad's construction undertakings during 1980–85 (Jihad-e Sazandegi, 1992, p. 44).

The questions that should be asked, bearing in mind its strong political support and generous supply of enthusiastic volunteers and financial resources, are how effective has the Jihad been and who has benefited from its programmes? Despite its numerous and varied activities, to date there has been no comprehensive evaluation of the Jihad's performance. (Part of the reason for this might be political and ideological in the sense that the Jihad is a revolutionary organisation, and any negative evaluation would put in doubt the ability of revolutionary institutions to solve rural problems.) The official reports are poor, fragmented and often contradictory, and consequently provide no concrete information on the quantity and quality of the Jihad's activities. For example an official report published in 1992, which was to have reviewed the past 16 years of the Jihad's activities, only compared the pre- and post-revolutionary situation in rural areas in respect of road construction and electrification over the decade 1980–90. According to this report, before the Islamic Revolution the total length of country roads was no more than 8000 kilometres, but by 1990 there were over 50 000 kilometres of gravelled roads and 6400 kilometres of asphalted country roads. During the decade 1980–90 Jihad took electricity to 10 680 villages and about 66 per cent of the rural population now have electricity, compared with just 5000 villages in earlier years. With regard to water, before the revolution only 6611 villages were supplied with drinking water, but by 1988 the number had risen to 18 139. Of these, 11 428 (63 per cent) had been supplied by the Jihad (Jihad-e Sazandegi, 1992, pp. 48–120).

Another report is that by Rafipour (1989) who conducted a survey of villagers' attitudes towards the Jihad in three provinces: Esfahan, Fars and Khorasan. The villages were selected on the basis of two criteria: population – villages with a minimum of 40 households; and the number of the Jihad's activities – villages in which a minimum of two projects had been carried out. The study sought to ascertain how well known the Jihad was among rural people, and the factors that affected the attitude of people towards the Jihad. Rafipour examined two sets of influences on people's attitude: environmental factors such as the size of the population, development facilities, religion and agricultural conditions; and personal factors such as sex, age, family background, social awareness, literacy, economic circumstances and so on. He found that the sample households were highly satisfied with the Jihad. For example, 85 per cent of the respondents believed that the Jihad had had a positive effect on their life (ibid., p. 197), and about the same percentage had a positive attitude towards the Jihad personnel (ibid., p. 197). Taking each province separately, 78.29 per cent of the sample households in Esfahan, 69.61 per cent in Khorasan and 67.27 per cent in Fars were satisfied with the Jihad's activities. Analysis of the other environmental variables provided similar results (ibid., p. 200). The reason for the slightly more positive result in Esfahan was the greater concentration of Jihad activities in that province (ibid., p. 201). It was found that variables such as sex, age, family background, social awareness, literacy, and economic circumstances had no significant bearing on the respondents' evaluation of the Jihad. However, variables such as interest in agricultural development, participation in the implementation of rural projects, and satisfaction with the village council and the national authorities did influence the results (ibid., pp. 200–2). My own observations in the districts in question indicated that although people did have a positive attitude towards the Jihad, they believed that it was becoming like an agricultural bureau:

> Another evaluation is that by the World Bank (1994, p. 57): the physical achievements are considerable. The watchword of popular participation in construction and maintenance is a useful link between responsibility and economic reality. The linkage of the construction programme to the ministry's extension and popular participation effort and to the structure of Islamic Rural Councils is a useful one.

This report is a description of the Jihad's activities and lacks critical analysis.

Other evaluations are based on simple observations. For example Farazmand (1989, p. 222) states that 'the developmental achievements of the Reconstruction Crusade have been impressive. By 1983, the organisation claimed to have built 8000 miles of roads, 1700 schools, 1600 public baths and 110 health centres'. He adds that:

> in a 1983 visit to more than 30 villages in the country of Foumenat in Gilan, I observed *an impressive change* in the face of these villages: access roads were built and others were in progress deep inside the villages, electrification and free electricity were being enjoyed by the villages, several new schools and public baths were in operation, credit and loans were easily available to peasants, fertilizers and machinery were accessible, and other services were being provided (ibid., emphasis added).

Similar observations have been reported by other researchers (Ferdows, 1983; Karimi, 1986; Loeffler, 1986). But Farazmand (1989, p. 222), while praising the Jihad for providing major developmental assistance, concludes that many rural people have been disappointed by the slow progress of its developmental services.

All of these appraisals are based mainly on the quantity and type of projects undertaken by the Jihad, and they do not examine whether they have been effective or the extent to which the Jihad has achieved its objective of alleviating rural problems. This is more clearly addressed by the Jihad itself:

> Despite the fact that the rural areas enjoy far more infrastructural facilities compared with the prerevolutionary era, the measures taken by the government in this regard have failed to eradicate rural poverty and to meet basic needs of the rural population. This was mainly due to the lack of a clear development strategy (both national and rural) and also due to concentration of the country's all developmental possibilities in urban areas (especially in Tehran) ... Moreover, the existence of parallel institutions in the same field of activities, and the lack of conformity of many of the activities with the basic needs of rural people have impeded efforts by the government to devise a coordinated mechanism for rural development (Jihad-e Sazandegi, 1992, pp. 48–9).

These thoughts were echoed by several senior officials at the Ministry of Jihad. For example the head of the Budget and Planning

Organisation, in response to the question 'to what extent do you think the Jihad has reached its objectives?' said:

> From the point of view of the activities carried out by the Jihad, I think it has done more than was expected. This owes much to the revolutionary zeal and sincerity of the forces who joined the Jihad voluntarily. From the point of view of economic rationality, I cannot say it has been successful. The reason for this is twofold. First, the Jihad's work has been based not on expertise, but more on trial and error. Second, the revolutionary atmosphere demanded such a rationality. The principle and aim were to serve the poor, so most of the work done by the Jihad was concentrated in poor areas and poor villages without taking into account the economic aspects of the activities (personal interview).

The same question was posed to the deputy in charge of the department of people participation who gave a similar answer: 'The answer is clearly no. The main reason is that we are moving away from revolutionary values and objectives. In my opinion we did not have any problems in fulfilling our duties, we were successful in solving the rural issues to some extent' (personal interview).

The Mosha cooperatives

Another government measure was the creation of a new form of cooperative (*mosha*) to replace the existing cooperatives and farm corporations. Their establishment proceeded apace with the transfer of estates by the seven-member Committee of Land Devolution.

The *mosha* system was introduced in 1980 (Azkia, 1986) and like the other state rural policies it was influenced by criticism of the Shah's agricultural policies, based on modern, capital-intensive farms and destruction of the traditional organisation of production (*boneh*). It was also argued that such cooperatives are indigenous and are based on the value of cooperatives in Islam. They would include the benefits of the large-scale use of machinery through the assistance and services which government would provide (Schirazi, 1993, p. 238). As a member of parliament demonstrated, 'the initiative aimed to establish an Islamic form of cooperative system differing from everything else known by this name in the rest of the world, especially from the monstrosities set up under the shah' (ibid, p. 237).

The basic purpose of these cooperatives was to minimise the disadvantages of small subsistence units without eliminating private landownership by the peasants. Each unit would consist of at least five members and operate as a council. They would be of medium size and their holdings would range from 20 to 60 hectares.

The basis of land transferral was the customary *mosha* system of land tenure. According to the Act of Islamic Land Reform, ownership of the land would be collectively transferred to the peasants. Thus the title received by each peasant would give him or her no absolute right to a defined piece of land but merely an equal share of the total land held by a *mosha* production cooperative (Azkia, 1992, p. 19). The members of the *mosha* would work cooperatively as a team, on the basis of traditional units of production (*boneh*) (ibid.). Each *mosha* cooperative would select an experienced peasant as director (*sarmosha*) and two advisors (*moshawer*) to deal with the *mosha*'s affairs outside the unit.

The aim was to regain the advantages of the traditional form of cooperative (*boneh*) (Schirazi, 1993), which were believed by some experts to have been destroyed by the Shah's land reforms. The members would have to have experience in farming and expertise in a particular facet of farming, or be farmers working on their own land (Azkia, 1986, p. 267). The range of skills should be such that, as far as possible, no labour would need to be hired from outside. The aim was to eliminate the exploitation of labour and to prevent the accumulation of wealth in the hands of a few individuals. The main objective was to increase production through cooperation without separating labour from ownership of the land and other means of production. All resources such as land, water, machinery and other inputs would belong to the cooperative. These units would only be concerned with farming activities, particularly cultivating 'strategic crops' such as wheat, rice, etc. These crops would be identified by the government every year. Fruit-growing and animal-husbandry units that belonged to peasants, would be operated individually (ibid.).

The establishment of the *mosha* cooperatives was based on the following objectives:

- To introduce new agricultural methods and machinery.
- To increase the per capita income of peasants.
- To utilise the maximum amount of manpower in each village.
- To solve the problem of uneconomic holdings and the excessive parcelling out of holdings.
- To increase output by the widespread use of farm machinery.
- To facilitate better investment in agricultural activities (ibid., p. 266).

According to official statistics, 12 399 *mosha* cooperatives with 87 243 households as members were established after the revolution

(Lahsaeiadeh, 1993, p. 267). There has been no comprehensive examination of the role of these units in agricultural development, but a number of case studies show that they have not proved a success. The main reasons for this are as follows.

Lack of land ownership leading to lack of motivation

In almost all *mosha* cooperatives, 'the members showed no understanding for the joint land ownership that had been forced on them and in fact preferred to parcel it out among themselves' (Schirazi, 1993, p. 240). The case studies showed that nearly 80 per cent of the land was informally subdivided among the members (Azkia, 1992, p. 21). According to the Ministry of Agriculture's Institute for Rural Studies (1985), the Rural Research Group of the University of Tehran (1986) and the Land Devolution Committee (1989) in the Garmsar region, in some areas all of the *mosha* cooperative members farmed individually (for example in Sabzevar, Fesa and Baft). In Fars province the members spilt into subgroups, consisting of two or three peasants who farmed jointly.

Shortage of capital

The *mosha* cooperatives were mostly given wasteland, and sometimes sandy or stony soil that needed a great deal of work and investment to make it arable. 'During the past ten years nearly 56 billion rials have been invested in the *mosha*s. The average loan received by each *mosha* during the past decade is estimated to be 4 965 000 rials. This amount is insufficient for infrastructural activities' (Azkia, 1992, p. 21). Peasants who received a plot of the 'local customary size' were either unable to make full use of it due to the inadequacy of the loan, or had to turn to private brokers who charged excessive interest rates. Another negative consequence of the latter was that the broker was able to dictate the farming plan (for example the type of crop grown and the required yield), and indeed the actual running of the *mosha*'s affairs. In most cases this threatened the cohesion of the cooperatives (Anoushirvani, 1982, p. 145; Bafekr *et al.*, 1985, p. 125; Azkia, 1986, pp. 272–3).

Management problems

The department responsible for supporting the *mosha* units on the eve of the revolution was initially independent and autonomous, but during mid 1980 it joined the Ministry of Jihad as a division dealing with the problem of land disputes. At the central, provincial and local levels it faced serious management and functional problems, such as a shortage of technical staff, a lack of transport facilities, an inadequate supply of key inputs to support the cooperatives, and insufficient farm credit to purchase farm machinery. All this resulted in a tendency among peasants to leave the cooperatives or to insist that the land be divided among the members (Azkia, 1992, p. 22). In addition the division of labour became unequal and collective work was gradually confined to just a few tasks (Azkia, 1986, p. 22).

Conclusion

Agricultural policy in Iran underwent a considerable change after the revolution. The new policies were mainly adopted as a reaction against the prerevolutionary policies, which were modernistic with a strong emphasis on mechanised and capital-intensive farming. Reorganisation of the prerevolution agricultural administration, the creation of the Jihad-e Sazandegi, the establishment of Islamic rural councils, the creation of *mosha* cooperatives and the implementation of land reform were the main rural policies.

The reorganisation of the prerevolutionary agricultural administration was a prime response by the government to pressure from a number of socioeconomic forces to deal with the rural problems of the country. The government first established the Centres of Services for Rural and Nomadic People, which was a significant measure in reforming the agricultural administration. The centres were responsible for practically all aspects of rural life, including the expansion of agriculture and the improvement of rural areas. The objectives were to encourage self-sufficiency, improve the welfare of rural people, ensure social justice and reduce the socioeconomic gap between city and village by meeting basic needs, minimising direct government interference and taking into account both top-down and bottom-up approaches in planning. The centres were organised at four levels: national, regional, county town and district. It was thought that this method of organisation would help to avoid the disadvantages of both top-down and bottom-up planning. An examination of performance of the service centres indicates that, in spite of the great emphasis on reform of the state's agricultural and rural organisations, they have far from achieved their objectives. Contrary to the spirit of the centres and their regulations, most of the planning has been imposed from above, not from below. Consequently no attempt has been made to use traditional skills and local knowledge. In many cases, regional particularities have been overlooked. Most of the district service centres are concentrated in prosperous areas of provinces and in areas where there was already access to services at the time of their establishment. Service provision tends to be given to the better-off villages. In most cases, due to bureaucratic and political struggles for survival, instead of cooperation and coordination there has been competition between the centres and other government organisations, particularly the Jihad, to prove their competence and prevent their dissolution or integration. The gradual transfer of the activities of the centres to the rural people has not materialised, and the tasks of the traditional agricultural organisation (the Ministry of Agriculture) have not been transferred to the centres. Instead a dualistic agricultural administrative system exists.

The setting up of village councils was part of a broad programme to create an administrative system for all organisations and regions at all levels, and in particular it was part of the service centres' programme to develop a bottom-up link in the planning and implementation of rural development programmes. But it was also political in that it was an attempt to disarm the leftist forces who had used the power vacuum that existed in the immediate aftermath of the revolution to set up their own councils in certain areas. The village councils were seen as offering a link between the government and the rural people. They were to be a means of identifying the needs of villages, and were to be responsible for technical, economic and production management. An examination of the councils indicates that they have seldom been able to fulfil their tasks. The main reason for this has been the unfamiliarity of the members of the village councils with both their own tasks and the work of the service centres, their principal point of contact in respect of rural development issues. In turn the members of the district councils know very little about the villages they supposedly represent. This, combined with the councils' lack of legal status, has resulted in the mandatory holding of periodic council elections being largely ignored, and many councils, particularly in remote areas, have been dissolved. Although the establishment of village councils resulted in changes to the political structure of villages, it did not eliminate the prerevolutionary power structures, and in most villages a dual power structure emerged.

The third measure after the revolution was the establishment of the Jihad organisation. This was a reaction against the traditional (prerevolutionary) administrative machinery, which had proved incapable of combating rural deprivation, and thus the tackling of rural issues urgently required a revolutionary administrative system. The Jihad was originally intended to be an interministerial organisation presided over by the Ministry of Agriculture, but due to the radicalisation of the political atmosphere in the country, the invasion of Iraq and the consequent outbreak of war, the responsibilities of the Jihad were increased. The radicalisation of the political atmosphere involved the growth of Islamic extremism, led by the Islamic Republic Party, which sought to reinforce the Jihad in order to obtain its bureaucratic status, and develop a coherent development ideology.

The expansion of the Jihad resulted in the *shoura* (council) system being converted into a ministerial system, and in the duplication or overlapping of its tasks with those of other organisations. For political reasons the Jihad enjoyed a generous supply of financial resources, and its responsibilities grew from merely implementing specific infrastructural and agricultural production programmes to formulating comprehensive development programmes. However, it never had a coherent strategy for rural development. All its efforts were based on past experience rather than scientific study, and despite the considerable infrastructural facilities and services it introduced, because of the lack of coherent planning the programmes carried out in rural areas failed to meet the basic needs of the population.

Land reform was another policy of the post-revolutionary era. With the fall of the Shah's regime the land question was raised by two main forces: the remnants of the former landowning class, who demanded the reversal of the prerevolutionary land reforms; and peasant and radical forces, who began to expropriate land. The latter provoked three responses: a conventional jurisprudential response based on the legitimacy of ownership; the conventional economic response, which was based on economic rationality; and the state legislative and executive response, which involved the preparation of a land reform bill. The bill was radicalised after the resignation of the provisional government and its implementation faced serious problems. A major problem was imposing a limit on the size of individual landholdings, which had its roots in the sanctity of private property in Islamic jurisprudence. Another was organised and highly effective resistance by commercial farmers, technocrats, traditionalist *ulama* and conservative merchants, who succeeded in blocking the implementation of a more radical reform. These factors, plus changes in the international and national politico-economic atmosphere, such as the failure to emerge victorious from the Iran–Iraq War, mounting economic pressure and the developments in the Soviet bloc, resulted in a loss of pressure for radical land reform. As a consequence only a limited reform was implemented, mostly involving barren land or land unsuitable for cultivation and benefiting only small segment of the rural poor.

Another measure was the creation of a new form of cooperative (*mosha*) to replace the existing cooperatives and farm corporations as a mode of production. The aim was to take advantage of both modern capital-intensive farming and the traditional organisation of production (*boneh*). The *mosha* were unsuccessful, due mainly to lack of motivation, shortage of capital and mismanagement of the units. In many cases the lack of motivation, arising from the fact that land ownership was communal rather than individual, resulted in the division of *mosha* land among the peasants. The inadequate provision of agricultural inputs and credit by the government, which was mainly a result of post-revolutionary administrative chaos, caused the peasants to turn to brokers, and this also damaged the cooperative nature of the *mosha* units.

To sum up, most agricultural and rural policies initiated after the revolution were politically motivated, and once the short-term political objectives had been attained most projects, such as the service centres, the village councils, the provisions laid down in the Land Reform Act and even the *mosha* cooperatives were either abandoned or left to fade away.

4
Agricultural Policies and Agricultural Growth

Introduction

This chapter discusses the government's agricultural policies and evaluates their contribution to agricultural development. The discussion is organised in two main sections. The first briefly examines the state of agriculture prior to the revolution of 1979. The second discusses the post-revolutionary agricultural policies and is divided into three subsections, the first of which deals with measures to increase agricultural growth, starting with a brief account of the government's investment and fiscal policies and their role in capital formation. It then turns to land and water-use policies to increase the area of cultivated and irrigated land. The second subsection considers the government's efforts to increase agricultural yields, including the provision of inputs and the implementation of price controls. The final subsection examines the impact of the government's policies on agricultural growth.

An overview of agriculture prior to the revolution

Although the agricultural sector accounted for a large proportion of the country's gross national product (GNP) between 1900 and 1970, over time this share decreased. As some studies show, while the total contribution of agriculture to GNP in the first quarter of the twentieth century ranged between 80 per cent and 90 per cent, from 1926 onward its share continuously declined to about 50 per cent in 1950, 23 per cent in 1968 and 8.9 per cent in 1978 (Bharier, 1971; Azkia, 1986; Razzaghi, 1989). A comparison of the per capita GNP of the various economic sectors (Table 4.1) reveals a similar picture, namely a decline in the importance of the agricultural sector. Between 1965 and

Table 4.1 Per capita GNP, 1962 and 1977 (thousands of rials)

	Agriculture	Industry*	Services
1962	24.2	42.1	75.6
1977	105.9	267.3	380.3

* Excluding oil.
Source: Katouzian (1981), p. 165.

1970, the growth rate of per capita income was about 40 per cent, and industrial products experienced an increase of over 14 per cent. The GNP increase between 1968 and 1973 remained at about 14 per cent (Azkia, 1986, p. 157).

The rise in the international price of oil in the 1970s makes the calculation of and conclusions about the growth rate of GNP difficult in subsequent years, but it is clear that the industrial sector enjoyed rapid growth: in 1977 its share of GNP was 15.5 per cent. The share of the services sector rose by 15.3 per cent, but the average annual growth rate of the agricultural sector was just 3 per cent, a dramatic decline (ibid.). Similarly, during the previous two decades (prior to the revolution), while GNP increased sixfold the agricultural sector's share merely doubled (ibid., pp. 157–8). According to official statistics, the growth rate of GNP during the fifth development plan (1973–78) was 17 per cent, increasing from $26 billion in 1973 to $53 billion in 1978, mainly due to oil revenues (Central Bank of Iran, 1956–96).

The rise in the price of oil and the government's modernistic policies prior to the revolution resulted in a change in the country's economic structure, which was manifested in a decline of the agricultural sector's share of GNP compared with other sectors (Table 4.2). These develop-

Table 4.2 The share of various sectors in GNP, 1963–78 (per cent)

	1959/60	1962/63	1967/68	1972/73	1977/78
Agriculture	32.0	27.4	21.6	10.3	9.2
Industry	17.0	17.8	20.7	12.6	18.5
Industry and mining	n.a.	12.8	14.2	8.5	12.6
Construction	n.a.	4.3	4.8	3.5	4.8
Water and electricity	n.a.	0.7	1.7	0.6	1.1
Services	41.0	40.0	36.4	23.9	34.6
Government services	n.a.	7.6	9.4	7.9	10.9
Oil	10.0	12.3	18.0	50.6	34.7

Source: Central Bank of Iran, annual reports (various years).

Table 4.3 Distribution of the urban and rural populations 1921–78 (per cent)

	1921	1941	1951	1961	1971	1976	1977	1978
Urban	28.0	28.7	29.4	30.4	34.5	41.3	47.0	48.0
Rural and nomadic	72.0	71.3	70.6	69.6	65.5	58.7	53.0	52.0

Source: Statistical Centre of Iran (various years).

Table 4.4 Average annual population growth rate, 1956–86 (per cent)

	Rural areas	Urban areas	Total population
1956–66	2.09	5.10	3.13
1966–76	1.10	4.93	2.71
1976–86	2.27	5.41	3.91

Sources: Statistical Centre of Iran (1970, 1980, 1991); Ministry of the Interior (1960).

ments also led to a rise in the urban population, particularly as a result of migration from rural areas, where population growth fell below the national average (Tables 4.3 and 4.4)

The decline in the agricultural sector's share of GNP, from 32 per cent in 1960 to 9.3 per cent at the end of the fifth five-year plan (1973–78), along with a 3 per cent increase in the population of the country, caused an increased of about 9 per cent in the demand for food (Azkia, 1986). It should be mentioned that between 1961 and 1976, total agricultural production rose from 7.0 million tons to 19.0 million tons and arable land expanded by about five million hectares. Overall production increased by 2.6 per cent, 4.0 per cent and 4.6 per cent per annum during the implementation of the third, fourth and fifth development plans respectively (1962–77), but this was insufficient to satisfy the demand (Schirazi, 1993, p. 8). However, the easy availability of foreign exchange, mainly from oil revenues, allowed food to be imported and helped alleviate the pressures on the supply side. In 1957 the government spent $2.6 billion on food importation (Azkia, 1986, p. 162), rising to $6.6 billion during the fifth five-year development plan (1973/74–1977/78) (Schirazi, 1993, p. 7). According to one estimate, in the 1970–77 period food imports rose by about 28 per cent per annum in real terms (Karshenas, 1990, p. 157).

Although the share of agriculture in GNP declined over time it continued to account for a large share of employment (Table 4.5). This could have been due to the lower productivity of agriculture, which in

Table 4.5 The share of non-oil sectors in production and employment, 1977 (per cent)

	Agriculture	Industry	Services	Total
Production	14.7	29.7	55.6	100
Employment	33.3	31.3	35.6	100

Sources: Katouzian (1981); Central Bank of Iran, annual reports (various years).

turn was partly due to the low productivity of the land. According to one estimate, during the period 1963–78 the rate of land efficiency in agriculture was zero or negative, showing that land reclamation did not result in commensurate increase in productivity (Katouzian, 1981, p. 304). The cultivation of additional land would not have naturally led to a decline in yield in per hectare, so the decline was probably due to other factors that nullified the effects of land reclamation, such as inefficient use of modern machinery and inputs (ibid.; Schirazi, 1993). This was despite the fact that in the 1963–77 period there was a rapid inflow of modern inputs such as chemical fertilisers and pesticides. For instance the use of chemical fertilisers grew from about 32 000 tons a year in the early 1960s to 675 000 tons by the mid 1970s. Investment in agricultural machinery increased sevenfold over the same period (Karshenas, 1990, p. 151).

Therefore it seems that the increased utilisation of non-traditional materials and technologies did not produce the expected results. The failure of mechanisation to increase the yields was 'particularly true of cereals, which accounted for 80 percent of arable land: at 810 kilograms per hectare (kg/ha), the yield for wheat in 1974 was only ten kg/ha more than in 1961, and at 610 kg/ha it was actually 120 kg/ha lower for barley' (Schirazi, 1993, p. 10). An intercountry comparison shows that the yield per hectare for cereals and many other agricultural products was much lower in Iran than the average in Asia and other developing regions (ibid.).

Part of the reason for this failure might have been technical in the sense that new machinery and suitability for the purpose to which it was to be put was introduced without considering related factors such as maintenance or training (ibid.). However, another important reason was the government's neglect of agriculture in favour of other sectors, as manifested in a reduction in the funds allocated to agriculture in the development plans, inappropriate use of the funds, the misdirection of agricultural investment and pricing policy.

A review of government funding reveals that agriculture accounted for about 30 per cent of the total in the first and second five-year plans, but fell to 20 per cent in the fourth plan and 7.5 per cent in the fifth, despite the fact that 52.2 per cent of the country's population were living in rural areas in 1986 – the final year of the fifth plan (ibid., pp. 8–9).

A large part (about 38 per cent) of the government's agricultural investment in the last three plans was allocated to projects such as the construction of dams to provide the towns with drinking water and electricity, which had little impact on agriculture (Azkia, 1986; Razzaghi, 1989; Schirazi, 1993). Much of the investment benefited highly modern enterprises – a large proportion of the credit granted by the specialist banks was awarded to corporations and agribusinesses, as discussed in the previous chapter, which proved unsuccessful and ineffective. The traditional agricultural sector, it should be noted included over 98 per cent of rural households (Katouzian, 1981, p. 309), which were farming over 90 per cent of the arable land but only received 10–15 per cent of the loans during the fifth plan (Schirazi, 1993, p. 9). According to one estimate the amount of annual loans granted to modern enterprises was 19 times higher than that granted to the agricultural cooperatives, which were composed of small farmers (Katouzian, 1981, p. 309). In addition the financial aid granted to the corporations was long term, while the small amount of credit given to the cooperatives was short term and irregular. Consequently 'the peasants used the loans granted primarily to bring their standard of living somewhat closer to the subsistence level' (Schirazi, 1993, p. 9).

Misdirected investment was also obvious in water projects for agricultural purposes. For instance priority was given to the drilling of new wells equipped with motorised pumps, which resulted in the destruction of the cheaper and move effective traditional irrigation systems (*qanat*), and new dams were sited inappropriately and built poorly. Neither of these efforts substantially increased the area of irrigated land and consequently had little effect on the total yield. 'While arable land expanded from 11.1 million hectares in 1960 to 15.4 million hectares in 1977, artificially irrigated land increased by a mere one million hectares' (Schirazi, 1993, p. 9).

The neglect of agriculture was also visible in pricing policy: 'the government bought the country's main product, wheat, at a fixed price that was below what it paid for imported wheat but was the same as the subsidised price at which it supplied the bakeries in the towns with flour – in effect, it subsidised urban consumers at the expense of the peasants' (ibid., p. 10).

The state's discriminatory policies were even more evident in the consumption disparity between urban and rural areas. While the rural population accounted for 60 per cent of the total population, rural consumption only amounted to 35 per cent of the total. The significant point here is that about 80 per cent of government provision was probably earmarked for the urban sector, which explains the great gap between the consumption patterns in rural and urban areas (Azkia, 1986, p. 159).

Likewise a relatively equal distribution of income between rural and urban areas was necessary to boost agricultural production, but the evidence indicates that in spite of the growth of the economy and the positive effect of this on per capita income, there were great disparities between different areas and social groups. According one survey, household expenditure was also highly unequal. The bottom 10 per cent of households (the lowest income group) accounted for only 2.5 per cent of total expenditure, while the highest 10 per cent income group was responsible for about 23 per cent of expenditure. The differentials among the regions were similar. For example per capita income in Tehran, the capital of the country, was 46 per cent higher than in other large cities and 20 per cent higher than in smaller cities (ibid.).

The neglect of the rural sector and the regional disparities led to the migration of thousands of peasant households to the cities from the mid 1960s onward, and there was also migration from the less prosperous to the more prosperous urban centres (Razzaghi, 1989; Karshenas, 1990; Consulting Engineers for Development and Regional Planning, 1993).

All in all it can be said that the prerevolutionary agrarian reforms were not successful in modernising the country's agriculture and boosting production. The failure to reform the country's traditional agricultural structure successfully precipitated the sector into deep crisis, causing agricultural development to be placed at the top of the agenda after the revolution.

Agricultural development policies after the revolution

As discussed in the previous chapter, agricultural development policy was changed after the revolution mainly as a reaction against the prerevolutionary encouragement of large and highly mechanised agribusiness and farm corporations. The policy makers of the post-revolutionary government focused their attention on strengthening the traditional small or medium-sized farms, and after a period of slow growth in the 1970s, agricultural value-added increased by 55 per cent in constant terms between 1980 and 1988. The new emphasis also resulted in a rise in the contribution of agriculture of about 19 per cent of GDP and more than 21 per cent of non-oil GDP over the period 1983–88 (World Bank, 1991b, p. 1).

The reorganisation of the agricultural administration and the establishment of the Jihad-e Sazandeghi can be seen as a manifestation of this change in government attitude towards agriculture after the revolution. These organisations absorbed a large share of the government's development disbursement at the expense of agribusiness and large agricultural units (Table 4.6).

In order to put agriculture on a new path the government formulated a detailed agenda as part of its first and second five-year plans aiming at food security and ultimate self-sufficiency within ten years through increased output; encouraging the consumption of farm products to meet physiological and nutritional requirements; a reduction in

Table 4.6 Structure of investment in the development of agriculture and natural resources, 1977–83 (per cent)

	1977	1978	1979	1980	1981	1982	1983
Preservation and exploitation of natural resources	7.0	5.9	6.8	5.5	9.0	8.4	15.9
Agro-business and large agricultural units	26.0	30.2	36.0	31.0	16.7	12.0	8.4
Improvement and increase of farm products	9.7	5.6	9.2	4.0	3.3	2.5	2.4
Improvement and increase of livestock	6.4	4.7	1.7	3.2	2.2	3.0	3.3
Farming and livestock services	7.0	5.9	5.1	6.8	5.8	3.3	20.7
Regulation of agricultural product markets	28.2	29.8	28.6	19.5	7.6	8.5	–
Development of agricultural cooperatives and corporations	11.0	13.6	10.1	1.3	1.7	0.9	1.0
Research and study	4.7	3.2	2.5	1.5	1.0	0.7	3.3
Establishment of the Service Centres for Nomadic and Rural People	–	–	–	5.9	22.0	26.0	20.0
Provincial allocation	–	–	–	21.3	30.6	34.4	24.8

Source: Central Bank of Iran, annual report and balance sheets 1977–83.

malnutrition; the conservation of natural resources; an improvement in rural income through enhanced output and employment opportunities; improvement of the water supply and expansion of the irrigation networks; the reclamation of barren and abandoned land; reform of the land tenure system; and the reversal of rural–urban migration (*Kayhan*, 1983, no. 11942, pp. 17–23; World Bank, 1991, p. 20).

The plans predicted an average annual growth rate of 9 per cent for the economy as a whole in the first years of the planning period, with a 7 per cent average annual growth in agriculture, 14.1 per cent in industry and 9.8 per cent in construction. Due to the significant part to be played by agriculture in the economic independence of the country, the plan projected an average value-added growth of 7 per cent for this sector per annum. Agriculture's contribution share to GDP was to increase from 18.9 per cent in the base year to a peak of 20.9 per cent, followed by a fall to 13 per cent by 2003 (Table 4.7). Total investment in the agricultural sector was set at 2133.6 billion rials – 16.4 per cent of the country's total investment. The investment growth rate, according to the five-year plan, would be 16.8 per cent. Of this, 1374.2 billion rials would be invested by the government and 1374.2 billion rials by the private sector (*Kayhan*, 1983, no. 11942, p. 22). Investment would be reduced in the subsequent five-year plans, from 6 per cent in the second plan to 4 per cent in the third and 3.1 per cent in the fourth (Table 4.8).

Before moving on to examine the new agricultural policies, it is necessary to note that the plans were designed in a revolutionary atmosphere and were based on an unrealistic estimate of the country's resources. Only total mobilisation of the economy or another large increase in the price of oil could bring about such results. Given the extreme dependence of the Iranian economy on oil revenues – in the early 1980s these accounted for 95 per cent of exchange earnings – it is

Table 4.7 The predicted share of domestic growth components, 1980–2003 (per cent)

	1980	1983	1984	1988	1993	1998	2003
Agriculture	20.9	18.9	19.2	20.9	19.0	16.0	13.0
Oil	10.6	18.1	17.5	15.6	11.7	8.5	5.1
Industry and mining	10.0	9.9	10.7	14.8	20.1	27.8	345.1
Construction	7.6	6.1	6.1	7.3	9.1	10.6	10.9
Services	50.9	47.0	46.5	41.4	40.1	37.1	36.7

Source: *Kayhan* (1983) no. 11942, p. 17.

Table 4.8 Planned investment growth, 1983–98 (per cent)

	1983	1988	1993	1998
Agriculture	16.8	6.0	4.0	4.0
Oil	30.2	−4.6	−4.6	−12.5
Industry and mining	10.2	10.7	9.6	9.5
Construction	9.7	14.7	12.0	11.9
Services	8.1	7.5	7.5	6.8
Total	11.5	8.5	8.0	8.0

Source: *Kayhan* (1983) no. 11942, p. 17.

clear that any fall in the price of oil would cause serious problems for the economy and the government. The plans also projected that even under the worst circumstances, the price of oil would remain at $29. Thus according to the plans, Iran had to export 2.2 million barrels per day in 1983, rising to 2.5 million barrels per day by 1987. Moreover non-oil exports were expected to grow by 48.7 per cent a year. All these projections proved totally unrealistic.

A most important factor in this was the Iraqi's invasion of Iran in September 1980, leading to a war that lasted eight years and had a devastating effect on the economy in general and agriculture in particular. The war was given the highest priority in all the state's political considerations and overshadowed all the government's economic policies. Development plans had to be deferred or were doomed to failure as the funds were diverted to the war effort. Indeed the entire country took on a warlike atmosphere and experienced a phase of destruction instead of construction. According to government documents the war accounted for 30–35 per cent of state expenditure each year.

By 1986/87 expenditure on development had fallen to 28.7 per cent. All ministries and state departments had to allot an undisclosed share of their budgets to the war. The State Budget Act of 1985/86 compelled several ministries to put 20 per cent of their funds at the disposal of the war effort. It is difficult to obtain precise data on the demands the war made on the funds of the executive organs of the state, but they have been estimated at over 20 per cent (Schirazi, 1993, pp. 80–3).

In addition to the war, the trade embargo imposed on Iran, the inflationary tendency in the international markets, political turmoil and the struggle among the various political factions for power all had a negative effect on post-revolutionary development policies. In order to minimise the harmful effect of these crises on the lower strata of the population the government adopted a distribution policy, rationing basic goods such as oil, rice, chicken, eggs, butter, cheese, sugar, washing powder, soup and fuel and keeping their prices low. After the ceasefire the price control on most goods was lifted and rationing was reduced.

The following subsections examine the government's policies, evaluate the effectiveness of these policies for the development of agriculture and consider the impact of the above-mentioned factors on the results of the agricultural policies.

The financing of agriculture and agricultural capital formation

The assignment of first priority to the agricultural sector raised expectations that investment in this sector would be increased. The available data indicate that there was a relative increase in government spending on agriculture compared with the prerevolutionary period and with spending on other sectors of the economy after 1983/84, particularly during the first five-year plan (1989–97). Nevertheless careful examination of the data shows that this increase was slow, particularly after 1995/96; and that in spite of the promise to prioritise the agriculture sector, in practice it ranked between third and sixth in terms of government investment (Table 4.9).

After comparing government investment in the agricultural sector with the inflation rate, the World Bank (1994, p. 2) concluded that 'between 1983 and 1989 . . . increases in government budgetary allocations for capital expenditures did not compensate for inflation and went through a steep decline in real terms (from 40 to 35 billion rials). In other words, government capital expenditure for agriculture is now below one third of what was in 1983'. A similar picture emerged in 1991–92 and 1994–96 (Table 4.10).

The decline of investment in the agricultural sector becomes more apparent if one examines total agricultural capital formation in the post-revolutionary era. According to one investigation of agricultural investment in the first development plan, some of the results of which are summarised in Table 4.11, the highest amount invested in the agricultural sector was 150.5 billion rials in 1984 and the lowest was 78.4 billion rials in 1990. Compared with the other major sectors, the agricultural sector received the least investment. The data indicate slow and irregular growth in agricultural capital formation. For example capital formation reached its highest level in 1984, then declined notably to 29 per cent in 1985 but rose again in 1990 (39 per cent growth), although it never returned to the 1984 level. The study also found that agricultural capital formation in 1990 and 1991 (31.7 per

Table 4.9 Government fixed investment by economic sectors, 1977–96 (per cent)

	Agriculture	Water	Electricity	Industry	Oil and gas	Mining	Transportation	Other
1977/78	6.2	6.8	27.7	17.3	17.1	2.2	15.2	3.6
1978/79	10.4	6.3	23.6	18.3	n.a.	3.9	30.0	2.6
1979/80	15.5	9.1	23.1	19.9	3.1	5.2	20.7	3.2
1980/81	8.3	12.1	20.7	21.9	6.8	6.4	5.8	3.9
1981/82	9.4	11.5	20.2	20.6	2.1	6.4	26.7	2.9
1982/83	9.1	9.3	20.3	22.2	9.9	5.0	21.4	2.9
1983/84	10.4	10.7	16.6	23.3	12.4	3.7	20.7	3.1
1984/85	13.1	12.7	18.8	17.9	9.5	3.6	23.8	0.6
1985/86	10.7	10.6	17.9	18.1	14.2	2.9	23.9	1.7
1986/87	12.3	8.7	14.0	14.8	24.3	3.1	21.5	1.3
1987/88	15.9	9.9	6.5	18.6	20.3	2.7	21.3	4.8
1988/89	16.8	16.4	3.3	29.4	n.a.	4.2	22.2	1.4
1989/90	18.7	15.7	4.4	24.3	–	4.8	30.5	1.5
1990/91	16.0	18.5	6.9	20.6	–	5.0	31.3	1.8
1991/92	13.0	27.6	6.6	14.1	0.2	6.2	30.9	1.4
1992/93	14.4	21.8	5.8	13.3	–	6.2	36.3	2.3
1993/94	11.7	19.4	8.8	4.5	24.7	2.7	26.4	2.0
1994/95	9.8	15.9	7.5	2.6	34.2	2.4	24.9	2.8
1995/96	7.8	18.1	14.1	2.2	32.8	1.9	18.8	4.3
1996/97	8.3	20.8	10.7	3.6	27.2	1.7	23.5	4.2

Sources: Central Bank of Iran (1991–99); Statistical Centre of Iran (1989).

Table 4.10 Comparison of the agricultural investment rate with the inflation rate, 1989–96)*

	1889/90	1990/91	1991/92	1992/93	1993/94	1994/95	1995/96	1996/97
Investment rate	38.3	50.9	20.0	16.8	123.1	12.0	11.2	23.6
Inflation rate	21.8	23.9	26.6	33.4	25.3	42.4	60.2	25.1

* The reason for the higher investment rate for the agricultural sector compared with the inflation rate in 1993 was probably due to a dramatic increase (176 per cent) in the credit allocated to the economic sectors. The total credit allocated in 1992 was 16.9 billion rials, but this figure had increased to 4458.6 billion rials by 1997 (for further details see Budget and Planning Organisation of Iran, 1997).
Source: Budget and Planning Organisation of Iran (1997).

Table 4.11 Domestic gross fixed capital formation, 1982–94 (billions of rials at constant 1983 prices)

	Agriculture	Oil and gas	Mining and industry	Electricity and water	Transportation	Services	Other
1982/83	108.9	167.9	298.5	138.5	240.8	39.6	304.7
1983/84	150.5	188.5	356.0	138.4	338.0	42.3	375.9
1984/85	106.6	139.6	424.3	187.5	396.4	62.1	370.4
1985/86	110.7	98.8	296.9	135.6	326.4	38.7	290.2
1986/87	94.0	89.6	233.4	110.4	170.6	34.9	229.0
1987/88	86.9	45.6	195.6	87.1	150.8	25.4	191.6
1988/89	83.4	47.2	168.5	57.4	149.5	11.8	174.5
1989/90	87.4	57.5	195.0	67.8	175.2	19.7	182.6
1990/91	108.9	48.0	254.5	83.5	175.5	15.8	283.2
1991/92	124.0	110.5	471.4	151.5	271.2	37.2	357.1
1992/93	108.5	73.2	507.2	130.2	288.5	36.3	479.4
1993/94	119.8	66.6	650.6	201.9	303.9	38.5	498.8
1994/95	95.1	100.1	622.2	144.1	n.a.	n.a.	n.a.

Sources: *Nashriyeh-e Barzgar*, no. 674 (1994) p. 24; Central Bank of Iran, annual balance sheet, 1991–6, annual reports, 1991–6.

cent and 6.7 per cent) was lower than predicted in the plan (*Nashriyeh-e Barzgar*, no. 674, 1994, p. 23). Another study, carried out by a research group at the Planning and Design Department of the Development and Handicraft Undersecretariat for the Ministry of Jihad in 1998, came to the same conclusion, stating that the share of agricultural and natural resources investment steadily declined from 11.3 per cent in 1988 to 4.2 per cent in 1996. In 1998 the parliamentary chairman said that the reduction of investment in the agricultural sector was disastrous (*Etellaat*, no. 21519, December 1998). The parliamentary agricultural commission stated that, according to note 77 of the Law of the Second Socioeconomic Plan, the government was required to allocate at least 25 per cent of bank credits to the agricultural sector, but in practice agriculture's share had been only 17 per cent. The proportion of credit allocated to the agricultural sector had fallen each year, from 10 per cent at the beginning of the second plan in 1995 to 3.2 per cent in 1999. The commission also stated that compared with 1998, the infrastructural credits of the economic sector in the 1999 budget indicated a reduction of 5.7 per cent, but the reduction for the agricultural sector was 11.2 per cent (*Etellaat*, no. 21519, December 1998).

Why, in spite of the increase in agriculture's contribution to GDP after the revolution, did it experience negative growth in respect of capital formation? There are a number of possible reasons: the contribution of other sectors to GDP had also increased; the weak role of the private sector in agricultural investment due mainly to land confiscation and lack of confidence in private property rights; large-scale capital flight; the comparatively low profitability of agricultural investment; and discrimination against this sector by the government in favour of the industrial sector (World Bank, 1991b; *Nashriyeh-e Barzgar*, no 676, 1993; Schirazi, 1993). While the share of agriculture in exports was often higher than that of other sectors, imports of capital goods for agriculture were proportionally lower (*Nashriyeh-e Barzgar*, no. 676, 1993). Even the foreign income obtained from agricultural exports was not ploughed back into that sector. In addition the government occasionally capped agricultural prices, thus subsidising consumers rather than producers. This further reduced the incentive to invest in the agricultural sector. Furthermore the large income gap between rural and urban areas and the higher productivity of non-agricultural sectors led to entrepreneurial forces deserting the agricultural sector (Nashriyeh-e Barzgar, pp. 23–4).

The government's policy of offering incentives in the form of loans to farmers was not successful. After the revolution there was nominal increase in loans by the Agricultural Bank to peasants for agricultural purposes (Table 4.12), but the benefit of these loans was largely negated by inflation, which caused production costs to rise. While in the prerevolutionary era the overall tendency had been to grant loans mainly to large-scale projects, loans were more diverse in the post-revolutionary period, in both number and the average amount. A review of loans between 1977 and 1997, based on a comparison of the growth rate of average loans with inflation, shows that the purchasing power of the loans increased yearly (Table 4.12). Nevertheless an examination based on the weighted mean index reveals that the real purchasing power of loans was lower than the inflation rate. As calculated from the data in Table 4.12, the weighted means for inflation was 33.48 per cent and that for the loan growth rate was 26.6 per cent, indicating that the loans did not offset the inflation rate.

In 1981 over 80 per cent of loans were under 500 000 rials, falling to 45 per cent five years later. There was also a fall in the number of loans granted to peasant smallholdings. One feature of these loans was that they were short term and at least half of them had to be repaid within two years. Long-term loans (over 10 years) constituted a tiny proportion of the total (2.1 per cent) (Schirazi, 1993, p. 278). This meant that the loans could be used for long-term investment. As a consequence borrowers tended to use the money for non-agricultural purposes. For example some borrowers spent up to 44 per cent of their loans on 'current expenses' (ibid.). The Agricultural Bank offered two types of loans: 'interest-free' loans, which were subject to a 2.5 per cent 'administrative fee'; and conventional loans at 6–9 per cent. However the bank deducted a total of 18 per cent from each loan, with 9 per cent or more going on tax and insurance. So all in all these loans were more expensive than the prerevolutionary era (ibid., p. 279).

Expansion of cultivated land

Another government measure to increase agricultural production was expansion of the area of arable land. It was thought that inadequate use of the available resources, for example land and water, had been one of the main reasons for the failure of agricultural policy in the prerevolutionary period. To maximise the country's agricultural potential the government launched a series of programmes aimed at repairing old irrigation plants and constructing new ones, covering open canals and waterways, levelling and draining potentially arable land, and consolidating the peasants' plots of land. A series of research projects was

Table 4.12 Agricultural Bank loans to peasants and farmers, 1977–96

	Total loans (billions of rials)	Number of loans (thousands of rials)	Average loans (thousands of rials)	Growth rate (%)	Inflation rate (%)
1977/78	51.7	382	135	–	–
1978/79	42.1	322	130	-3.7	9.2
1979/80	81.7	552	148	13.8	20.0
1980/81	116.3	573	203	37.2	30.8
1981/82	148.4	634	234	15.3	19.1
1982/83	183.7	626	293	25.2	14.0
1983/84	219.9	581	379	29.4	7.6
1984/85	155.7	325	479	26.4	7.7
1985/86	200.0	339	589	23.0	7.2
1986/87	201.9	297	679	15.3	25.3
1987/88	279.0	335	835	23.0	29.7
1988/89	382.0	420	911	9.1	21.8
1990/91	624.4	551	1132	6.7	18.5
1991/92	956.9	560	1710	16.5	23.9
1992/93	1076.5	458	2348	51.1	26.6
1993/94	1752.1	588	2980	37.3	33.4
1994/95	2363.7	583	4530	26.9	25.3
1995/96	3361.9	567	5929	52.0	42.4
1996/97	3695.2	598	6177	30.9	60.2

Sources: Ministry of Agriculture, *Agricultural Report*, 1985/6, 1986/7; Central Bank of Iran, *Statistical Yearbook 1980/1* and *1988/9*, economic reports and balance sheets, 1996, 1998–9.

also planned. In 1987 other measures were added, such as the prevention of soil erosion and water loss.

The area under cultivation, both irrigated and non-irrigated, was increased not only through greater utilisation of pastures and fallow land, and more extensive mechanisation but also through large occupation of the lands by new farmers and redistribution of the land by the seven-member committees (Razzaghi, 1989; World Bank, 1991; Amuzegar, 1993; Schirazi, 1993). There is no precise information on the contribution of the above-mentioned programmes to the expansion of the cultivated area, but Schirazi (1993, p. 281), based on statistics from the Statistical Centre of Iran and the Self-Sufficiency Plan, provides some data on the amount of arable, fallow, irrigated and non-irrigated land in 1986–88 (Table 4.13). His data indicates that arable land increased about 455 000 hectares between 1974–5 and 1988–90.

The World Bank presents a similar picture. It estimates that the increase was about 13.5 million hectares, with 5.9 million hectares under irrigation, 7.6 million hectares of non-irrigated land and about 8 million hectares lying fallow. Pasture land amounted to about 10 million hectares, and 19 million hectares were forests or scrubland. This left some 28.5 million hectares of marginal but potentially usable land. The irrigated area increased by 19 per cent and non-irrigated land by 12 per cent (World Bank, 1991, p. 3). However, we must be cautious about the validity of these statistics as arable land within city limits was counted in the 1988/89 agricultural census but not in 1974/75 and 1982/83 (Schirazi, 1993).

A significant but undetermined proportion of arable land has been used for non-agricultural purposes in recent years (Razzaghi, 1993). There has also been some destruction of arable land as a result of incorrect usage (*Nashriyeh-e Barzgar*, no. 674, 1989). According to the Minister of Agriculture, each year between 50 000 and 60 000 hectares

Table 4.13 Arable land area, 1986–88 (millions of hectares)

	Arable	Fallow	Irrigated	Non-irrigated
1974–5	16.416	5.955	4.095	6.366
1978–9	14.868	5.683	3.825	5.360
1982–3	14.777	4.929	3.979	5.869
1985–6	18.500	6.314	4.265	7.921
1987–8	n.a.	n.a.	6.562	5.262
1988–9	16.871	5.364	5.626	5.881

Source: Schirazi, 1993, p. 281.

of pastureland and forestry is destroyed and 300 000 hectares of arable land degenerates into desert (quoted in Schirazi, 1993, p. 282). According to another source, around two billion tons of fertile soil is eroded each year, causing an additional 800 000 hectares of desertification and preventing full use of dam waters because of sedimentation (Amuzegar, 1993, p. 191).

One of the aims of the 1983 development plan was to consolidate 17 067 hectares of fragmented peasant plots by 1987/88 but in 1989 only 450 hectares had been consolidated (in the Qazwin area). High costs and insufficient government funding were said to be the main reasons for the failure of this endeavour (Schirazi, 1993, p. 282).

With regard to water use, there had been no significant advancements in the case of irrigation plants by 1987/88, and only four of the nine dams started before the revolution had been completed by 1978. The rest of them, along with two major dams (including Pishan Dam in Sistan and Baluchestan province and Saveh Dam in Tehran province), which were designed in 1982, were gradually completed by 1992. The completion of these dams increased the total storage capacity of dams from 13 billion cubic metres to 270 million cube metres (Ministry of Energy, 1993, pp. 1–3). However, the number of wells, springs and subterranean channels (*qanat*, did increase several fold between 1976/77 and 1986/87. Only 53.3 per cent of the 229.3 billion rials allotted to the projects was spent and the state's plan to cover the open canals remained largely unfulfilled, with only 1078 out of 25 983 kilometres completed. According to the Minister of Agriculture, full use of dam waters could not be expected before 1989 (ibid.). In 1993 the minister summed up the situation regarding water and land use as follows:

> the [agricultural] possibilities of the country are high, however we have not been able to exploit them effectively. For the maximisation of these possibilities investment and planning should have started a century ago, since the implementation of infrastructural schemes takes a long time and requires considerable capital. Such efforts have not been made [and] therefore our agriculture is limited to 7.2 million hectares of irrigated farmland . . . and six million hectares of non-irrigated farmland. Of the 120 billion cubic metres of water available we have only been able to control 70 billion cubic metres, unfortunately efficiency still is under 35 per cent (*Nashriyeh-e Barzgar*, no. 652, 1993, p. 8).

Support policies

Input provision

In addition to the measure discussed above, the mechanisation of production, the provision of seed, fertilisers and pesticides, and the expansion of training and research were also undertaken to improve agricultural conditions and increase the yield.

An examination of the post-revolutionary government's mechanisation programme shows that the number of tractors in use increased from 78 000 in 1979 to 135 000 in 1985, while the number of ploughs and combine harvesters increased by 15 per cent during the same period (Amuzegar, 1993, p. 190). However, tractor sales dropped off dramatically after 1985 (Table 4.14), mainly because of the reduction in dollar revenues from oil but also because agricultural funds were diverted to the war effort, and only 30 per cent of tractor capacity was being utilised, compared with 53 per cent in 1982. The amount of foreign currency earmarked for agricultural machinery fell from $240 million to $18 million between 1984/85 and 1986/87 (Schirazi, 1993, p. 286). This resulted in fewer machines being imported from abroad and a drop in domestic food production. In 1989 Ministry of Agriculture reported that 'only 20 of the 1000 tractors and 30 of the

Table 4.14 Number of tractors and combines purchased, 1981-86

	Tractors	Combines
1981/82	14 727	320
1982/83	28 977	15
1983/84	32 918	10
1984/85	23 881	428
1985/86	15 840	377
1986/87	1 269	286
1987/88	3 278	149
1988/89	1 757	85
1989/90	6 290	473
1990/91	7 499	487
1991/92	7 753	309
1992/93	5 144	224
1993/94	2 364	88
1994/95	1 952	21
1995/96	1 737	62
1996/97	877	54

Source: Statistical Centre of Iran, *Statistical Yearbook*, 1981/2-196/7.

200 combine harvesters planned for production in Tabriz were actually delivered' (quoted in ibid., p. 286). Though there was a rise in food imports this did not compensate for the drop in domestic production (ibid.). The price index for agricultural machinery fell considerably in the early 1980s. Indeed the increase in the number of tractors, ploughs and combines until the mid 1980s (Table 4.14) was due to heavy subsidisation. However, the government's post-war economic liberalisation policy, which was supposedly aimed at reducing the cost of production and improving productivity, instead caused the price of agricultural machinery to soar by up to tenfold. From 1992 the subsidies were gradually removed (Table 4.15).

With regard to the supply of artificial fertilisers, there was rapid growth in the post-revolutionary period, followed by a decline from 1984 onwards. The government heavily subsidised fertilisers and pesticides for farmers, keeping prices constant for several years (World Bank, 1991b, p. 8). However, the targets set in the 1983 development plan to achieve agricultural self-sufficiency were not attained. Lack of foreign currency and the destruction of domestic fertiliser factories during the war have been cited as the main reasons for the shortfalls. One consequence was the emergence of a black market in fertilisers because it was more profitable for farmers to sell the subsidised fertiliser than to enrich their fields with it (*Nashriyeh-e Barzgar*, 1988). A two-tier fertiliser and pesticide distribution system developed, with farmers buying a proportion of their requirement from government agencies, mainly at subsidised prices, and the rest in the open market. It should be noted that the price of fertilizer was increased from 9 rials a kilo to 95 rials a kilo during 1992–94, while the guaranteed price for wheat rose from 150 to 225 rials a kilo, barley from 115 to 172 rials a kilo, grain from 130 to 195 rials a kilo, sugar beet from 27 to 52 rials a kilo and cotton from 400 to 513.5 rials a kilo (*Nashriyeh-e Barzgar*, no. 671, 1992, pp. 16–7).

Table 4.15 Comparison of major agricultural machinery in profiles of subsidisation the price of (1988) and liberalisation (1992) (thousands of rials)

	1988	1992
Romanian tractors (Model 650)	700	7 600
Ferguson tractors (model 285)	1 300	9 600
Combines	4 500	29 000

Source: *Nashriyeh-e Barzgar*, no. 671 (1992), p. 17.

Table 4.16 Government investment in agricultural research, 1983–86 (million rials)

	1983/84	1984/85	1985/86	1986/87
Planned investment	14 343	13 746	9 165	4 494
Actual investment	2 436	2 678	4 244	5 943

Source: Schirazi (1993), p. 288.

With regard to research, there was a large gap between the work that needed to be done and that which was actually done. A comparison between Iran and developing countries such as India and Turkey reveals that India has ten times more research personnel than does Iran, and Turkey invests one and half times more in research than does Iran (Schirazi, 1993, p. 288). The neglect of research becomes even more apparent if one examines the difference between government investment in research and the amounts earmarked for it in the 1983 development plan (Table 4.16).

The available data for subsequent years show a similar picture, with expenditure constantly falling below the planned investment. In 1989/90 and 1994/95, when a considerable expenditure was planned, no research at all took place.

The poor research performance was publicly addressed by the Ministry of Agriculture; for example in 1993 the minister of agriculture, Kalantari, stated:

> the fact that we have natural advantages in the field of farming, such as seasonal variation and other geographical attributes, promises great success for the country's future agricultural development, however at the present time the lack of research and training does not permit us to make optimum use of these potentialities . . . . [R]esearch [in] our country is [very] young . . . most of the work in this field has been done since the revolution . . . [and] we still have a long way to go (*Nashriyeh-e Barzgar*, no. 652, 1993, p. 8).

Pricing policy

Government control on agricultural prices has been partial and irregular. In the post-revolutionary period the policy for major food staples involved a combination of subsidisation/controlled pricing and two-tier pricing, with coupon allocation for certain categories of the population.

Wheat was considered important by the government, and controlling and promoting its production was seen as the best route to economic independence. The government fixed the price of wheat each year and, in an attempt to establish a purchasing monopoly, purchased whatever the farmers produced in excess of their own needs. As a result the price fixed by the government largely determined the farmers' inclination to grow wheat. The price was set by the Supreme Economic Council on the basis of costs calculated by the Ministry of Agriculture.

Compared with other types of grain, the government's subsidy on wheat was high, for example in 1988/89 the price paid to the farmer was 91 rials a kilo and the selling price to flour mills was 17.5 rials a kilo. There was also an element of subsidisation in the amount charged by mills when selling flour to bakeries. Bread is a principal staple in the diet of the population and its price was kept constant throughout the 1980s (30 rials a kilo) (World Bank, 1991b, p. 43). In 1991 the government started to rationalise the producer and consumer subsidies. Starting with wheat, the guaranteed price for producers was adjusted to the world price and the price of bread was increased by 50 per cent. The consumer price of most non-basic staples such as barley, fruit and vegetables was not subsidised or controlled (ibid.).

The main reason for continuing to keep the price of wheat low is political. The government subsidises bread in the towns at a price far below that fixed for wheat, which induces the peasants, especially those in villages close to towns, to become customers of the municipal bakeries, which in turn drives up the demand for wheat and allows farmers to sell more wheat to the state (Schirazi, 1993, pp. 290–1).

Barley is mainly used for animal fodder, and since it is in great demand the market price is much higher than the guaranteed price, which does not even cover the production costs. It costs 10 per cent less than wheat to produce but has the same price in the open market (Schirazi, 1993, p. 291), which is why its production is increasing faster than that of wheat (Table 4.17).

Table 4.17   Yields of selected crops (in thousands of tons)

	Wheat	Barley	Rice	Potatoes	Onions
1979–81	1063	1000	3215	14 324	15 491
1985–86	1140	1200	3547	15 792	19 297
Increase (%)	724	20	13	10	25

Source: World Bank (1991b), p. 12.

Rice is another staple food in Iran, but unlike bread it has been subject to very little subsidisation (only for sales through cooperative stores), and most of the harvest is sold and distributed at open market prices. In 1989 the retail price of rice was 1450 rials a kilo, in 1980 it was 220 rials. In 1986 the wide gap between its production cost (280 rials a kilo) and the wholesale price (440 rials a kilo) ensured that as much land as possible was given over to rice growing (85 per cent in the Caspian Sea area). While, the producers benefited from the price fluctuations, the brokers were the main beneficiaries of the high profit margins (Ministry of Agriculture, *Agricultural Report*, 1988). The government unsuccessfully attempted to contain the upsurge in the price of rice by using an inconsistent import policy and controlling domestic sales. One of the main reasons for its lack of success, according to Schirazi (1993, p. 291), was that the price of rice was the subject of 'a struggle . . . between those elements in the government favouring the consumer, and influential wholesalers who have lobbyists in the government and among the clergy'.

The prices of vegetable oils, sugar beet and potatoes have been subject to similar irregular fluctuations as the prices are dictated by the state processing plants.

For other major food staples such as meat and milk there has been a dual market. The Meat Organisation purchases carcasses and sells subsidised meat at a much lower price, but animals are also slaughtered by cooperatives and the meat sold on the open market. A similar two-tier market exists for milk. Fruit and vegetables are not controlled or subsidised (World Bank, 1991b, p. 44).

The government's pricing policy has been sharply criticised by experts at the Ministry of Agriculture. For example its 1986/87 report on the agriculture situation called the policy contradictory, inconsistent and opportunistic. 'The government considers prices to be a political instrument for pacifying the consumers. Its measures to control production and prices have been largely unsuccessful' (quoted in Schirazi, 1993, p. 293).

Agricultural output growth

Despite the drop in production discussed earlier in this section, the rate of growth of agricultural production in the post-revolutionary period has been notable, averaging 5–6 per cent per acre (World Bank, 1991b, p. 7). Depending on the accuracy and reliability of official data, it seems that almost all major crops experienced a steady rise in yield after the revolution, especially cereals, potatoes and onions. This trend can also be seen in the case of tobacco, tea, citrus fruits and other crops. However, output growth tended to be relatively slow and irregular (Table 4.18), and was mainly due to expanded acreage, the use of fertilisers and pesticides, and higher-quality seeds rather than improvements in productivity (Mojtahed and Esfahani, 1989; Amuzegar, 1993). According to the chairman of the Advisory Reconstruction Organisation, 'with respect to agriculture we have shouted more slogans in the past ten years than achieved performances' (quoted in Schirazi, 1993, p. 295).

An appraisal of per capita agricultural production in the postrevolutionary era provides a grim picture. According to one evaluation, per capita agricultural production fell from 106.63 per kilo in 1981 to 98.42 per kilo in 1986. That for cereals dropped from 110.87 per kilo to 105.43 per kilo and the total production of cotton plants from 112.21 per kilo to 104.75 per kilo (Mojtahed and Esfahani, 1989, p. 845). According to another assessment, per capita wheat output dropped by 70 kilos between 1976/77 and 1988/89, even though wheat accounted for over half of the arable land under cultivation and the major part of government expenditure. Per capita growth was positive only for barley, legumes and potatoes, that is, crops whose production was determined by market forces and to which the government made no positive contribution (Schirazi, 1993, pp. 296-7).

The decline in per capita production was accompanied by population growth, which caused a steady increase in total demand and an increase in food imports after the revolution. According to the World Bank (1991b, p. 46), food imports reached $2.5 billion in 1989. Between 1980 and 1989 imports of wheat and flour rose from 2.6 million tons to 3.4 million tons, and rice from 570 000 tons to 700 000 tons.

It should be added that a profound change in the structure of consumption following a return to traditional basic foods and a turning away from high-protein products was another reason for the increase in food imports (Table 4.19). The scarcity of most food products at affordable prices and the heavy subsidisation of wheat simultaneously caused a reduction in per capita consumption of protein products, for example meat and milk, and an increase in that of wheat and potatoes.

Conclusion

An examination of the state of agriculture prior to the revolution indicates that over time, due mainly to the rise in world oil prices and the

Table 4.18 Crop production, 1977–96 (thousands of tons)

	Wheat	Barley	Rice	Sugar beet	Vegetable oil	Cotton	Potatoes	Onions	Tobacco
1977/78	5 517	1230	1399	4187	105	557	697	392	15
1978/79	5 660	1217	1527	3660	126	427	735	393	13
1979/80	5 946	1262	1271	3814	99	322	998	515	20
1980/81	5 744	1265	1181	3917	110	219	1270	631	24
1981/82	6 610	1700	1624	2331	105	275	1540	675	27
1982/83	6 660	1903	1605	4321	138	358	1814	965	25
1983/84	5 956	2034	1215	3648	188	300	1740	736	21
1984/85	6 207	2293	1474	3392	118	351	1784	844	22
1985/86	6 631	2297	1772	3924	137	324	1725	719	28
1986/87	7 556	2505	1784	4965	137	359	2349	824	28
1987/88	7 600	2731	1803	4456	229	341	2348	923	25
1988/89	7 265	3394	1419	3454	298	380	1443	612	21
1989/90	6 010	2847	1854	3535	236	395	2033	692	15
1990/91	8 012	3548	1681	3641	145	437	2516	1213	19
1991/92	8 793	3102	2357	5000	137	412	2612	1200	20
1992/93	10 179	3065	2364	6005	267	330	2708	1125	22
1993/94	10 732	3058	2281	5408	316	275	322	1305	20
1994/95	10 870	3045	2259	5295	288	387	3185	1112	10
1995/96	11 228	2952	2301	5521	234	523	3074	1130	14
1996/97	10 015	2736	2685	3687	210	598	3140	1200	17

Sources: FAO (1979, 1980, 1992); Central Bank of Iran, various years.

Table 4.19 Annual rise/fall in food consumption, 1961–86 (per cent)

	1961–70	1970–80	1980–86
Wheat	5.36	4.81	5.82
Rice	3.86	6.37	1.47
Maize	–11.77	43.40	–0.46
Barley	2.95	–0.31	35.56
Potatoes	3.44	14.84	8.97
Sugar	4.64	7.95	2.74
Pulses	6.95	2.64	6.80
Vegetables	11.30	5.83	0.82
Citrus fruit	–2.55	0.56	0.22
Other fruit	4.91	4.94	3.89
Vegetable oil	9.54	5.49	8.23
Coffee	–6.59	15.15	–21.18
Tea	5.06	7.20	11.09
Beef	–0.01	11.35	0.30
Mutton	3.51	5.86	0.82
Poultry	9.25	13.57	4.00
Milk	1.73	7.74	0.49
Eggs	5.84	15.10	4.29

Source: World Bank (1991b), p. 32.

state's modernisation policies, the country's economic structure changed, resulting in a decline in the agricultural sector's share of GNP and per capita GDP compared with other economic sectors. The high growth rate in the non-agricultural sector led to rural–urban migration and hence a fall in the rural population. In spite of the government's emphasis on the mechanisation of agriculture and modern inputs, the agricultural sector failed to meet the demand for food. This poor productivity was partly because of technical issues related to mechanisation; however, it was mainly due to the government's increasing neglect of the traditional agricultural sector in favour of mechanised, capital-intensive farming, as well as its adoption of a discriminatory pricing policy for domestic agricultural products compared with imported ones. The poor productivity of agriculture and a population increase resulted in the need for even more imported food. The government's policies also led to greater regional and social disparities. In sum, the prerevolutionary rural policies were unsuccessful and caused the agricultural sector to fall into what could be called a deep crisis.

The failure of the prerevolutionary policies meant that rural and agricultural reforms were put at the top of the agenda in the post-revolutionary era and agricultural policy underwent a considerable change.

The post-revolutionary government focused more on strengthening the small and medium-sized farms. Its policies were based on the assumption that agriculture was the 'axis' of development and consequently the five-year plans gave the agricultural sector top priority. The ultimate aim was to achieve self-sufficiency within 10 years. The government participated indirectly in agricultural production through investment in agricultural infrastructure, support measures such as pricing policy, supplying inputs (fertilisers, pesticides, farm machinery) and granting loans.

However, these government activities soon lost momentum and capital formation in the agricultural sector remained low. This was also due to weak private sector participation in agricultural investment because of lack of confidence of private investors, extensive capital flight and the low profitability of agricultural investments compared with the returns to be had from the business and industrial sectors. The inadequacy of the loans available to peasants and the shortness of their duration served to deter long-term investment by peasants.

While the area under cultivation was expanded after the revolution, the extent of this was far below the target set in the first five-year plan. A similar situation existed in the case of water supply.

The provision of agricultural inputs such as fertilisers, seed, pesticides and agricultural machinery was reduced due to a shortage of foreign currency after the fall in the international price of oil and the decline in oil production as a consequence of the Iran–Iraq War. The cost of inputs was kept more or less constant during the 1980s, but when the liberalisation policy was introduced in 1991 their prices rose.

At the consumer level, pricing policy involved a combination of subsidised/controlled prices for major staples (wheat, barley and rice), two-tier pricing with rationed distribution (rice, plus other foods such as meat, butter and so on), and open-market prices for fruit and vegetables. However, the combined effect of widely fluctuating exchange rates and subsidisation created substantial distortions relative to the open market, and as a consequence farmers withdrew their resources and available inputs from food-grain production and channelled them towards more profitable crops.

5
Rural Development at the Micro Level

Introduction

The discussion in the previous chapters was mostly concerned with rural development at the macro level. In this chapter we shall examine rural development at the micro or village level by focusing on five variables: participation, mobility, income, wealth and well-being. The aim is to ascertain the effect of the post-revolutionary rural reform policies on rural people. Three dimensions are considered: the degree to which rural communities have been changed by the implementation of rural development programmes; the degree to which this change has been influenced by the socioeconomic background of villagers (such as age, education, occupation and so on) and the developmental potential of the villages (in respect of soil fertility, population size, remoteness from cities and so on); and the degree of inequality in villagers' share of the benefits of the programmes. These factors were examined using an *ex-post-facto* comparative method in six villages in Eastern Azerbaijan. The villages were selected in pairs from three distinct categories. The villages in each pair were similar from the perspective of developmental potential but differed in respect of the number of rural development programmes they received, as shown in Table 5.1. The data are based on interviews with 381 households, which were selected through random proportionate sampling, and interviews with rural reform officials in 1998. (For a detailed discussion of the method of selecting the sample of villages and villagers see Shakoori, 1998.)

This chapter first provides a brief description of the socioeconomic and geographical characteristics of the province, district and villages under study. Next the five variables listed above are discussed, followed by an investigation of inequalities within and between the selected vil-

Table 5.1 Characteristics of the selected villages in terms of programme provision, developmental potential and sample size

	Rural programme provision			Developmental potential			
	Jihad	Centres	Land reform	Geographical	Remoteness	Population	Sample size
Pair one:				geographical			106
1. Duwlat Abad	Maximum	Maximum	Yes	High	Very remote	Large	88
2. Dizaj-e Hossein Bayk	Minimum	Minimum	No	High	Very remote	Large	88
Pair two:							
3. Gharajeh-Fayzullah	Maximum	Maximum	Yes	High	Average	Medium	60
4. Livar-e-Paeen	Minimum	Minimum	No	High	Average	Medium	60
Pair three:							
5. Ghermezi Gheshlag	Maximum	Maximum	Yes	Low	Average	Small	30
6. Babreh-e-Sofla	Minimum	Minimum	No	Low	Average	Small	35

Notes: The service centre programmes included the provision of agricultural machinery, the implementation of irrigation scheme and the provision of agricultural inputs such as pesticides, fertilisers, seed and water pumps. Jihad's programmes consisted of building public baths, constructing schools, supplying piped drinking water, building gravelled or asphalted roads and implementing physical upgrading projects (*behsazi*).

lages to identity the extent to which the post-revolutionary rural reforms changed the distribution of resources among rural groups.

The socioeconomic and geographical characteristics of the province, district and villages under study

The province: Eastern Azerbaijan

Eastern Azerbaijan is situated in the north-west of the Iranian plateau and covers a total area of 46 929.9 square kilometres. The River Aras forms the northern border of the province and separates it from the former Soviet republics of Azerbaijan, Nakhjovan and Armenia. In the west, the River Ghotour and Lake Urumiyeh form the borders between Eastern and Western Azerbaijan. In the south, a chain of mountains, valleys and plains connect the province with Western Azerbaijan and the province of Zanjan. In the east, the river valley, the mountains of Sabalan, Chahil Nour and Saeen and the River Ghizell-Ozan separate the territory from the province of Ardabil. In terms of geographical coordinates, the province lies between latitudinal zone 36° 45' to 39° 43' and longitudinal zone 45° 50' to 48° 55'.

The province has 1.1 million hectares of agricultural land, of which 420 000 hectares are irrigated. The area covered by pastures and forest amounts to 23 million hectares and 170 thousand hectares respectively.

In general the terrain in Iran can be divided into four types: plains and valleys (30.5 million hectares), plateaus (47 million hectares), Caspian piedmont (350 000 hectares) and slopes and mountains (86.2 million hectares). The soil in the plains and valleys is mainly fine or coarse-textured alluvial soil. Over 80 per cent of soils on the plateau are associations of brown, chestnut and *sierosem*. (*Sierosem* is a kind of premature soil which belong to temperate zones. The characteristic of the *sierosem* mostly depends on the kind of bedrock. Therefore in order to categorise the *sierosem* into various sorts the kind of bedrock is taken into consideration and if the proportion of the stone is high it is called skeleton soil. *Sierosems*, which are made of unstable and soft bedrock, fall into *regosol*, and those made of hard and tight ones are called *lithosol*. *Sierosom* is found mostly in the mountainous areas over the new sediments and where the soil has been eroded.) The Caspian piedmont has various types of forest soil, including grey podzol. The soil of the slopes and mountains is mainly lithogenous and calcareous (Aresvik, 1976, p. 1). All but the Caspian soils are present in Eastern Azerbaijan, in varying proportions.

Most of the mountain chains in the Azerbaijan region run from north-west to south-east, and the eastern mountains separate the region from the Caspian Sea. The altitude of the province ranges from 160–4811 metres, giving rise to a difference of about 20° centigrade in the mean temperature.

Three air flows govern the climate of Azerbaijan. The first, the 'Mediterranean flow', is mild, humid and the main source of Iran's rainfall. However a large part of the water content is lost before it reaches Eastern Azerbaijan. The second flow comes from Siberia and Central Asia and is cold and dry. The third flow comes from the Atlantic and Scandinavian and is cold and humid. Although the bulk of its water content is lost in Europe and Russia, bands of high pressure moving from the north and north-west of the country into the province bring heavy snowfalls.

Thus Eastern Azerbaijan has a mixed climate, but most of the province is cool and dry or cold and dry. Even the north-eastern corner of the region, which is lowland and has a more moderate climate, has an average of 50 days of frost a year. At higher altitudes (2000 metres or more) there is frost for up to nine months a year. It can be intensely cold at the higher altitudes, falling below −30°C, but in the summer the temperature can rise to 40°C in some parts of the province, such as Jolfa and Miyaneh. The average annual rainfall varies from 250 millimetres to 600 millimetres.

The people of the province speak Azari-Turkish. The official language is Persian, but according to the Plan and Budget Organisation (1989) only 40.7 per cent of the people in the province are able to speak Persian. Ethnically the province is relatively homogeneous and most of the people are of Aryan descent. In the beginning of the eleventh century, Ghaz Turks occupied Azerbaijan and gradually converted the language to Turkish. Agriculture, horticulture and livestock breeding are the principal means of subsistence for the majority of people.

Demographically, 79.6 per cent of families are nuclear in nature and 20.4 per cent live as an extended family (ibid., p. 4). Families of seven members or more constitute 34.7 per cent of total households in the province, 6.4 per cent higher than the national average (Plan and Budget Organisation of Eastern Azerbaijan, 1990, 1993).

According to the agricultural census of 1987 (the most recent available), 52.38 per cent of people aged six and over are literate, compared with the national average of 61.8 per cent. The rates for urban areas, rural areas and nomads are 64.96 per cent, 40.22 per cent and 10.81 per cent respectively. Tabriz, the capital of the province, has the highest literacy rate – 60.22 per cent. According to the available data, out of 809 692 students, 381 550 come from rural areas and the rest from urban areas (Appendix 1, Table A1.1).

According to the 1986 national census the rate of economic activity, particularly in rural areas, has fallen and at the provincial level it is 38.6 per cent. A review of the trends between two national censuses (1976 and 1986) shows that the unemployment rate in the province, in both rural and urban areas, has increased. According to the Plan and Budget Organisation of Eastern Azerbaijan (1993, p. 5) it rose from 2.8 per cent in 1976 to 13.1 per cent in 1987, putting Eastern Azerbaijan in fifteenth place in national terms. In particular the participation of women in economic activities has declined. In 1986 only 6.7 per cent of employed people in the region were female.

According to the 1986 national census, Eastern Azerbaijan is home to 8.3 per cent of Iran's population. With a growth rate of 2.52 per cent, between 1976 and 1986 the population of the province increased to 4 114 084. The national growth rate in that decade was 3.2 per cent (excluding Afghanistani refugees). This difference between the growth rates of the province and the country as a whole indicates that emigration has taken place (Statistical Centre of Iran, 1991). In 1990, 4 494 713 of the total national population of 57 million people were living in Eastern Azerbaijan.

The sex ratio in the province during 1976–86 declined from 107.2 to 104.9, suggesting that males were migrating elsewhere in search of work. The ratio for the whole country during this decade fell from 106 in 1976 to 105 in 1986 (ibid.). With regard to age structure, in 1976 42.72 per cent of the province's inhabitants were under fifteen years, rising to 46.4 per cent in 1986. The national averages in these years were 44.53 per cent and 44.45 per cent respectively.

A review of the population distribution in rural and urban areas indicates that between 1960 and 1989 the proportion of urban dwellers rose from 31.4 per cent to 52.3 per cent, while the proportion of rural dwellers fell from 68.6 per cent to 47.67 per cent. This population shift is particularly apparent if one examines of the rural population of the cities of the province between the two censuses (1976–86) (Appendix 1, Table A1.2)

In 1976, of the total economically active population aged 10 years and over, 92.85 per cent were employed. By 1986 this figure had fallen to 87 per cent, representing a rise in unemployment from 7.15 per cent to 13 per cent (Plan and Budget Organisation of Eastern Azerbaijan, 1995). The total area of the town (*sharestan*) is 4907 square kilometres, equal to 8.6 per cent of the total area of Eastern Azerbaijan. According to territorial divisions, Marand is divided into two major districts. It consists of 16 counties (*dehestan*), and 203 villages (Appendix 1, Table A1.3).

This towns lies to the south of the Republics of Armenia and Nakhichevan, to the west of the towns of Ahar and Kalibar, to the east of Western Azerbaijan and to the north of the town of Shabestar (Plan and Budget Organisation of Eastern Azerbaijan, 1993, p. 120). The area is semi-mountainous, consisting of two-thirds highlands and one-third low and/or plains (Syeedzonouzi, 1979, p. 2).

According to a survey conducted in 1991, 276 836 people were living in Marand at that time, or 8.4 per cent of the total population of Eastern Ajerbaijan. Of this figure, 43.8 per cent were living in towns and the remaining 56.2 per cent in villages. The town's growth rate in 1976–86 was 1.75 per cent. In towns the rate was 3.17 per cent and in villages 0.71 per cent (Appendix A1, Table A1.3). The proportion of urban dwellers increased from 3.21 per cent in 1976 to 40.8 per cent in 1986 and 43.8 per cent in 1989. In 1989, of the total 50 598 households, 45 per cent were situated in urban areas and 54.4 per cent in towns. The average size of households was 5.47 individuals or 5.26 in towns and 5.65 in villages. The literacy rate among those aged six years and over was 70.2 per cent in 1989 or 77.7 per cent in town areas and 64 per cent in villages (Statistical Centre of Iran, 1991).

Farming and horticulture are the major agricultural activities in Marand. According to the 1987 national agricultural census, agricultural land in Marand amounted to about 98.7 thousand hectares, or 6.8 per cent of the agricultural land in Eastern Azerbaijan. Farmland accounted for 84.5 thousand hectares and 14.2 thousand hectares were devoted to horticulture. Of the 84.5 thousand hectares of farmland, 26.9 thousand hectares were irrigated, 23.5 thousand hectares were unirrigated and the remaining 34.1 thousand hectares were lying fallow. In 1987, 73 per cent of agricultural land was devoted to the cultivation of cereal, 23 per cent to fodder and 3.8 per cent to other crops (Statistical Centre of Iran, 1989).

The characteristics of the selected villages and the sample population

As mentioned above, six villages were selected for the study: Duwlat Abad, Dizaj-e Hossein Bayk, Gharajeh-Fayzlullah, Livar-e-Paeen, Ghermezi Gheshlag and Babreh-e-Sofla.

Duwlat Abad is situated six kilometres east of the city of Marand and has a population of 4567. On the basis of a recent territorial division (1992), Duwlat Abad was designated as the centre of the county. It has three primary schools, two secondary schools (one for female students and one for males) and one high school. (In Iran, the educational system is divided into two broad categories: *school* and *university*. School is divided into three levels: primary school, guidance school and high school. Actually the high school consists of two levels: guidance and high school. In this book secondary school refers to guidance school.) The village's flat agricultural land is extensively irrigated, but the more mountainous land – which constitutes less than 30 per cent of the village's agricultural land – has to rely on rainfall. Deep wells with motorised pumps are the main source of irrigation. The village has five minibuses for transportation to Marand, and about eight of the village's 25 private cars are also used for transportation.

The village of Dizaj-e Hossein Bayk, which has a population of 4237, is situated in the east of the Koshsarayh county, eight kilometres from the city of Marand and four kilometres from the international highway, enabling easy access to the outside world. The village lies on a plain and has an abundant supply of water from the mountains to the north of the village. About 60 per cent of the water used for irrigation comes from these natural flows, and the rest is obtained from three deep wells or seasonal streams. Over 90 per cent of the land is irrigated. The village has three primary and two secondary schools. According to local people and the district education bureau, although the village has sufficient students of high-school age to warrant a high school, because of its closeness to the school in Koshsarayh, three kilometres distant, at the time of the study no need had been felt and no attempt had been made to establish a high school. The village has three minibuses for public transportation and some 50 private cars. About five of the latter are used as public transport.

Gharajeh Fayzullah is situated 22 kilometres to the west of Marand and has a population of 1650. About two fifths of the village's land is situated on the plain and the remaining three fifths is mountainous. Only the flat land is irrigated. Five deep wells and a natural stream are the main water sources. The village has two primary schools and one secondary school. The main means of transportation are two minibuses and a few private cars.

Livar-e-Paeen is located 19 kilometres to the south-west of Marand and has a population of 1470. About half of the village's land is sloping or mountainous and the rest lies on the plain. Two natural streams and three deep wells are the major source of water for irrigation. The village has a primary and a secondary school. One minibus, two intervillage minibuses and four private cars are available to transport people to and from Marand.

Ghermezi Gheshlag lies 31 kilometres to the north-east of Marand, and has a population of 950. The village is situated on the plain and is poorly supplied with water, thus conditions are poor for both daily living and agricultural activities. A natural stream flowing down from the northern mountains only provides enough water to irrigate about 20 per cent of the land. The village has a primary school but no secondary facilities. Just one private car is available for transportation, but the village is close to the international highway so the villagers are able to use intercity or intervillage vehicles to travel to the city. A considerable number of the villagers are engaged in transportation activities, particularly lorry driving.

Babreh-e-Sofla is located 35 kilometres to the south of Marand in hill country. It has a population of 1056. A stream and a canal are used to irrigate about 60 per cent of the village's agricultural land. The village has a primary and a secondary school. The secondary school is shared by one other village: Babreh-Olia. A minibus and two private cars are available to transport people to the city.

All six villages are supplied with electricity. Dizaj-e Hossein Bayk and Livar-e-Paeen have private telephone lines, but the other villages only have one public telephone each. With the exception of Ghermezi Gheshlag, all the villages have health clinics.

The characteristics of the sample households

The male:female sex ratio in the sample households was 119:110 at the time of the study, which was close to the average for the whole province (Appendix 1, Table A1.4). About 40 per cent of the sample population were under 15 years, around 50 per cent were aged 15–64 and 7 per cent were 64 or over. Again this more or less conformed with the provincial average (Appendix 1, Tables A1.5 and A1.6). The majority of households had more than five children and a notable proportion (over 20 per cent) had eight or more. A comparison of family size in the villages under study (and in other rural areas of the province) with that in urban areas shows that the rural families were far larger (Appendix 1, Table A1.7).

In all the villages a considerable number of the villagers were either illiterate or could just about write and read. This tendency was greater in the poorer villages than in the more prosperous ones. Although the number of respondents with secondary school education was higher in the better-off villages than in the poorer ones, the overall percentage was not considerable (Appendix 1, Table A1.8).

Agriculture and animal husbandry were the main occupations of the sample households. On average, 50 per cent of the households in all six villages were engaged in agriculture, but there were more wage labourers in the poor villages than in the better-off ones. Only a small number of respondents had clerical jobs. A notable percentage of the non-agricultural workers were engaged in business, lorry driving, carpet weaving and so on (Appendix 1, Table A1.9).

Participation

Participation is seen as providing a "moral incentive" and a new avenue in development allowing the powerless poor to negotiate new "material incentives" for themselves, and as a leverage point permitting successful micro actors to get into macro arenas of decision-making' (Goulet, 1989, p. 165).

With regard to involving people in the process of development, two approaches can be identified in the rural development literature. The first is based on the assumption that there is little wrong with the direction of development efforts and that past failures are mainly due to neglect of the 'human factor'. That is, people do not want to get involved in projects about which they have insufficient information. This has led to the elaboration of extension strategies, whose aim is to fill the gap by providing information and expanding the knowledge base (Oakley and Marsden, 1984). The second approach grew out of a rethinking of development strategies, where participation is seen as a strategy to provide opportunities to those who are traditionally the objects of development (Freire, 1972; Wignaraja, 1993; Burkey, 1993; Chambers, 1994). The stress in both approaches is on the significance of participation in the process of social change.

The key point in the latter approach is whether people who have hitherto been treated as mere objects to be acted upon, can act for themselves and determine their own social fate. When people are oppressed or reduced to a culture of silence they do not control their own destiny. However, if they participate they become active subjects of knowledge and action; they begin to construct their own history and become involved in the process of development (Freire, 1973, 1975). There is general agreement among an increasing number of development practitioners and the largest aid agencies (United Nations, 1975a; World Bank, 1991a) that the participation of beneficiaries makes them more committed to development projects, improves project performance and enhances project maintenance (Oakley and Marsden, 1984, 1996).

The need for participation in the process of social change in Iran was put forward by some experts and academicians before the revolution, along with an overall rethinking of development paradigms. This need was strongly endorsed immediately after the revolution, so much so that many considered it to be the cornerstone of the blueprint for an Islamic society (Schirazi, 1993). This strong conviction is reflected in the constitution of the Islamic Republic, which explicitly guarantees 'the participation of all people in the determination of their political, economic, social, and cultural fate' (Article 3.8). The preamble to the constitution stresses that 'the extensive and active participation of all members of society' is the *sine qua non* for the 'development of human beings'. The promotion of the sovereignty of the people in various aspects of social life led to the guaranteed participation of excluded people, including the majority of the rural population, in the post-revolutionary agricultural and development programmes: 'from the stage of passing resolutions to bringing in the harvest, the planning of agriculture and rural development will soon be based on the . . . cooperation and participation of the rural population and nomads' (Schirazi, 1993, p. 261). The greatest possible participation of the population in reaching individual plan targets was repeatedly emphasised in the agricultural section of the 1983 development plan and in the 1987 self-sufficiency plan. Likewise the participatory approach was the cornerstone of rural development policy in respect of the Centres for Agricultural, Rural and Nomadic Services, the *mosha* cooperatives and the Construction Ministry (Jihad). With regard to project evaluations, it was insisted that the involvement of the people in the development process must be considered a key indicator of the success of the project.

In this study, participation is defined and examined at four distinct but interrelated levels: decision making, cooperation, satisfaction and awareness. Decision making relates to the degree of people's involvement in the process of decision making and planning. Awareness refers to the degree of familiarity of the target population with the regulations, procedures and duties of the organisations and officials working for or in the villages. Cooperation refers to the involvement of villagers in government projects and activities conducted by rural organisations.

Satisfaction is defined as the ability of people to evaluate both the activities of external organisations and the effectiveness of these activities. In order to ascertain the degree of the sample population's participation in the rural development process, aggregate participation is discussed first, followed by an evaluation of their participation at the four levels listed above.

Aggregate participation

On average, half of the sample households participated very little in the rural development programmes, under a quarter participated a little and about a quarter participated to a considerable degree (Table 5.2). Taken separately, there was variation not only between the three pairs of villages but within the pairs. The respondents in villages 1, 3 and 5, which benefited from a larger number of programmes, had a higher participation rate than those in villages 2, 4 and 6, which received

Table 5.2 Degree of participation in rural development programmes in the six villages (per cent)

Degree of participation	1	2	3	4	5	6	Average
Aggregate participation							
Considerable	28.8	21.0	31.7	24.0	23.3	10.0	23.0
Little	25.4	27.0	26.7	26.2	30.0	25.0	26.0
Very little or none	45.8	53.0	53.0	49.5	45.5	65.0	51.0
Awareness							
Considerable	25.0	13.2	13.3	10.0	13.0	10.0	14.0
Little	32.5	28.6	39.1	31.0	38.0	28.5	33.0
Very little or none	42.0	56.9	47.3	59.0	69.0	61.3	52.5
Decision making							
Considerable	32.6	17.0	36.0	17.7	19.0	11.0	22.0
Little	21.2	24.0	23.0	26.6	28.0	26.7	24.0
Very little or none	46.0	59.0	41.0	56.1	53.0	61.0	52.4
Cooperation							
Considerable	51.6	32.0	45.0	32.7	38.8	9.4	35.0
Little	20.6	19.3	22.0	30.5	31.0	26.0	25.0
Very little or none	27.8	48.0	33.0	36.4	30.0	63.4	35.0
Satisfaction							
Considerable	31.0	23.0	33.0	23.0	23.0	13.0	24.0
Little	24.0	25.0	15.0	17.5	20.0	20.0	20.0
Very little or none	45.0	52.0	52.0	59.5	57.0	67.0	56.0
Size of sample	108	88	60	60	35	30	38

Source: Shakoori (1998), pp. 224–50.

fewer or no programmes. For instance, of the two prosperous villages, village 1 (maximum number of programmes) scored 29 per cent in the 'considerable participation' category while village 2 (minimum number of programmes) scored 21 per cent. Similarly, of the less prosperous villages, village 3 (maximum number) scored 32 per cent in that category while village 4 (minimum number) scored 24 per cent. Of the poorer villages, village 5 (maximum number) scored 23.3 per cent and village 6 (minimum number) scored 10 per cent (Table 5.2).

Analysis of the respondents' socioeconomic background revealed that the variables income, wealth and literacy had a strong influence and age, occupation and family size had a weak influence on their participation (Appendix 2, Table A2.1). The analysis also revealed that the correlation between income/wealth and participation tended to be stronger in the poor villages than in the others, and that the correlation between literacy and participation was strong in the prosperous villages and weak in the poor villages.

The higher impact of income and wealth on participation in the poorer villages may be due to the fact that, as these villages were more remote and less incorporated into wider society, socioeconomic and political power had not been separated. Consequently those individuals who enjoyed economic power, mainly in the form of land, usually enjoyed sociopolitical leverage in the community and occupied higher positions in the village hierarchy. Our observations in the selected villages and other villages in the district revealed that in many remote and small villages, those who acted as representatives of the people – or were members of the rural councils – were large landowners and elders, while in the better-off and prosperous villages the situation was very different. In most of these villages, the majority of the members of the councils set up immediately after the revolution and the officials of village institutions were young or middle aged and educated. One explanation of the situation in the remote villages might be that land in rural society is the major means of production and therefore land ownership confers prestige and political power, and is consequently a determining factor in social relations. There are two reasons for this. First, unlike in prosperous villages, where the sources of income and production have been diversified and people have access to job opportunities in the urban economy, remote villages lack or have limited access to the urban market, leaving them with restricted sources of income based mainly on the land. Second, the arrival of bureaucratic institutions in these villages created a number of new positions, many of which required full time engagement and certain qualifications in respect of education and skills. In the prosperous villages the newly created positions might not have offered landowners higher benefits compared with the costs, and therefore they declined to take up these positions.

A number of factors are responsible for the perpetuation of the hierarchical relations in remote villages.

First, according to our observations there was a strong tendency in remote villages for influential people to be asked to communicate with outsiders (officials, researchers and rural development workers), resulting in their having a greater awareness of new issues. Second, one of the state's rural policies after the revolution was to change the village political structure by replacing the village headman system with elected village councillors. But in remote areas the council members were often appointed by the developmental or revolutionary organisations rather than being elected. For example in villages 5 and 6 we were told by some people that 'we did not know about the rural council. A long time ago officials came from the bureau and introduced somebody as our representative and asked us to inform the other villagers about the representative.' An official at the Jihad district bureau confirmed this:

> It was difficult to set up an election system in the less populated areas, where people were reluctant to cooperate with officials and still had a negative attitude towards governmental organisations. It required time. We tried to find and introduce the most respected people in these villages as their representative for a transitional period, and we asked for the agreement of people who were present at the time. Our assumption was that after a short period of training and familiarising the villagers with councils tasks they would be able to elect their own council members. But for many reasons – particularly the existence of different parallel organisations engaged in the same field [mainly the Jihad and the Agricultural Bureau concerning rural issues] and the councils' uncertain status in the legal system of the country – council elections were not often held, and in many cases the councils were dissolved (personal interview).

Third, there was a general tendency among officials to deal only with villagers who were influential and well-informed. As Sjoberg *et al.* (1966, p. 73) argues, local bureaucrats preferred to avoid lower-class people as they might have handicapped the attainment of development goals, and development workers thought that better results could be achieved by visiting a few big farms rather than hundreds of scattered farms owned by small farmers. Our field study observations confirmed these arguments. For example a peasant in village 4 said:

> It always happens that I and a few others are called by the Agricultural Bureau or they come to the village and ask questions about the village, the quality of the soil and the amount of yield, and consult about seeds and pesticides and other agricultural issues. [The reason for this is that] they know that we cultivate a considerable amount of land and keep livestock, consequently we are asked more than others about agricultural issues in the village (personal interview).

Part of the reason for such inclinations among officials and villagers is the nature of the administration system and its incompatibility with the grass roots. We can distinguish two types of rationality: bureaucratic rationality and peasants' rationality. Bureaucratic rationality is based on the division of functions, rules and regulations, organisational hierarchy, specialisation, efficiency, impersonality and so on.

The rationality of rural people (excluding wealthy or large-scale farmers) is shaped by sheer poverty, lack of education, the unequal social structure and, in Freire's (1975) words, 'the culture of silence'. The majority of rural people do not have the ability to speak the language of bureaucrats or deal with administrative organisations, and hence are marginalised. Peasants' lives are governed by the powerful and unpredictable effects of nature, the market and state policies. Such factors as high socioeconomic positions, political influence, personal knowledge and information play important roles in providing a secure life for rural people and enabling them to deal with outside world. The bureaucracy, which emphasises a particular ethos and rationality, is not compatible with the majority of rural people who are in a lower status of the socioeconomic hierarchy.

While the government's policy after the revolution was to rectify the overbureaucratic nature of rural affairs by reorganising the prerevolutionary agricultural administration and establishing the Jihad (Schirazi, 1993), in the event administration became even more bureaucratic. As a senior official at the Centre of Services for Rural and Nomadic People stated, the only thing that:

differentiates this bureau from the prerevolutionary bureau is its name. In that time it was called the Agricultural Bureau, now it is called the Centre of Services for Rural and Nomadic People. You can even see this in the Jihad. . . . After years of rejecting a bureaucratic administrative system the Jihad has started to adopt our system, even though we have always complained about it (personal interview).

Participation at the awareness level

Analysis of participation at the awareness level revealed that only about a quarter of households were fully aware of the objectives and duties of the rural organisations, and over half of the respondents had no knowledge of this at all (Table 5.2).

The intervillage comparisons indicated that although the degree of awareness among people in villages with the maximum number of rural programmes was higher than among those in villages with fewer or no programmes, the difference was not significant. For example, of the prosperous villages, village 1 (maximum number of programmes), scored 57 per cent awareness in the 'considerable' and 'little' categories, while village 2 (minimum number of programmes scored 43 per cent. Similarly, of the less prosperous villages, village 3 (maximum number) scored 52 per cent in these categories, and village 4 (minimum number) scored 41 per cent. Of the poorer villages, village 5 (maximum number) scored 51 per cent, and village 6 (minimum number) scored 38.5 per cent (Table 5.2).

The analysis also revealed that most of the respondents knew more about the Jihad than the service centres. This was mainly because of the nature and comprehensiveness of the Jihad's activities, which targeted the majority of rural people, while the service centres concentrated mainly on farmers and horticulturists

Contrary to our expectations, only 16 per cent of the respondents were very familiar with the duties of the village councils, while those with less awareness thought of the councils as a communication instrument between the government and the village, and a village institution to deal with people's disputes. One significant finding was the correlation between age and awareness in that the elderly respondents were seemingly unaware of or had little knowledge about the postrevolutionary rural reform organisations. This might have been due to scepticism or cynicism about outsiders (researchers or officials) or a reluctance to get involved in the process of change and the associated institutions (Dawson and Prewitt, 1969; Dowse and Hughes, 1986).

Another reason could be related to the economic consequences of the revolution. Except during the first stages of the revolution, when material inequalities and poverty were reduced, during the second and subsequent periods economic inequality increased and the poverty rate often surpassed that in the prerevolutionary period. (This was a common feature of many of the European revolutions, so the Iranian revolution was not exceptional in this respect.) The economic situation was exacerbated by disastrous events such as the invasion by Iraq and the imposition of economic embargoes, which made living conditions worse. Since older people had lived much of their lives in the prerevolutionary era they were in a better position than the young to make comparisons, and were not often satisfied with the new developments. At the same time they were unable to protest against these changes and so preferred not to be involved in the process of change.

Participation at the decision-making level

Similar to the awareness level, over half of the respondents took no part in decision making and only 22 per cent were fully involved (Table 5.2). While 37 per cent of the respondents believed that their opinions were considered seriously in the rural elections and 19 per cent said they had been informed by the rural development organisations that programmes were to be implemented in their village, only about 9 per cent said that their opinions had been sought on the matter. For instance a villager in village 5 said of a large, expensive school built a few years after the revolution:

> If our opinions had been sought or considered before . . . building this school, to which we cannot send our children because of our need for their contribution to the household budget, we would have said first of all, solve our subsistence problems such as infertile soil and the lack of water for irrigation (personal interview).

In village 3 it was pointed out that the irrigation canal that had been built as part of one project was not suitable for flood situations: 'If we had been asked before the start of the project, the canal would have been totally different and more useful and we would not have lost our crops in the flood that took place a few days ago'. An official at the Jihad bureau concurred:

> Although the idea of taking people's views into consideration was on the agenda of the Jihad, before the flood occurred nobody had

actually realised the importance of people's knowledge. If local knowledge had been taken into consideration we may have had less damage in the flooded villages . . . [we] were going to implement a huge project in the area, but because of financial problems it was fortunately postponed, otherwise we would have lost all our investment because we did not know the area was in the flood zone and we had never asked the local people (personal interview).

Indeed the involvement of local people in the planning and formulation of projects was of paramount importance (Cohen and Uphoff, 1977; Pearse and Stiefel, 1979; Oakley and Marsden, 1984; Goulet, 1989; Burkey, 1996) but in practice they received little attention.

Participation at the cooperation level

Compared with the two previous categories a relatively large number of the respondents were involved at the cooperation level: 35 per cent of the respondents cooperated extensively, 25 per cent a little and 35 per cent did not get involved (Table 5.2). This could mean that contrary to the technocratic idea that peasants are resistant to change and innovation, and are therefore reluctant to cooperate with rural development agents, they are likely to welcome development efforts if they see these as benefiting their lives. Compared with the other levels of participation, socioeconomic background did not seem to play a notable part in the respondents' tendency to cooperate with rural organisations and respondents from all strata expressed their desire to be involved in rural issues.

Among the indicators of cooperation, involvement in discussions with the rural organisations scored the lowest and local discussions scored the highest. For instance, while almost 50 per cent of the respondents said that they always participated in the rural council elections, only 19 per cent were extensively involved in discussions on rural issues with the rural organisations. However 38 per cent said that they regularly visited the Jihad bureau.

Satisfaction

Less than one third of the respondents were highly satisfied and over half were not satisfied with the process of rural change after the revolution (Table 5.2). The significant finding in this category was the negative correlation between education and satisfaction (Appendix 2, Table A2.1): that is, the higher the education, the lower the satisfaction. This could have been due to the worsening economic situation in Iran as a result of the Iran–Iraq War, the economic embargo and declining oil revenues. This situation affected moderately educated people in two ways. First, there were now fewer job opportunities for high school graduates. After the start of the war, parliament passed a law that prevented governmental organisations from recruiting new officials, although some exceptions were made in the case of skilled and highly educated people in that they could be employed as temporary contract workers. However, the majority of educated rural people did not have a university degree. Second, even in the case of secure government employment the employees' fixed salaries could be devalued by economic crises, so employment did not provide them with adequate financial security. Therefore they did not see themselves as beneficiaries of the post-revolutionary changes. Farmers and livestock breeders, on the other hand, sometimes benefited from the post-revolutionary fluctuations. It should be mentioned that the war provided considerable job opportunities for rural people at the frontiers. However, such engagements were temporary, and even if they resulted in permanent employment they too were vulnerable to economic fluctuations. Having one or two part-time jobs on top of their permanent job became a common means for fixed-salary employees to supplement their income.

Most of the respondents in the study wanted to leave their village and live in the city, but two groups were more likely to do so than the others: those who were rich enough to change their livelihood by investing in the urban sector; and those whose poverty and unemployment (mostly the younger generation) meant they had nothing to lose by leaving the village. The data showed that the majority of respondents would like to invest in non-agricultural sectors, particularly in business.

Most believed that their living conditions had worsened, mainly because of economic pressures, but that in general their standard of living was better than it had been 20 years ago. They considered that although the diversification of living facilities, such as the development of infrastructure, enlargement of job chances, the possibility of access to refrigerators, cars, etc., the possibility of access to markets and suchlike had brought new opportunities, they had not been able to benefit from these opportunities. Two factors seem to be important in explaining the villagers' attitude towards their living conditions: (1) the changes in the national economy and society since the revolution; and (2) the effect of this on the respondents' villages and households. It might be argued that the living conditions in most villages, in aggregate terms, had improved, either because of the rural development programmes or as a result of the overall changes in society in the previous 18 years, resulting in better facilities and improved life chances. In other words, these developments had facilitated the incorporation of rural areas into society at large. Nevertheless the deteriorating economic circumstances of the country had put notable economic pressure on households. Hence, given the increasing dependency of the rural economy on the national economy, it would be reasonable to say that the changes at the macro level had not necessarily had a positive effect on individual households.

Social mobility

Social mobility has been the subject of much attention in social change and development studies, mainly because social mobility says something about the life chances of individuals in society and has a significant effect on class formation, in the sense of distinctive class subcultures and class identification (Giddins, 1974, 1993). An important concern in this respect is people's response to the experience of social mobility. Their satisfaction or lack of satisfaction with the process can have significant consequences for the stability of society. This is particularly important politically owing to the fact that a relatively high rate of upward mobility acts as a 'political safety value' in society (Parkin, 1968; Haralambos and Holborn, 1995).

The availability of opportunities is a central question in mobility debates. Many mobility studies have focused on the extent to which modern stratification systems are 'open' and they allow a high incidence of social mobility (Coxon and Jones, 1975, p. 10). There are many processes that affect the availability of opportunities and the diversification of life chances, but the main ones are as follows.

The first is related to the structural changes that result from changes in social formations, which in turn have their roots in economic development and technological advancement. The latter results in a steady broadening of the opportunity for upward mobility, a change in the occupational structure and the growth of higher-level occupations.

The second process is related to rapid changes in society as a result of events such as revolution and war, which break down the old system or deform the structure of society, and consequently provide opportunities for various social strata to move beyond 'the conventional orderings of status'. According to Sorkin (1967, pp. 234–5), rapid changes such as those brought about by revolutions weaken or eliminate the existing structure by deforming 'the structure of the social aggregate'. During a revolution:

> the structure of the social aggregate suddenly becomes weak, formless and crumbles to pieces, social borderlines suddenly disappear. The processes of change in the composition of social groups and of circulation of individuals . . . go on much quicker and affect a larger number of people . . . . The amplitude of fluctuations in . . . social groups is much wider, old groups are extinguished and new ones formed.

During revolutionary periods both downward and upward mobility can be high, but it is often temporary.

The third process is related to mobility as the result of planned change. The main objectives of development policies are to increase people's choices and improve their capabilities so that they can make a better life for themselves. This is made possible by eliminating such obstacles as differential knowledge and unequal opportunity structures, as well as distributing material resources (Olson, 1963; Pye, 1966; Sen, 1977, 1983; Clements, 1995).

The reasons for examining social mobility in Iran in general and rural areas in particular are as follows. First, the revolution and the consequent politico-economic changes should have resulted in a more fluid and mobile society. Second, great emphasis was put on enhancing the status of the poor and improving the plight of the lower stratum – the Islamic economic order was defined as 'one in which the poor and deprived stood at the centre' (Amuzegar, 1993, p. 17). Third, a major objective of rural development policy was to diversify the economic activities of villages by improving their physical infrastructure in order to upgrade 'the living standards and welfare of villages and to bridge the gap between villages and cities' (Ministry of Jihad-e Sazandegi, 1992, p. 49).

The measurement of social mobility in rural areas can serve as a proxy for changes in the circumstances of the lower stratum. In this study, mobility is defined as a movement towards or away from existing occupational positions. Two aspects of occupational mobility are examined: (1) intergenerational mobility, involving a comparison between the position of an individual and that of his or her parents; and (2) intragenerational mobility, or a change in the position of an individual at two or more points in his or her lifetime or career (Miller, 1975a, 1975b; Hamilton and Hirszowicz, 1993; Giddens, 1993).

The field study revealed the following. In general, occupational mobility tended to be higher in the villages that received the most rural development programmes than in those which received fewer or no programmes. In all villages there was a tendency for offspring to opt for the same occupation as their fathers (50 per cent), and 71 per cent of the respondents were in the same occupational category after the revolution as they had been before it, giving an average score of 23 per cent for intragenerational mobility and 28 per cent for intergenerational mobility (Tables 5.3–5; see also Appendix 2, Tables A2.2–3). Given the fact that mobility occurs over the long term, and taking into account the fact that the revolutions potentially provide a greater chance for larger mobility the higher figure for intergenerational mobility appears reasonable.

Of the various occupational categories examined in this study, in general the lowest levels of intra- and intergenerational mobility were found in the labourer category. In other words, more respondents in this category had moved away from their father's status or changed their prerevolutionary status.

In general, most movement tended to be to the adjacent category, usually from labourer to farmer or from farmer to farmer and livestock breeder. This means that while there was some diversification of household activities there was no real occupational mobility. The tendency of respondents to engage in these occupations was greater in villages with a larger number of rural programmes than in those with fewer programmes. The higher degree of movement, both intra- and intergenerational between the 'farmer' and 'farmer and livestock breeder' categories could be due to the land redistribution policy after the revolution, a scarcity of opportunities in the other categories, or the fact that these two groups were by far the largest. The lesser degree of upward mobility is reflected in the lower and weak correlation coefficients (Tables A2.2 and A2.3).

A comparison of the paired villages showed that in the prosperous villages the tendency to move to the 'functionary' category was greater than in the poorer villages. There was no great difference between the villages in each pair concerning mobility towards the 'urban job' category, but the tendency was far less in the poorer villages than in the better-off and prosperous villages. In general, the poorer the village, the more lowly the occupations.

An examination of the effect of the respondents' socioeconomic circumstances on their intra- and intergenerational mobility showed that, apart from the income variable in villages 1 and 3, none of the independent variables was significantly associated with mobility. The correlation coefficient for income was around 40 per cent (a moderate association),

Rural Development at the Micro Level 147

Table 5.3 Comparison of the occupation of the respondents with that of their fathers (intergenerational mobility) (per cent)

	Labourer	Farmer	Farmer and livestock breeder	Shopkeeper	Functionary	Other (urban jobs)
Village 1						
(1)	1	9	49	1	10	20
(2)	–	11	22	3	19	46
(3)	–	11	82	–	–	–
(4)	37	42	19	23	–	–
(5)	–	–	17	71	11	–
(6)	19	15	20	17	28	–
Village 2						
(1)	2	–	35	7	–	54
(2)	–	–	25	9	–	64
(3)	13	–	87	–	–	–
(4)	28	35	20	16	–	–
(5)	–	13	–	87	–	–
(6)	25	24	26	23	–	–
Village 3						
(1)	7	18	48	–	1	22
(2)	–	–	67	2	–	30
(3)	29	71	–	–	–	–
(4)	30	48	11	11	–	–
(5)	–	16	54	10	–	–
(6)	14	15	19	22	28	–
Village 4						
(1)	–	20	18	–	–	60
(2)	–	20	19	–	–	60
(3)	–	100	–	–	–	–
(4)	35	25	40	–	–	–
(5)	–	–	100	–	–	–
(6)	25	25	20	–	30	–
Village 5						
(1)	16	3	32	–	–	17
(2)	–	37	41	–	–	21
(3)	66	–	44	–	–	–
(4)	58	33	8	–	–	–
(5)	–	–	100	–	–	–
(6)	18	24	24	33	–	–
Village 6						
(1)	–	53	12	14	–	20
(2)	–	26	31	22	–	42
(3)	–	100	–	–	–	–

Table 5.3 Comparison of the occupation of the respondents with that of their fathers (intergenerational mobility) (per cent) *(Continued)*

	Labourer	Farmer	Farmer and livestock breeder	Shopkeeper	Functionary	Other (urban jobs)
Village 6 (*contd*)						
(4)	–	88	12	–	–	–
(5)	–	–	100	–	–	–
(6)	–	25	16	29	30	–
Total number in sample	108	88	60	60	35	30

Notes:
(1.) Absolute mobility rate for each category.
(2.) Upward mobility rate for each category.
(3.) Downward mobility rate for each category.
(4.) Background of upward mobility rate for each category.
(5.) Background of downward mobility rate for each category.
(6.) Self-recruitment rate for each category. *Background* in intragenerational mobility refers to the occupation of the respondents before the revolution, and in intergenerational mobility refers to the occupation of the respondents' fathers.
Source: Shakoori (1998), pp. 356–9.

and for the rest of the variables it was below 25 per cent (a weak or very weak association). There were no significant variations between villages, but income, wealth and literacy were higher in the prosperous villages, particularly those with more rural programmes, than in the poorer villages (Appendix 2, Tables A2.2 and A2.3). From the data we may conclude that the respondents with higher levels of income and wealth in the villages under study had a better chance of changing their status. Although most of the socioeconomic variables examined in this study had a weak effect on the respondents' social mobility, they did not prevent the respondents from changing their occupational status.

From the foregoing points we may conclude that most of the observed mobility was short range. Second, the background of the respondents – the status of their fathers and their own status before the revolution – played an important part in mobility. Although the higher upward mobility in villages with more rural programmes confirms the assumption of this study that the higher the number of rural reforms the greater the mobility, the fact that a significant proportion did not change their employment status and that mobility was largely concentrated in the farming categories shows that the rural programmes did

Rural Development at the Micro Level 149

Table 5.4 Comparison of the occupational status of the respondents with their status before the revolution (intra-generational mobility) (per cent)

	Labourer	Farmer	Farmer and livestock breeder	Shopkeeper	Functionary	Other (urban jobs)
Village 1						
(1)	3	20	44	8	1	23
(2)	–	9	46	13	16	32
(3)	10	49	40	–	–	12
(4)	46	28	12	–	–	50
(5)	–	–	6	13	40	–
(6)	7	23	32	37	–	–
Village 2						
(1)	2	–	57	13	16	11
(2)	–	13	27	21	15	24
(3)	4	–	15	51	31	–
(4)	35	39	25	–	–	–
(5)	–	–	6	–	63	30
(6)	–	38	37	–	24	–
Village 3						
(1)	–	38	35	16	4	22
(2)	–	17	35	10	5	30
(3)	–	60	20	20	–	–
(4)	36	40	10	–	10	–
(5)	–	–	12	25	61	–
(6)	–	19	43	26	11	–
Village 4						
(1)	–	34	36	–	18	19
(2)	–	25	29	–	16	29
(3)	–	17	83	–	11	20
(4)	44	24	30	–	–	–
(5)	–	–	17	83	–	–
(6)	–	32	24	44	–	–
Village 5						
(1)	17	17	49	–	–	–
(2)	–	15	63	–	21	–
(3)	75	25	–	–	–	–
(4)	61	43	3	–	–	–
(5)	–	–	100	–	–	–
(6)	9	21	26	43	–	–
Village 6						
(1)	–	27	46	16	2	7
(2)	–	24	49	17	2	7
(3)	–	100	–	–	–	–

Table 5.4 The comparison of the occupational status of the respondents with their status before the revolution (intra-generational mobility) (per cent) *(Continued)*

	Labourer	Farmer	Farmer and livestock breeder	Shopkeeper	Functionary	Other (urban jobs)
Village 6 (*contd*)						
(4)	60	24	14	–	–	–
(5)	–	–	100	–	–	–
(6)	–	26	29	43	–	–
Total number in sample	108	88	60	60	35	30

Notes:
(1.) Absolute mobility rate for each category.
(2.) Upward mobility rate for each category.
(3.) Downward mobility rate for each category.
(4.) Background of upward mobility rate for each category.
(5.) Background of downward mobility rate for each category.
(6.) Self-recruitment rate for each category.
Source: Shakoori (1998), pp. 359–62.

Table 5.5 The main indices of intra- and intergenerational mobility (per cent)

	Village 1	Village 2	Village 3	Village 4	Village 5	Village 6	Aggregate
Intragenerational mobility							
Upward	21	12	20	15	16	9	23
Self-recruitment	66	87	71	81	80	80	71
Downward	13	2	9	4	4	10	6
Integenerational mobility							
Upward	36	31	32	28	32	34	28
Self-recruitment	43	48	48	57	57	63	40
Downward	21	21	20	15	11	2	32
Total number in sample	108	88	60	60	35	30	381

Source: Shakoori (1998), pp. 260–74.

not have a significant effect on the occupational mobility of the respondents. The fewer occupational differences between the paired villages in most job categories confirms the notion that mobility was influenced more by the developmental potential of the villages, particularly their geographical situation, than by the rural programmes.

One reason for this might be that mobility takes place over generations and two decades is too short a time to detect overall change in occupational mobility. However, the main reason lies in the nature of the rural programmes. Employment creation was centred mainly on farming – the land redistribution programme encouraged the inhabitants of the target villages to engage in the categories 'farmer' or 'farmer and livestock breeder', with further encouragement being provided by the output delivery programmes. While such programmes as the provision of piped water, electrification, school construction and road building created temporary jobs for the villagers, particularly for construction workers, they did not offer a sustained change in their employment status. Indeed measures to improve professional skills for project planning and implementation benefited urban citizens more than rural people. Given the limited employment opportunities in the rural economy, any sharp changes in people's occupational status required investment in sectors other than purely agricultural ones, but this was rare in the villages under study.

In addition to these factors, a fundamental reason for the lower mobility in rural areas in general and the villages under study in particular is the historical powerlessness of villagers. This is particularly related to the low literacy levels in the village which prevents the villagers from gaining access to new opportunities in rural areas and from benefiting from opportunities in urban areas.

Mention should be made of the physical upgrading projects (*behsazi*), whose main objective was to provide the groundwork for a better service distribution system in the villages, raising the employment rate by establishing industries and paving the way for investment and market expansion (Ministry of Jihad-e Sazandeghi, 1992, p. 29). In village 1 this project had not had a significant effect on job opportunities at the time of the field study (two years after the project's completion), but it may have been too soon for the full benefits to have emerged. Some benefits were visible in the business sector of the village, but only for the few who could afford to invest. Even if the project proves a success, the trickle-down benefits will take a long time to materialise.

Income

This section examines the effect of the rural development programmes on the income of the sample households. In this study income refers to the total earnings of a person from his or her product, trade or investment.

The finding of the study, based on an analysis of variance, is that income varied significantly among the villages. The F-statistics for income in all six villages strongly bear out the hypothesis of the study that income is affected by rural development programmes and the developmental potential of the villages (Appendix 3, Table A3.1).

A comparison of the village pairs (Table 5.1) revealed that the average annual income in the villages with more rural programmes (villages 1, 3 and 5) was higher than in their pairs (villages 2, 4 and 6), and that the difference was statistically significant. Similarly, a comparison between villages with the maximum number of programmes but with different potential developmental conditions revealed that the difference between the average annual income in the villages of the latter group was critically higher than in the villages of the former group.

The variables age, literacy, family size, occupation, land and assets together were found to have a relatively strong effect on income, especially in the villages with more development programmes. These variables together explained over 40 per cent of the changes in the income of the respondents. In general the impact of age on households' income was very weak and in some villages it was negative. The highest contribution to income in the villages with most programmes was made by the variables agricultural land and orchard, indicating that the income of those with a larger amount of agricultural land, orchard assets and a higher job position was improved by the process of rural change. Finally, the effect of education and orchard sized gardens in the poorer villages was far lower than in the better-off and prosperous villages.

The F-ratios for the poorest pair of villages was low, which does not lend support to the hypothesis that income would be significantly affected by the measures of socioeconomic background examined in the study (Appendix 3, Table A3.2). These measures together accounted for 40 per cent of the variation in income of the respondents in village 1, 30 per cent in village 2, 59 per cent in villages 3, 45 per cent in village 4, 30 per cent in village 5 and 23 per cent in village 6.

It should be noted that it was expected that the role of the explanatory variables in household income in the poorer villages would be greater because of the more simple economic relations in these villages. That is, in the prosperous villages the larger population, proximity to the city and so on enabled greater diversity in respect of income sources, often outside the rural economy (which may not been included in data gathered for the regression model), while the remote villages had more limited sources and these were mainly within the village economy. Thus the variables included in the regression model were expected to account for a higher proportion of the variations in household income in the remote villages. However, the analysis provided the opposite result (Appendix 3, Table A3.2). One possible explanation for this, and particularly for the lack of a statistically significant correlation between socioeconomic background and income in the poorer villages, might be the small sample size in these villages. Another might be that the average income was lower because the land was less productive as a result of poor-quality soil. We were told in these villages that a considerable number of people worked in neighbouring villages as labourers during the farming season. This could mean that income from labouring or other activities might have accounted for a significant part of household income but was not included in the data.

The higher contribution of land in villages 1, 3 and 5 (those with the maximum number of rural reform programmes) might have been due to the land redistribution programme. This was particularly obvious in village 3 where the land was of higher quality and distributed in greater quantities.

One possible explanation for the higher correlation coefficient for literacy in the prosperous villages compared with the poorer villages could be the higher proportion of educated people in the former. As for the very weak or negative correlation between age and household income, because of the high dependence of the majority of rural people on manual work and the declining ability of ageing people to carry out such work, lower or negative correlation coefficients are understandable. The lower contribution of horticulture in the poorer villages could be because fewer engaged in horticulture due to a shortage of water for irrigation and lack of funds to invest in horticulture, which requires a higher investment than farming and the financial returns take longer to come.

Wealth

Here, wealth refers to all the assets of a household, including land, buildings, livestock, vehicles, water, the material used in building housing such as brick, stone, and so on. Analysis of the effect of the rural programmes on household wealth in the selected villages revealed a similar effect to that on income and was statistically significant. A comparison of the pairs of villages showed that apart from the first pair, where contrary to the research assumption average wealth in village 2 was higher than in village 1, in the other pairs the average wealth in the villages with the maximum number of rural development programmes (villages 3 and 5) was higher than in the villages with fewer programmes (villages 4 and 6), as expected. Nevertheless the differences were not statistically significant. A comparison of the villages with the maximum number of programmes but different developmental potential conditions (villages 1, 3 and 5) revealed that, apart from the first pair, the average wealth difference between the villages in the third and second pairs was not statistically significant (Appendix 3, Table A3.3). Broadly speaking, the small difference between the villages with most programmes and the others could mean that the wealth of the sample households in both groups had increased, but this was due to overall societal changes rather than the development programmes. The higher average wealth in village 2 compared with village 1 might have been due to the higher percentage of lorry owners in village 2, because lorries and other motor vehicles had a higher value than the main forms of wealth in rural areas, such as land.

Taking into account the fact that there was a greater difference between the annual incomes of the sample households compared with their wealth, it may be argued that although the rural development programmes had a more positive effect on wealth and living standards in the villages with the maximum number of development programmes, the effect was not so great as to make the difference between the villages in the pairs statistically significant. It may also be argued that the increase in the income of the sample households served to increase their wealth, although the extent of this was not the same as in the case of income.

Part of the reason for the smaller difference between the paired villages might be the nature of the rural development programmes. As already mentioned, the programmes were very diverse and included land redistribution, agricultural input delivery programmes, road building, electrification, provision of piped drinking water, education facilities and physical upgrading (*behsazi*) projects. Of these the land distribution programme could have had a positive and direct effect on household wealth, for the following reasons. First, the amount of land in question was not large enough to change the average wealth of the villages, but as only a small percentage of households received land it did have a positive effect on wealth distribution within the villages, and to some extent between the villages of the pairs. Other programmes, particularly the agricultural input programme, had a direct effect on income and in the long term resulted in increased household wealth, but the effect was not dramatic.

The *behsazi* projects were designed to improve the physical and spatial infrastructure of the targeted areas, integrate scattered villages, create rural industrial areas and provide for the settlement of nomads. The aim of the physical upgrading projects was to provide the basis of a better service distribution system in villages, and to pave the way for socioeconomic development in rural areas by improving their physical and environmental conditions in order to attract agricultural and commercial investment. The projects were only implemented in villages with over 100 households, so in our sample only village 1 benefited from this programme. At the times of the study the projects had not had a significant effect on household wealth, but as we shall see below, housing quality had improved markedly.

An examination of the effect of socioeconomic background on wealth indicated that the variables income, literacy and occupation, together with age and family size, had a relatively strong impact on the wealth of the sample households in all the villages, particularly in the case of the first and second pairs, suggesting that those with higher socioeconomic positions gained greater wealth during the process of rural change. These variables explained about 40 per cent of the variations in the wealth of the respondents in village 1 and 50 per cent in village 2. The figures for second pair of villages were 40 per cent for village 3 and 32 per cent for village 4, while for the third pair (villages 5 and six) they were 38 per cent and 35 per cent respectively (Appendix 3, Table A3.4).

In the first pair of villages the effect of these variables was greater in village 2 (with minimal rural programmes) than in village 1 (maximum number of programmes), but for the other pairs their effect followed the same pattern as that for income. Although the sample households with a higher socioeconomic position had greater wealth, the statistical difference was not great (Appendix 3, Table A3.4). One possible reason might be the small sample size in the poorer villages. Another could be the lower level of wealth and the similarity of the forms of the wealth among the sample households in these villages.

The major differences between the pairs relate to the variables literacy and occupation, whose effect in the poorer villages was weaker than in the prosperous and middle-ranking villages. This could be due to the larger number of educated individuals with non-agricultural occupations in the first and second pairing (Table 5.3).

Well-being

Well-being is defined here according to the 'basic needs' approach: that is, people are deemed to have an adequate level of well-being if their basic needs are met. In this study three basic needs – housing, food and clothing – are proxied by (1) expenditure on food and clothing, and (2) quality of housing.

Analysis of expenditure on food and clothing in the six villages produced a similar finding to that for income and wealth. Level of expenditure was positively correlated with the number of development programmes, which in turn depended on the original development potential of the villages. In other words expenditure was higher in the villages with the most development programmes. The impact of this variable on the poorer villages (5 and 6) was not statistically significant. This might be due to cultural consumption differences, lower income and small sample size compared with the better-off or prosperous villages (Appendix 3, Table A3.5).

An examination of the effect of socioeconomic background expenditure revealed that those with higher socioeconomic positions spent more on food and clothing. This effect was not significant in the poorer villages, perhaps due to the small degree of socioeconomic differentiation in these villages. In percentage terms, socioeconomic background explained 75 per cent of the variation in living expenses in village 1, about 58 per cent in village 2, 50 per cent in village 3, 40 per cent in village 4, 30 per cent in village 5 and 20 per cent in village 6 (Appendix 3, Table A3.6). Of the socioeconomic variables, income, family size and wealth had the greatest effect, while literacy and age, particularly in the poorer villages, had a very weak effect on expenditure.

Quality of housing was examined in terms of status: that is, high-status, medium-status and low-status housing. Of the 381 sample households, 17 per cent had high-status housing, 43 per cent had medium-status housing and 38 per cent had low-status housing (Table 5.6). In general, housing quality in the villages that received the most rural development programmes (villages 1, 3 and 5) was higher than in those villages which had received fewer or no programmes (villages 2, 4 and 6). High-status housing was enjoyed by 29 per cent of the sample households in village 1, 16 per cent in village 2, 18 per cent in village 3, 10 per cent in village 4, 12 per cent in villages 5 and 8 per cent in village 6. For medium-status housing the figures were 46 per cent in village 1, 41 per cent in village 2, 45 per cent in village 3, 37 per cent in village 4, 40 per cent in village 5 and 30 per cent in village 6.

As Table 5.6 makes clear, there were notable variations between the villages in the first pair in respect of high-status housing, and between the villages in the second and third pairs in respect of medium-status housing. Assuming that the higher percentages in villages with a higher concentration of rural programmes were the result of these programmes, one may conclude that the programmes in village 1 – a prosperous village with the maximum number of programmes – served to increase the amount of higher-quality housing, while those in village 3 (moderately prosperous, maximum number of programmes) and village 5 (poor, maximum number of programmes) boosted medium-quality housing. Indeed, according to the respondents in village 1 the physical upgrading (*behsazi*) project had enabled most of the villagers to rebuild their houses.

Analysis of the correlation between socioeconomic background and housing status revealed that most of the independent variables were positively correlated with housing status. In general the impact of these variables was stronger in the villages with many programmes than in those with fewer or no programmes. In most villages, income, wealth and education exerted the greatest effect (Appendix 3, Table A3.7). This could mean that respondents with a higher socioeconomic status, particularly in the villages with many rural programmes, were able to take greater advantage of the programmes than those with a lower socioeconomic status, both within their own villages and in the counterpart villages.

The direction of rural change

The direction of rural change was calculated using the Gini index and decile distribution. The aim was to see how the rural development programmes changed the distribution of income, wealth and well-being among rural people. The Gini index and decile distribution were calculated on the basis of ratio and interval data but among the components

Table 5.6 Distribution of respondents in terms of housing status (per cent)

Status	Village 1	Village 2	Village 3	Village 4	Village 5	Village 6	Average
Low	24.5	43.0	36.7	53.3	52.0	61.1	42.4
Medium	46.3	41.1	45.0	36.7	38.0	30.6	38.7
High	29.2	15.9	18.3	10.0	10.0	8.3	17.9

Source: Shakoori (1998), p. 307.

of change considered in this study, only income, wealth and well-being qualified in this respect. Consequently intra- and intercommunity inequality refer to differences in these variables. (There are three main levels of measurement: *nominal, ordinal* and *interval/ratio*. A nominal variable is one where we can distinguish between categories of a variable but cannot rank the categories in any order. Sex or religious affiliation are examples of nominal level variable. An ordinal variable is one where it is meaningful to rank the categories, however it is not possible to quantify precisely how much difference is between the categories. The categories can be rank ordered in terms of the strength of agreement they reflect toward a statement or attitude. If people were asked to what extent they are in paid work with the responses of 'not at all', 'part time only' and 'full time', this would be an ordinal variable. An interval/ratio is one on which the categories have a natural ranking and it is possible to quantify precisely the differences between the categories. Age, if it is measured in years is an interval variable. For further details of the methodological rationale and calculation method see Shakoori, 1998.)

Income distribution

The results of the analysis are shown in Table 5.7. As can be seen, income was unequally distributed within and between the six villages. A comparison of the paired villages shows that income inequality was greater in the villages with the maximum number of rural programmes (villages 1, 3 and 5) than in those with fewer or no programmes (villages 2, 4 and 6). The greatest difference was observed in the poorer villages: 0.38 for village 5 and 0.33 for village 6, compared

Table 5.7 Gini coefficients for income, wealth and expenditure

Village	Income	Wealth	Expenditure (well-being)
One	0.46056	0.32465	0.24850
Two	0.41010	0.39608	0.20413
Three	0.40293	0.36694	0.23400
Four	0.37433	0.33361	0.19579
Five	0.38663	0.31419	0.20276
Six	0.33094	0.28629	0.18622
Aggregate	0.54685	0.40561	0.25982

Source: Shakoori (1998), pp. 313, 317, 322.

with 0.46 for village 1 and 0.41 for village 2. The least difference was observed in the middle-ranking villages (0.40 for village 3 and 0.37 for village 4). A comparison of the villages within maximum number of programmes but different development potential (villages 1, 3 and 5) revealed a significant degree of income inequality between villages 1 and 5, with income being more unequal in the former than in the latter.

A detailed examination of decile income distribution clarified the above points (Table 5.8). There was a remarkably wide gap between the top and bottom deciles, with the aggregate share of the top 10 per cent accounting for over 50 per cent of the total income of the sample households, and the share of the bottom 10 per cent amounting to less than 2 per cent. A similar pattern could be observed between the top 40 per cent (80 per cent of total income) and the bottom 40 per cent (about 10 per cent of total income). There was not a dramatic gap between the fifth and sixth deciles, so income distribution among this group was more equal. In general there was little income variation between the six villages, apart from in the top decile. The greatest difference was between the first pair of villages (40.07 per cent for village 1 and 36 per cent for village 2) and the third pair (27.25 per cent for village 5 and 22.7 per cent for village 6). The income share of villages with the maximum number of programmes tended to be higher than that of their paired villages. For example the share of the lowest 20 per cent in village 1 was 6.01 per cent but in village 2 it was 3.51 per cent. Likewise the shares of the lowest 20 per cent in villages 3 and 4 were 7.1 per cent and 3.1 per cent respectively, and in villages 5 and 6 they

Table 5.8 Decile distribution of income (per cent)

Decile	Village 1	Village 2	Village 3	Village 4	Village 5	Village 6	Aggregate
0–10	2.84	0.45	2.70	0.45	3.82	1.34	1.97
10–20	3.17	3.06	4.40	2.65	3.33	2.57	2.37
20–30	3.26	5.66	5.10	3.00	4.13	5.07	3.17
30–40	4.56	6.96	5.18	5.41	5.61	6.09	3.71
40–50	4.71	7.13	5.80	9.52	6.76	10.05	3.13
50–60	5.47	8.30	6.21	11.81	8.58	12.53	4.00
60–70	7.44	10.02	6.33	12.64	10.15	12.60	6.64
70–80	11.44	10.31	10.31	14.06	12.29	13.40	9.82
80–90	17.04	12.10	20.23	15.72	18.08	13.65	15.01
90–100	40.07	36.00	32.70	24.74	27.25	22.70	50.18

Source: Shakoori (1998), p. 314.

were 7.15 per cent 3.91 per cent respectively. The slightly higher figures for villages 1, 3 and 5 might have been the result of the land redistribution programmes and some output distribution programmes for the lower classes in these villages (the landless and small landowners).

The differences between the lower quintiles might also have been due to the quality and quantity of the land redistributed among the poorest rural strata. In other words the post-revolutionary land reform was not comprehensive and did not include all of the rural poor. As we will show later in relation to the distribution of wealth, although the rural programmes increased the income, wealth and so on of the villagers in aggregate terms, the benefits for the lower stratum were far less tangible.

Wealth distribution

Similar to income distribution, wealth was unequally distributed within and between the six villages. A comparison of the paired villages revealed that, apart from in the first pair of villages (the prosperous ones), where the Gini index for village 2 (minimum number of programmes) was higher than for village 1 (maximum number of programmes), inequality of wealth was higher in the villages that received the maximum number of rural programmes than in those which received fewer or no programmes. As shown in Table 5.7, the Gini coefficients were 0.32 for village 1 and 0.39 for village two. The figures for villages 3 to 6 were 0.36, 0.33, 0.31 and 0.28 respectively. As can seen from these figures, the highest difference was between the villages of the first pair.

An examination of decile wealth distribution showed that the top decile owned over 29 per cent and the bottom decile only 2 per cent of the wealth. There was also a wide gap between the top and bottom 40 per cent – the top 40 per cent owned 67 per cent of the wealth of the sample households while the bottom 40 per cent owned just 14 per cent (Table 5.9).

In general this aggregate trend also held for the individual villages, but with slight variations. With regard to the first pair of villages, the share of the top decile in village 2 was higher than in village 1 (20 per cent and 15 per cent respectively), while the top 40 per cent in both villages owned almost 65 per cent of the total wealth the sample households. As already noted, the higher share of the top decile in village 2 (which was reflected in a higher Gini coefficient for this village, contrary to the assumption of the research) might have been

Table 5.9 Decile distribution of household wealth (per cent)

Decile	Village 1	Village 2	Village 3	Village 4	Village 5	Village 6	Aggregate
0–10	2.24	1.13	2.59	0.76	1.85	1.56	2.01
10–20	4.13	1.14	4.78	3.06	5.08	4.01	2.61
20–30	5.84	5.47	5.21	6.65	7.10	5.20	4.78
30–40	6.05	8.01	6.36	6.20	7.11	7.07	6.73
40–50	8.59	9.66	7.19	9.44	8.60	11.62	7.83
50–60	9.37	9.57	8.17	10.05	9.35	11.66	8.87
60–70	9.46	10.44	8.22	12.84	9.43	12.75	10.78
70–80	11.87	10.48	12.31	12.89	11.96	12.63	12.99
80–90	16.28	13.20	15.57	13.53	12.56	12.97	14.29
90–100	26.17	30.90	29.60	24.58	26.96	20.53	29.11

Source: Shakoori (1998), p. 318.

due to the larger number of vehicle owners, while the higher share of the lowest 40 per cent group in villages with the maximum number of rural programmes might have been due to the benefits reaped by the poorer villagers from these programmes, particularly the land redistribution programme. A comparison of the second and third pairs gave a similar picture of wealth distribution among the deciles.

Distribution of living expenditure

According to the Gini coefficients (Table 5.7), in general inequality in expenditure (as a proxy for well-being) was greater in the villages with the maximum number of programmes than in their paired counterparts, the coefficients ranging between 0.18 and 0.24. However, the differences between the villages were very small compared with the those observed for income and wealth. This might be because an increase in the income or wealth of a household did not necessarily mean an increase in its well-being, as reflected in expenditure on food and clothing. It is reasonable to assume that households with a higher income saved a higher proportion of that income, given the vulnerability of the rural economy and the uncertainty of villagers about their future. Second, from a historical perspective, it can be argued that some of the government's post-revolutionary distribution policies, whose coverage ranged from basic necessities (rationing goods such as oil, rice, sugar and so on) to industrial goods (refrigerators, tape-recorders, fans and so on), resulted in similar consumption and living costs among the classes. Third, given the simplicity of life in rural areas

Table 5.10 Decile distribution of expenditure (per cent)

Decile	Village 1	Village 2	Village 3	Village 4	Village 5	Village 6	Aggregate
0–10	4.28	4.56	3.47	3.75	4.64	5.06	4.18
10–20	5.99	5.91	6.38	5.84	6.05	5.64	5.09
20–30	6.89	7.40	7.57	7.43	7.25	6.24	6.87
30–40	7.33	8.81	8.16	8.00	8.61	7.31	7.39
40–50	7.60	8.57	8.53	10.67	8.67	11.53	7.73
50–60	9.52	10.33	9.04	11.53	9.71	11.81	7.73
60–70	10.46	11.31	9.93	11.68	11.78	11.82	8.39
70–80	13.63	11.97	11.74	12.55	12.86	12.22	10.41
80–90	14.18	13.62	13.46	13.83	13.89	13.90	17.51
90–100	20.12	17.52	21.72	14.72	16.54	14.47	24.70

Source: Shakoori (1998), p. 323.

compared with the complexity of urban life and the drastic gap between social groups, all classes might have tended to live similar lives and shared similar expenditure patterns.

However, Gini coefficients can be misleading because the Gini index gives an absolute figure for the entire society. It does not provide detailed information and even when a coefficient is low, inequality may still exist. Indeed a close examination of the decile distribution of expenditure revealed a similar trend to that for income and wealth. For instance the top decile accounted for 24 per cent and the bottom decile less than 5 per cent of total expenditure (Table 5.10). The expenditure of the top 40 per cent is greater than the bottom 40 per cent. A comparison of the first pair of villages revealed that the expenditure shares of the top decile and the top 40 per cent were higher in village 1 than in village 2, suggesting that the wealthier inhabitants of village 1 (maximum number of rural development programmes) benefited most from the process of rural change. An examination of the second and third pairs produced similar results. Among the lower deciles there were no significant differences between the villages.

Summary

In general the Gini coefficients indicate that, in spite of the government's distribution policies, inequality was greater in the villages where the maximum number of rural programmes were carried out than in those which received fewer or no programmes. The decile distributions show clear differences in respect of income, wealth and well-being between the richest and poorest groups. Although some of the programmes were targeted at the poor and benefited the lowest social groups, on the whole it was the upper classes who gained most from the rural efforts.

6
Conclusion

This book has investigated the long-term impact of Iran's post-revolutionary rural reform policies at the macro and micro levels. The rural sector became a major developmental concern after the 1979 revolution and the government attempted to increase agricultural production and enhance the well-being of the rural population by implementing a series of programmes. The post-revolutionary state inherited a rural economy that, despite a prolonged period of modernist reforms and land redistribution, still suffered a high degree of poverty and inequality.

The revolution of 1979 was the consequence of long-term discontent in Iranian society, and had a similar background to the constitutional revolution of 1909. Its ideology was based on nationalism, and its anti-imperialist character reflected the bitter hostility of the petit bourgeoisie towards the modern capitalist world. The revolution was a mass protest against the social and economic policies of the monarchical regime, as well as the relations of power and authority that sanctioned the regime's policies. Hence the revolutionaries had specific social demands and policy expectations, with great emphasis on indigenous policies.

The post-revolutionary rural and agricultural policies reflected these realities, as did the process of reforming the state. The agricultural reforms were mainly adopted as a reaction against the prerevolutionary policies and attempted to reverse their effects. The prerevolutionary agricultural administration was reorganised and a number of new organisations were set up to implement the rural development programmes: the service centres, the revolutionary organisation (Jihad-e Sazandegi), Islamic rural councils and the *mosha* cooperatives.

The Centres of Services for Rural and Nomadic People were part of a comprehensive programme to improve all aspects of rural life, including the expansion of agriculture and the comprehensive development of rural areas. The idea was to use these facilities to provide basic needs without the intervention of government officials in the daily lives of the peasants, but in the event most of the planning was imposed from above. There was no sign of local planning, and no attempt was made to use traditional skills and local knowledge. In many cases, regional particularities were overlooked. Most of the district service centres were concentrated in prosperous areas, and within these areas, more services were provided to the better-off villages.

The post-revolutionary administrative organisations went through a period of competition and duplication of responsibilities, rather than cooperating with each other and coordinating their efforts. This was mainly due to technocratic and political struggles for survival. There was no gradual transfer of the activities of the centres to the rural people, nor were the tasks of the traditional agricultural organisation taken over by the centres. In practice a dualistic administrative system emerged to replace the old system, and all in all the post-revolutionary reorganisation of agricultural administration was not a success.

The Islamic village councils were part of the service centre programme and their ostensible purpose was to act as the grass-roots link in the planning and implementation of development programmes. But the fundamental reason for their establishment was political – it was an attempt to disarm the leftist autonomists who had used the power vacuum in the immediate aftermath of the revolution to set up leftist rural councils in certain areas. The village councils were to have been fully participatory and to have linked the government with the rural population, but in general this failed to happen. The main reasons for their failure were the unfamiliarity of the council members with both their own tasks and those of the organisations set up to deal with rural development issues, and the councils' lack of status in the legal system of the country. This led not only to the neglect of council elections, but also to the dissolution of councils in many areas, particularly in remote regions. Although the establishment of the village councils changed the political structure of villages, it did not eliminate the pre-revolutionary structures of power and influence. In most villages a dual power structure came into existence.

Another significant measure after the revolution was the establishment of the Jihad-e Sazandeghi, which was part of the reaction against the traditional (prerevolutionary) administrative machinery, and was based on the idea that the fundamental and rapid tackling of rural issues required a revolutionary administrative system. The Jihad was to have been an interministerial organisation, but due to the radicalisation of the political atmosphere in the country and the war with Iraq it became a ministry in its own right, with some of its work duplicating that of other organisations. The Jihad progressed from merely implementing infrastructural and agricultural programmes to initiating its own programmes, but it never had a coherent strategy for rural development and all its efforts were based on past experience rather than on new scientific knowledge. For political reasons the Jihad enjoyed a generous supply of financial resources, but apart from providing some notable infrastructural facilities and services, it failed to meet the basic needs of the rural population.

Land reform was another important measure in the post-revolutionary era. The land reform programme was a response by the post-revolutionary government to pressure by a number of social forces, such as the remnants of the former landowning class, who called for the reversal of the prerevolutionary land reform, and peasants and radical forces, who started to expropriate land. The programme was radicalised after the resignation of the provisional government. In spite of several revisions and amendments to the reform programme by parliament, its implementation faced serious problems. One major obstacle was opposition to the imposition of a limit on the size of landownership, which had its roots in the sanctity of private property in Islamic jurisprudence. Another obstacle was the organised and highly effective resistance by commercial farmers, traditionalist *ulama*, conservative merchants and a section of the petit bourgeoisie. These factors plus changes in the polito-economic atmosphere at the international and national levels, particularly Iran's failure to win the Iran–Iraq War, mounting economic pressure and the developments in the Soviet bloc served to deter the implementation of radical land reform and gave rise to a very limited and conservative one.

Part of this reform was the creation of *mosha* cooperatives to replace the prerevolutionary cooperatives and farming corporations. The intention was to take advantage of both modern capital-intensive farming and the traditional organisation of production (*boneh*). But the *moshas* were not successful, for three reasons. First, they were based on a misconceived picture of traditional production, which had evolved over centuries and accorded with the geographical and social features of the regions where it existed. The *moshas*, however, were uniform in design and took no account of regional differences. Second, their establishment was influenced by revolutionary illusions and optimistic faith in the ability of the government to finance or provide the necessary agricultural inputs. But in practice the government lacked this ability and from the start the *moshas* suffered from a shortage of capital. Finally, due to the lack of effective supervision the units were subjected to mismanagement, and the unpopularity of joint ownership resulted in the *mosha* members dividing the land into separate parcels.

A review of the post-revolutionary agricultural performance reveals that, compared with the prerevolutionary era, the government's investment in agriculture increased slowly but never reached the level intended. Capital formation in the agricultural sector remained low, mainly due to the weak participation of the private sector in agricultural investment, discrimination by the government against this sector in favour of the industrial sector, and the existence of large urban–rural income differentials.

Despite the utilisation of fallow land, more extensive mechanisation and expansion of the area under cultivation, agricultural production remained far below the targets. The government's incentive provisions at the producer level, including price support and the subsidisation of agricultural inputs, had to be reduced when the fall in international oil prices and declining oil production as a consequence of the Iran–Iraq War led to a shortage of foreign currency.

A review of the agricultural policies shows that they were far from successful. First, they did not serve to increase the production of cereal. Second, where the yields were increased they did not match the increase in demand. Third, the pricing policy and other support measures brought about price distortions relative to the open market. The consequence was that farmers withdrew from food-grain production and concentrated on more profitable crops.

The micro-level study reported in this book assessed of the effects of the rural development programmes on village life. Three dimensions were considered: the degree to which the villages were changed by the implementation of the programmes; the degree to which the changes were influenced by the socioeconomic background of the villagers and the developmental potential of the villages; and the degree of inequality the changes caused among the villagers. The study was conducted in six typical Iranian villages in Eastern Azerbaijan. The villages were divided into pairs and three distinct categories. The villages in each pair were similar in terms of their potential for development but were different in respect of the number of rural development programmes they attracted.

Five variables were taken into consideration when examining these changes: participation, social mobility, income, wealth and well-being. Participation was measured at four levels: awareness, decision making, cooperation and satisfaction. Social mobility was examined in terms of intra- and intergenerational occupational mobility.

The analysis revealed that in terms of participation at the awareness level, one third of the sample households were fully aware of the objectives and duties of the rural organisations, but more than half had absolutely no knowledge of these organisations. Most of the respondents knew more about the Jihad than about the service centres mainly because of the comprehensiveness of the Jihad's activities, which involved all rural people.

Half of the sample households did not take part in the process of decision making. However, a relatively large number of households (more than one third) were involved at the cooperation level. This could mean that, contrary to the idea that peasants are resistant to change or innovation and are therefore reluctant to cooperate with rural development agents, they are likely to welcome developmental efforts if they see them as fruitful to their own lives. This was confirmed by the weak correlation between the socioeconomic background of the respondents and their participation at the cooperation level compared with the other levels. Among the indicators of cooperation, involvement in discussions on rural issues had the lowest percentage.

With regard to satisfaction, analysis of the data revealed that only one third of the households were highly satisfied with the progress of rural change after the revolution. The variables income, wealth and well-being were positively and significantly correlated with satisfaction, while education was negatively correlated with satisfaction. Most of the respondents believed that their living conditions had deteriorated in recent years, mainly because of economic pressures, but that in general they were better than they had been 20 years earlier. The access to rural infrastructures (road, electericity, etc.), the enlargement of job opportunities, easier access to markets and the like had brought new opportunities, although the villagers themselves might not benefit from these developments.

The examination of participation in aggregate terms showed that nearly half of the sample households had very little or no involvement in the process of rural development. The review of the effects of socioeconomic background on participation showed that income was strongly and positively correlated with aggregate participation and that wealth, literacy and well-being had a modest but positive effect. The other variables – age, family size and occupation – were not found to have a significant effect on participation in aggregate terms. All in all, the sample households in the villages that had received more rural development programmes tended to participate more than those that had received fewer or no programmes.

In general terms there are two reasons for the low level of participation. First, the rural development programmes were rooted in the centralised administrative system of the country and in order to fit in with the overall system the service centres and rural development planning were themselves centralised, despite the original intention to adopt a participatory bottom-up approach. For its part the Jihad may have had contact with the grass roots in that most of its workers came from a rural background but its activities were unscientific and based on revolutionary zeal and trial and error. While the principle of participation was put at the top its agenda it adopted no procedure to realise this. Furthermore, its work was backed up by more traditional organisations and bureaucratic procedures, and consequently the top-down approach tended to dominate its activities.

The second reason for the low level of participation was the lack of effective and appropriate organisation at the village level, which compounded the above problems. The village councils were set up for this purpose, but in practice they showed little interest and failed to undertake the tasks laid down in the executive regulations. Most were dissolved, and those that remained became dysfunctional.

Returning to the results of the field study, the data on social mobility show that in terms of both intra- and intergenerational mobility the majority of respondents did not change their status and occupied the same position as they had before the revolution. Although the greater upward mobility in the villages that received the most rural programmes conforms with the assumption of the study, the high degree of self-recruitment and the tendency for mobility to occur within the farming categories does not indicate a great change in occupational structure. A comparison of the three groups of villages showed that mobility was lowest in the poorer villages. Most of the upward mobility was short range, and indeed in many cases it represented a diversification of activities rather than a real change in job status. From the data it appears that the respondents' past status had a considerable influence on their mobility.

Hence the opportunities created after the revolution in the villages studied did not radically change the employment status of the respondents. There were two main reasons for this, the first of which had to do with the nature of the programmes implemented. The land reforms created real job opportunities, but only in agriculture, while the output delivery programmes encouraged people to take up agriculture-related occupations. The infrastructural programmes, however, only created temporary labouring jobs in construction projects. Indeed the latter were more beneficial for urban citizens than for rural people. The second reason was related to the powerlessness of the villagers to seize opportunities, particularly as a result of poor literacy and other inequalities.

The examination of annual income, wealth and expenditure on food, clothing and living expenses (as a proxy for well-being) showed that in general all of these variables were higher in the villages with the most development programmes and developmental potential. In all the villages the socioeconomic background of the respondents was strongly correlated with growth in income, wealth and expenditure as a result of the programmes, and again this was stronger in the villages with the most programmes. Hence while the process of rural change did produce concrete benefits if failed to alleviate the income, wealth and expenditure discrepancies between the prosperous and poor villages.

The review of the direction of change confirmed the existence of income, wealth and expenditure inequalities in all the villages, particularly in those where the maximum number of rural programmes were carried out. Income distribution was particularly unequal, followed by wealth. Inequality of well-being was not so marked. In spite of the government's distribution policies and programmes targeted specifically at the poor, on the whole the higher social groups benefited most from the process of rural change. From results of the data analysis based on the positive and mostly significant effect of the rural development programmes on the variation of rural development indicators (income, wealth, well-being, participation and social mobility), the positive correlation of the socioeconomic backgrounds of the sample household with the rural development indicators, and the unequal distribution of these indicators within and between the villages, we can conclude that, first, rural reforms changed rural life positively. Second, this change was strongly affected by the potential developmental conditions of the rural areas and the socioeconomic backgrounds of rural people. Third, because of differential potentialities between rural people and between rural communities, rural development programmes did not have identical impacts for all villages and all villagers. That is, the villages with high potential developmental conditions and the villagers with better socioeconomic positions could benefit most. In sum, the pre-existing geographical and socioeconomic structures still play a significant role in the distribution of the benefits of rural policies in the post-revolutionary era.

Appendix 1: Socioeconomic Characteristics of Eastern Azerbaijan, Marand and Sample Households

Table A1.1   Number of students enrolled in Azerbaijan, 1987

	Number	Per cent
Primary	590 672	72.6
Secondary	150 071	18.4
High school	64 220	7.9
Technical and professional	8 799	1.1
Total	813 762	100.0

Source: Plan and Budget Organisation of Eastern Azerbaijan (1990, 1993).

Table A1.2   Fall in the rural population of Azerbaijan, by township, 1976–86 (per cent)

	1976	1986	Change in rural population 1976–86
Sarab	85.0	75.1	–9.9
Aahar	89.2	79.5	–9.7
Miyaneh	81.9	72.9	–9.0
Marand	67.3	60.2	–7.1
Tabriz	33.4	26.6	–6.8
Hasht rude	96.1	90.7	–5.4
Maragheh	60.7	57.0	–3.7

Source: Plan and Budget Organisation of Eastern Ajerbaijan (1995).

Socioeconomic Charateristics 173

Table A1.3 Number of towns and communities, Marand, 1996

District/country	Area (km²)	Number of communities		
		Residential	Non-residential	Total
Central district (Marand)	3.814	112	21	133
County districts	3308.8	112	21	133
Bonab	373.1	10	1	11
Duwlat Abad	193.8	10	0	10
North Mishab	370.0	15	1	16
Koshsarayh	583.1	21	1	22
Zolbianin	379.4	15	9	24
Zonuozagh	355.6	6	2	8
Eastern Harazand	305.0	11	0	11
Western Harazand	285.0	13	1	14
Yekanat	463.8	11	6	17
Central district (Jolfa)	825.5	55	15	70
County districts	1591.2	55	15	70
Irsi	190.6	6	1	7
Shojah	471.9	16	8	24
Western Dizmar	353.7	6	0	6
Nojeh Mehr	375.6	22	4	26
Daran	199.4	5	2	7

Source: Plan and Budget Organisation of Eastern Azerbaijan (1996).

Table A1.4 Sex ratio in rural areas of the province and in the sample population, 1976–86

Province (1976)			Province (1986)			Sample population		
Males	Females	Ratio	Males	Females	Ratio	Males	Females	Ratio
1 030 838	978 555	105	1 077 991	1 033 587	104	1694	1538	110

Source: National population census, 1976, 1986. The sex ratio is calculated as follows: SR = (males ÷ females) × 100.

Socioeconomic Charateristics   175

Table A1.5   Age distribution in rural areas of the province and in the sample population, 1976–86

	Province (1976)	(%)	Province (1986)	(%)	Sample population	(%)
0–14	991 406	48.7	1 048 388	49.6	1 390	43.8
15–64	948 708	46.5	1 005 505	47.6	1 588	49.2
65+	69 279	3.4	56 579	2.7	258	7.0
Total	1 017 987	100.0	2 111 578	100.0	3 238	100.0

Source: Shakoori (1998), p. 219.

Table A1.6   Age distribution (per cent)

Age	Village 1	Village 2	Village 3	Village 4	Village 5	Village 6	Total
0–30	14.3	11.4	24.6	10.3	24.1	14.3	16.9
31–40	31.7	33.0	43.9	32.8	41.4	22.9	36.2
40–50	26.0	33.0	21.1	39.7	24.1	37.1	28.1
51+	28.0	22.7	10.5	17.2	10.3	25.7	19.0
Sample size	106	88	60	60	35	30	381

Source: Shakoori (1998), p. 219.

Table A1.7 Distribution by size of family (per cent)

Family size	Village 1	Village 2	Village 3	Village 4	Village 5	Village 6	Total	Rural areas of the province (1986)	Urban areas of the province 1986
0–1	3.7	2.3	5.0	6.7	8.1	8.5	5.0	3.5	3.8
2	3.8	9.1	5.0	10.0	12.0	13.9	8.4	8.3	10.2
3	3.8	3.4	9.0	11.7	13.3	7.2	8.1	8.5	13.3
4	8.5	14.8	13.7	11.7	6.7	13.9	11.3	10.9	17.4
5	15.1	20.5	10.0	15.0	16.7	5.6	16.3	12.6	16.7
6	32.1	14.8	17.3	15.0	13.3	20.5	18.6	13.2	13.8
7	11.3	13.6	13.3	11.7	10.0	5.6	10.8	13.3	10.4
8+	21.7	21.6	23.3	19.2	20.0	25.0	21.2	29.7	14.4
Sample size	106	88	60	60	36	30	381	351 278	396 325

Source: Shakoori, (1998), p. 219.

Table A1.8 Educational level (per cent)

	Village 1	Village 2	Village 3	Village 4	Village 5	Village 6
Illiterate	13.3	14.9	26.7	30.7	45.3	50.0
No schooling but able to read and write	20.3	25.3	27.7	26.7	21.7	25.0
Primary school	27.0	25.0	19.0	20.6	26.7	16.7
Secondary school	19.8	16.3	17.0	13.3	6.3	5.6
High school	16.6	18.5	9.7	6.7	0.0	2.8
University	0.0	0.0	0.0	0.0	0.0	0.0
Sample size	106	88	60	60	36	30

Source: Shakoori (1998), p. 220.

Table A1.9 Occupational distribution (per cent)

	Village 1	Village 2	Village 3	Village 4	Village 5	Village 6
Labourer	12.1	15.9	17.7	18.0	23.0	29.4
Farmer and livestock breeder	31.7	32.0	30.7	20.3	20.3	12.8
Farmer	19.9	14.6	24.7	36.7	30.0	33.9
Shopkeeper	11.7	13.6	42.1	3.0	3.3	11.1
Clerical	12.8	5.1	9.3	1.7	6.7	0.0
Urban job	12.7	18.8	13.7	20.3	16.7	12.8
Sample size	106	88	60	60	36	30

Source: Shakoori (1998), p. 220.

Appendix 2: Correlation Coefficients for Participation and Mobility

Table A2.1 Correlation coefficients (Spearman) for participation

Variable	Village 1	Village 2	Village 3	Village 4	Village 5	Village 6
Income	0.5881	0.4869	0.6919	0.6890	0.7125	0.7479
	Sig. 0.000	Sig. 0.000	Sig. 0.000	Sig. 0.000	Sig. 0.000	Sig. 0.000
Wealth	0.4251	0.3229	0.4864	0.3066	0.6766	0.6289
	Sig. 0.000	Sig. 0.003	Sig. 0.000	Sig. 0.009	Sig. 0.000	Sig. 0.000
Literacy	0.4358	0.4050	0.3444	0.1556	0.0724	0.0349
	Sig. 0.000	Sig. 0.000	Sig. 0.004	Sig. 0.118	Sig. 0.340	Sig. 0.427
Occupation	0.1348	0.1205	0.4062	0.2684	0.1369	0.0787
	Sig. 0.126	Sig. 0.152	Sig. 0.001	Sig. 0.020	Sig. 0.235	Sig. 0.327
Family size	−0.0593	−0.1931	0.1792	−0.0369	0.2472	0.3188
	Sig. 0.308	Sig. 0.048	Sig. 0.085	Sig. 0.390	Sig. 0.094	Sig. 0.03
Age	−0.1571	−0.1738	−0.0105	−0.0978	−0.0751	−0.2723
	Sig. 0.094	Sig. 0.068	Sig. 0.469	Sig. 0.233	Sig. 0.349	Sig. 0.057
Sample size	108	88	60	60	35	30

Source: Shakoori (1998), p. 225.

Table A2.2 Correlation coefficients (Spearman) for intragenerational mobility

Variable	Village 1	Village 2	Village 3	Village 4	Village 5	Village 6
Income	0.4605	0.3220	0.4470	0.3106	0.2296	0.1952
	Sig. 0.000	Sig. 0.001	Sig. 0.000	Sig. 0.009	Sig. 0.111	Sig. 0.131
Wealth	0.2135	0.2447	0.2471	0.2099	0.1571	0.1446
	Sig. 0.051	Sig. 0.006	Sig. 0.028	Sig. 0.133	Sig. 0.072	Sig. 0.204
Education	0.1805	0.1125	0.1087	0.0976	0.0813	0.0823
	Sig. 0.032	Sig. 0.148	Sig. 0.204	Sig. 0.229	Sig. 0.335	Sig. 0.317
Family size	0.0446	0.0268	0.1087	0.0456	0.0738	0.0651
	Sig. 0.346	Sig. 0.393	Sig. 0.204	Sig. 0.367	Sig. 0.349	Sig. 0.355
Age	0.0603	0.0798	0.0807	0.0598	0.0924	0.0373
	Sig. 0.271	Sig. 0.212	Sig. 0.270	Sig. 0.329	Sig. 0.196	Sig. 0.416
Sample size	108	88	60	60	35	30

Source: Shakoori (1998), p. 267.

Table A2.3 Correlation coefficients (Spearman) for intragenerational mobility

Variable	Village 1	Village 2	Village 3	Village 4	Village 5	Village 6
Income	0.3774	0.1619	0.3916	0.2990	0.1982	0.1652
	Sig. 0.000	Sig. 0.066	Sig. 0.001	Sig. 0.011	Sig. 0.147	Sig. 0.168
Wealth	0.2200	0.1972	0.2152	0.1525	0.1296	0.1050
	Sig. 0.012	Sig. 0.067	Sig. 0.049	Sig. 0.124	Sig. 0.226	Sig. 0.290
Education	0.1069	0.1345	0.1485	0.1192	0.0881	0.0743
	Sig. 0.210	Sig. 0.106	Sig. 0.129	Sig. 0.269	Sig. 0.325	Sig. 0.333
Family size	0.0509	0.1032	0.0711	0.0684	0.0680	0.0040
	Sig. 0.302	Sig. 0.169	Sig. 0.295	Sig. 0.302	Sig. 0.361	Sig. 0.491
Age	0.0808	0.1605	0.2043	0.0456	0.0729	0.0441
	Sig. 0.208	Sig. 0.068	Sig. 0.064	Sig. 0.367	Sig. 0.353	Sig. 0.401
Sample size	108	88	60	60	35	30

Source: Shakoori (1998), p. 275.

Appendix 3: Statistical Results (Analysis of Variance, Multiregression and Correlation) for Variables Income, Wealth, Expenditure and Housing Status

Table A3.1 Comparison of income

Variance Source	DF	Sum of squares	Mean squares
Between groups	5	94073289.2	18814657.83
Within groups	372	224829511.4	604380.4069
Total	377	318902800.5	
F ratio	31.1305		
F prob.	0.0000		

One way Mean	Village	6	4	5	3	2	1
480.3429	6						
605.1356	4						
892.2333	5	*					
917.2833	3	*	*				
1239.6705	2	*	*	*	*		
1870.5943	1	*	*	*	*	*	

* Indicates significant differences.
Source: Shakoori (1998), p. 281.

182 Income, Wealth, Expenditure and Housing

Table A3.2 Multiregression analysis: income by measures of socioeconomic background (beta coefficients)

Variable	Village 1	Village 2	Village 3	Village 4	Village 5	Village 6	Aggregate
Age	−0.0163	−0.0515	−0.0695	−0.0274	−0.0826	0.01453	−0.047
Garden	0.2407	0.2206	0.0801	0.1034	0.1333	0.0054	0.232
Land	0.3556	0.2952	0.2002	0.2180	0.3544	0.3440	0.249
Family size	0.2063	0.2094	0.3764	0.2989	0.1535	0.1789	0.072
Occupation	0.1291	0.1205	0.1444	0.1507	0.1364	0.0959	0.202
Literacy	0.2479	0.1277	0.2530	0.2533	0.01453	0.0182	0.059
Assets	0.2008	0.2023	0.1438	0.1123	0.1885	0.2659	0.441
Multiple R	0.66395	0.55224	0.77203	0.67737	0.54178	0.48192	0.66477
R^2	0.4408	0.3046	0.5960	0.4588	0.2935	0.2322	0.4419
F-statistic	10.81	5.01	9.69	4.96	1.246	1.166	32.69
Signif. F	0.0000	0.0001	0.0000	0.0004	0.3228	0.3537	0.0000
Sample size	108	88	60	60	35	30	381

R: Multiple regression
F: Significant F statistics
Source: Shakoori (1998), pp. 281–7.

Table A3.3 Comparison of wealth

Source	DF	Sum of squares	Mean squares
Between groups	5	160372955.3	32074591.05
Within groups	374	683834979.3	1828435.774
Total	379	844207934.6	

Variance

F ratio 17.5421
F prob. 0.0000

One way Mean	village	6	5	4	3	2	1
1234.9722	6						
1480.3000	5						
1528.3167	4						
1649.6500	3						
2626.7264	1	*	*	*	*		
2936.7955	2	*	*	*	*		

* Indicates significant differences.
Source: Shakoori (1998), p. 294.

Table A3.4 Multiregression analysis: wealth by socioeconomic background (beta coefficients)

Variable	Village 1	Village 2	Village 3	Village 4	Village 5	Village 6
Income	0.4787	0.6264	0.5847	0.5015	0.5297	0.4205
Literacy	0.2014	0.1757	0.1405	0.1099	0.1082	0.1382
Age	0.1383	0.0430	0.1109	0.1244	0.0485	0.0104
Family size	0.1927	0.0987	0.1730	0.1831	0.1536	0.1437
Occupation	0.1421	0.1974	0.1795	0.2104	0.1160	0.0479
Multiple R	0.66129	0.72203	0.63705	0.57334	0.62158	0.59981
R^2	0.4373	0.5213	0.4058	0.3287	0.3863	0.3597
F-statistic	15.23	17.86	6.96	4.99	2.89	3.25
Signif. F	0.000	0.000	0.0001	0.0008	0.0359	0.0186
Sample size	108	88	60	60	35	30

Source: Shakoori (1998), pp. 295–9.

184 Income, Wealth, Expenditure and Housing

Table A3.5 Comparison of expenditure

Variance Source	DF	Sum of squares	Mean squares
Between groups	5	2368583.569	473716.7137
Within groups	374	7700888.671	20590.6114
Total	379	10069472.240	

F ratio 23.0064
F prob. 0.0000

One way Mean	Village	6	5	4	3	2	1
229.5278	6						
297.1333	5						
313.8000	4	*					
379.7833	3	*	*	*			
406.3636	2	*	*	*			
478.3491	1	*	*	*	*	*	

* Indicates significant differences.
Source: Shakoori (1998), p. 301.

Table A3.6 Multiregression analysis: expenditure by socioeconomic background (beta coefficients)

Variable	Village 1	Village 2	Village 3	Village 4	Village 5	Village 6
Age	0.0128	0.0787	0.0121	0.0061	−0.1455	−0.0523
Assets	0.2231	0.1739	0.3242	0.1046	0.1812	0.1062
Income	0.5678	0.6087	0.6227	0.5572	0.3435	0.3556
Family size	0.2501	0.2299	0.1879	0.1247	0.2896	0.1411
Literacy	0.1799	−0.1120	0.0614	0.0633	0.0990	0.0078
Multiple R	0.68735	0.76255	0.71751	0.61275	0.54928	0.45493
R^2	0.7523	0.5814	0.5148	0.3754	0.3017	0.2069
F-statistic	59.52	22.78	10.82	6.13	1.98	1.51
Signif. F	0.0000	0.0000	0.0000	0.0002	0.1186	0.2163
Sample size	108	88	60	60	35	30

Source: Shakoori (1998), pp. 302–6.

Table A3.7 Correlation between housing status and socioeconomic background

	Village 1	Village 2	Village 3	Village 4	Village 5	Village 6
Literacy	0.2581	0.2100	0.1857	0.1796	0.0302	0.0906
	Sig. 0.004	Sig. 0.025	Sig. 0.078	Sig. 0.085	Sig. 0.437	Sig. 0.300
Age	0.0981	0.1060	0.0711	0.0314	0.1764	0.1872
	Sig. 0.161	Sig. 0.163	Sig. 0.300	Sig. 0.407	Sig. 0.180	Sig. 0.141
Occupation	0.2356	0.1953	0.2717	0.1479	0.2512	0.1866
	Sig. 0.008	Sig. 0.034	Sig. 0.018	Sig. 0.130	Sig. 0.090	Sig. 0.138
Family size	0.3006	0.1659	0.2261	0.1234	0.1063	0.0906
	Sig. 0.001	Sig. 0.061	Sig. 0.041	Sig. 0.174	Sig. 0.288	Sig. 0.300
Income	0.7471	0.5643	0.6043	0.4560	0.4805	0.3689
	Sig. 0.000	Sig. 0.000	Sig. 0.000	Sig. 0.000	Sig. 0.004	Sig. 0.013
Wealth	0.5322	0.4443	0.5640	0.4230	0.4117	0.3887
	Sig. 0.000	Sig. 0.000	Sig. 0.000	Sig. 0.000	Sig. 0.012	Sig. 0.010
Sample size	108	88	60	60	35	30

Source: Shakoori (1998), p. 309.

Bibliography

Abrahamian, E. (1982) *Iran Between Two Revolutions*, Princeton, NJ: Princeton University Press.
Adamiyat, F. (1961) *Fekr-e Azadi wa Moqaddame-ye Nehzat-e Mashrutiyat* [The Idea of Freedom and Prelude to the Constitutional Revolution], Tehran: Entesharat-e Kharazmi.
Adamiyat, F. (1976) *Idi'olozhi-ye Nahzat-e Mashrutiyat-e Iran* [The Ideology of the Constitutional Movement in Iran], Tehran: Payam.
Adamiyat, F. and Nateq, H. (1976) *Afkar-e Ejtema 'i wa Siyasi dar Asar-e Montasher Nshode-ye Douran-e Qajar* [Social and Political Ideas in the Unpublished Writings of the Qajar Era], Tehran: Payam.
Afshar, H. (1981) 'An Assessment of Agricultural Development Policies in Iran', *World Development*, vol. 9, nos 11/12, pp. 1097–108.
Agency for International Development (1975) 'Strategies for Small Farmer Development: An Empirical Study of Rural Development Projects', a report prepared for the AID under contract AID/CM/ta-c-73–41, 2 vols, Washington, DC: Development Alternatives Inc.
Agricultural Development Bank (1981) unpublished material, Tehran: Bureau of Economic Studies.
Ahluwalia, M. S. (1974) *Income Inequality: Some Dimensions of The Problem*, Oxford: Oxford University Press.
Ahluwalia, M. S. (1976) 'Inequality, Poverty and Development', *Journal of Development Economics*, vol. 3, pp. 307–42.
Ahluwalia, M. S. (1978) 'Rural Poverty and Agricultural Performance in India', *Journal of Development Studies*, vol. 14, pp. 298–323.
Ajami, I. (1975) *Agrarian Reform, Modernisation of Peasants and Agricultural Development in Iran*, Shiraz (Iran): University of Shiraz.
Alavi, H. (1976) 'Rural Elite and Agricultural Development in Bangladesh', in R. D. Stevens, H. Alavi and P. J. Bertocci *et al.*, *Rural Development in Bangladesh and Pakistan*, Honolulu: the University of Hawaii Press.
Alexander, J. and Alexander, P. (1992) 'Protecting Peasants from Capitalism: the Subordination of Japanese Traders by the Colonial State', *Comparative Studies in Society and History*, vol. 33, no 2, pp. 370–94.
Alfonso, F. B. (1986) 'Empowering Rural Communities', in J. C. Ickis, E. de Jesus and R. Maru, *Beyond Bureaucracy, Strategic Management of Social Development*, New York: Kumarian.
Alimorad, M., Hadipaur, M. and Karimi, M. (1984) 'Gozaresh-e Moqadamati-ye Mas'al-ye Wagozari-ye Zamin, Waheda-ye Toulidi-ye Mosha 'dar Sharestan-e Fasa' [Preliminary Report on the Problem of Land Transfer and on the Work of the Moshas in the County Town of Fasa], Tehran: Ministry of Agriculture.
Alizadeh, M. (1989) 'Estratezhi-ye Eshteghal-e Keshawarzi' (Employment Strategy in Agriculture). *Ettela'at-e Siyasi-Eqtesadi*, vol. 27, pp. 58–60.

Allison, D. (1978) 'Measures of Inequality', *American Sociological Review*, vol. 43, pp. 865–80.
Amin, G. A. (1980) *The Modernization of Poverty: A Study in the Political Economy of Growth in Nine Arab Countries, 1945–1970*, Leiden: Brill.
Amin, S. (1974a) *Historical Studies of Chile and Brazil*, New York: Monthly Review Press.
Amin, S. (1974b) *Accumulation on a World Scale*, Sussex: Harvester.
Amin, S. (1976) *Unequal Development*, Hassocks and New York: Harvester Press and Monthly Review Press.
Amirahmadi, H. (1988) 'War Damage and Reconstruction in the Islamic Republic of Iran', in H. Amirahmadi and M. Parvin (eds), *Post-Revolutionary Iran*, Boulder, CO. Westview Press.
Amirahmadi, H. (1990) *Revolution and Economic Transition: The Iranian Experience*, Albany, NY: State University of New York Press.
Amuzegar, J. (1993) *Iran's Economy Under The Islamic Republic*, London: I. B. Tauris.
Anderson, B. (1992) 'The New World Disorder', *New Left Review*, vol. 193, pp. 3–14.
Anoushirvani, A. (1982) *Negareshi Bar zera atha-ye Jam'i-ye dasht-e arzu'iye* [A Survey of Collective Field Works in the Arzu'iyeh Plain], Tehran: Ministry of Agriculture.
Apter, D. (1965) *The Politics of Modernization*, Chicago, IL: Chicago University Press.
Apter, D. (1987) *Rethinking Development: Modernisation, Dependency, and Postmodern Politics*, Newbury Park, CA: Sage.
Arce, A., Villarreal, M. and Vries, P. (1994) 'The Social Construction of Rural Development: Discourse, Practices and Power', in D. Booth, *Rethinking Social Development Theory, Research and Practice*, Harlow: Longman.
Aresvik, O. (1976) *The Agricultural Development of Iran*, New York: Praeger.
Aron, I. (1982) *Modernisation of Agriculture in Developing Countries; Resources, Potentials and Problems*, New York: John Wiley.
Arsanjani, H. (1962) 'Implementation of Iran's Land Reform Programme', pamphlet issued by the Ministry of Agriculture, Tehran.
Asayesh, H. (1996) 'Nabrabari va Shekaf bain-e Shahr va Rousta' [Inequality and Gab Between City and Village], *Mohnameh-e Jihad* [Jihad Monthly], vol. 16, nos 184/5, pp. 33–43.
Ashraf, A. (1978) 'The Role of Rural Organisations in Rural Development: The Case of Iran', in E. Inayatullah (ed.), *Rural Organisations and Rural Development: Some Asian Experiences*, Kuala Lumpur: APDAC.
Ashraf, A. (1982) *Dihqanan, Zamin, va Enghilab* [Peasants, Land, and Revolution], *Ketab-e Agah*, vol. 1, no. 1, pp. 6–49.
Ashraf, A. (1985) 'The States, Classes, and Modes of Mobilisation in the Iranian Revolution', *State, Culture, and Society*, vol. 1-2, no. 3 (Spring), pp. 5–25.
Ashraf, A. (1991) 'State and Agrarian Relations Before and After the Iranian Revolution: 1960–1990', in F. Kazemi and J. Waterbury, *Peasant and Politics in the Modern Middle East*, Miami, F. A: International University Press.
Ashraf, A. and Banuazizi, A. (1980) 'Policies and Strategies of Land Reform in Iran', in E. Inayatullah (ed.), *Land Reform: Some Asian Experiences*, Kuala Lumpur: APDAC.

Bibliography

Atavenhagen, R. (1977) 'Basic Needs, Peasants and the Strategy for Rural Development', in M. Nerfin (ed.), *Another Development: Approaches and Strategies*, Uppsala: The Dag Hammarskjold Foundation.

Axinn, G. H. (1978) *New Strategies for Rural Development*, Nepal: Rural Life Associates.

Ayatullahi, A. R. (1998) *Shoura hayeh Keshvari va Amayesh-e Shar va Rousta* (Civil Councils and Rural and Urban Logistics, Tehran: Zohal.

Azar, G. (1980) 'Mubarizat-e Dihqani dar Iran' [Peasants Struggle in Iran], *Dunya*, vol. 7, pp. 74–7.

Azar, G. (1981) *Junbishha-yi Dihqani dar Iran* [Peasant Movements in Iran], Tehran: Nika'in.

Azimi, H. (1982) 'Twazi-e Zamin va Daramad dar Astana-yi Islahad-e Arzi' [Distribution of Land and Income on the Eve of Land Reform], *Ketab-e Aghah*, vol. 1, no. 1, p. 75–95.

Azimi, H. (1992) *Madar hayeh Toseah Naftegi-e Iran dar Eqtesad-e Iran* [Developmental Bottlenecks in Iran's Economy], Tehran: Nashr-e Ney.

Azkia, M. (1980) 'The Effect of Rural Development Programmes on the Iranian Peasantry between 1962 and 1978 with Special Reference to Farm Corporations', PhD dissertation, University of Aberdeen.

Azkia, M. (1986) *Jameh Shenasi-e Tousehyeh Roustaei va Touseh-na-yafteghiyeh Jamehyeh Raustaei Iran* [Sociology of Rural Development and Underdevelopment of Iranian Rural Societies], Tehran: Entesharat-e- Ettlaat.

Azkia, M. (1992) 'Markaz-e Khadamate Keshavarzi ba Masabehe Olghuyeh Touseh-e Roustaei' [The Centres of Services for Rural and Nomadic Population as a Rural Development Strategy], *Nameh-e Ulom-e Ejtemaei* [Letter of Social Sciences Journal], vol. 2, pp. 113–33.

Azkia, M. (1993a) 'Agrarian Structure of Iranian Society with Special Reference on Post-revolutionary Era' working paper, Tehran: University of Tehran.

Azkia, M. (1993b) 'The Modes of Production in Contemporary Iran: A Critical Review', working paper, Tehran: University of Tehran.

Aziz, S. (1978) *Rural Development: Learning From China*, London: Macmillan.

Bafekr, H. Niyazi, J., Heydari, G., Yazdani, N. and Zahediabghari, I. (1985) *Barrasiyeh-e Masael-e Marbout beh Vaghouzariyeh Zanmin va Vahedhayeh Toulidiyeh Mosha dar Ghonbad va Ghorgan* [A Study of the Problems in Relation to Land Redistribution and the Mosha Cooperatives in Ghonbad and Ghorghan], Tehran: Ministry of Agriculture, Centre for Rural and Agricultural Studies.

Bahrier, S. (1971) *Economic Development in Iran 1900–1970*, London: Oxford University Press.

Baily, F. G. (1969) *Stratagems and Spoils*, Toronto: Coppclark.

Bajaj, J. L. and Shastri, C. (1985) *Rural Poverty: Issues and Options*, Lucknow, India: Print House.

Baker, C. (1975) 'Invading the Government's Privacy: Problems of Research on National Security Issues', in P. Nejelski, *Social Research in Conflict with Law and Ethics*, Cambridge, MA: Ballinger.

Bakhash, S. (1978) *Iran – Monarchy, Bureaucracy and Reform under Qajars*, London: Ithaca Press for the Middle East Centre.

Bakhash, S. (1984) *The Reign of the Ayatollahs*, New York: Basic Books.
Bakhash, S. (1989) 'The Politics of Land, Law, and Social Justice', *The Middle East Journal*, vol. 43, no. 2, pp. 186–201.
Baldwin, G. B. (1967) *Planning and Development in Iran*, Baltimore, MD: Johns Hopkins University Press.
Banani, A. (1961) *The Modernisation of Iran*, Stanford, CA: Stanford University Press.
Bashiriyeh, H. (1984) *The State and Revolution in Iran, 1962–1982*, London: Croom Helm.
Bawden, R. (1992) 'Systems Approaches to Agricultural Development: the Hawkesbury Experience', *Agricultural Systems*, vol. 40, pp. 153–76.
Bazargan, M. (1985) *Enghelab-e Iran dar Dou Harakat* [Iranian Revolution in Two Movements], Tehran: Nehzat-e Azadi-yeh Iran.
Behdad, S. (1989) 'Winners and Losers of the Iranian Revolution: A Study in Income Distribution', *International Journal of Middle East Studies*, vol. 21, no. 3, pp. 327–58.
Belcher, J. C. (1972) 'A Cross-Cultural Household Level of Living Scale', *Rural Sociology*, vol. 37, no. 2, pp. 208–21.
Bendix, R. (1967) 'Tradition and Modernity Reconsidered, Comparative Studies', *Society and History*, vol. 9, pp. 292–346.
Benvenuti, B. (1975) 'General Systems Theory and Entrepreneurial Autonomy in Farming: Towards a New Feudalism or Towards Democratic Planning', *Sociologia Ruralis*, vol. 15, nos 1/2, pp. 46–64.
Bernstein, H. (1971) 'Modernisation Theory and the Sociological Study of Development', *Journal of Development Studies*, vol. 7, pp. 141–60.
Bernstein, H. (1977) 'Notes on capital and peasantry', *Review of African Political Economy*, vol. 10, pp. 60–73.
Bernstein, H. (1990) 'Agricultural Modernisation and the Era of Structural Adjustment: Observations on Sub-Saharan', *Journal of Peasant Studies*, vol. 18, no. 1, pp. 3–36.
Berry, S. (1984) 'The Food Crisis and Agrarian Change in Africa: A Review Essay', *African Studies Review*, vol. 27, no. , pp. 59–112.
Berry, S. (1989) 'Social Institutions and Access to Resources', *Africa*, vol. 59, pp. 41–55.
Bertocci, P. J. (1970) 'Elusive Village: Social Structure and Community Organisation in East Pakistan', PhD thesis, East Lansing: Michigan State University.
Bertocci, P. J. (1976) 'Social Organisation and Agricultural Development in Bangladesh', in R. Stevens, H. Alavi and P. Bertocci (eds), *Rural Development in Bangladesh and Pakistan*, Honolulu: University of Hawaii.
Biggs, S. (1979) *Villagisation and the 1974–76 Economic Crisis in Tanzania*, London: Cambridge University Press.
Bill, J. (1972) *The Politics of Iran, Groups, Classes, and Modernisation*, Columbus, Ohio: Charles E. Merrill.
Birou, A., Henry, P. and Schelegel, J. P. (eds) (1977) *Towards a Redefinition of Development – Essays and Discussions on the Nature of Development in an International Perspective*, Oxford: Pergamon Press for the Development Centre of the Organisation for Economic Co-operation and Development, Paris.

Bisset, R. (1988) 'Developments in EIA Methods', in P. Wathern (ed.), *Environmental Impact Assessment: Theory and Practice*, London: Allen & Unwin, pp. 47–60.
Blalock, H. M. (1978) *Social Statistics*, New York: McGraw-Hill.
Blomstrom, M. and Hettne, B. (1984) *Development Theory in Transition – The Dependency Debate and Beyond: Third World Responses*, London: Zed Books.
Blua, P. M. and Duncan, O. D. (1975) 'Measuring the Status of Occupations', in A. P. M. Coxon and C. L. Jones, *Social Mobility*, Harmondsworth: Penguin.
Blau, P. M. (1977) *Inequality and Heterogeneity: A Primitive Theory of Social Structure*, New York: The Free Press.
Boeke, J. H. (1953) *Economic Policy of Dual Societies*, New York: Institute of Pacific Relations.
Booth, D. (1985) 'Marxism and Development of Sociology: Interpreting the Impasse', *World Development*, vol. 13, no. 7, pp. 761–87.
Booth, D. (1994) *Rethinking Social Development Theory, Research and Practice*, Harlow: Longman.
Brand, W. (1958) *The Struggle for a Higher Standard of Living*, Chicago, IL: The Free Press.
Brookfield, H. (1975) *Independent Development*, London: Methuen.
Browett, J. (1984) 'On the Necessity and Inevitability of Uneven Spatial Development under Capitalism', *International Journal of Urban and Regional Research*, vol. 8, no. 2.
Buchanan, N. S. and Ellis, H. S. (1955) *Approaches to Economic Development*, New York: The Twentieth Century Fund.
Burkey, S. (1993) *People First: A Guide to Self-Reliant, Participatory Rural Development*, London: Zed Books.
Buttel, Frederick H. and Flinn, L. (1977) 'Conceptions of Rural Life and Environmental Concern', *Rural Sociology*, vol. 42, (Winter).
Byres, T. J. (1981) 'The New Technology, Class Formation and Class Action in the Indian Countryside', *The Journal of Peasant Studies*, vol. 8, no. 4, pp. 405–54.
Byres, T. J. (1982) 'Agrarian Transition and the Agrarian Question', in J. Harriss (ed.) *Rural Development: Theories of Peasant Economy and Agrarian Change*, London: Hutchinson.
Cardoso, F. H. (1970) 'The Structure of Dependency', *American Economic Review*, vol. LX (May).
Central Bank of Iran (1956–96) *Hasabha-ye Melli-ye Iran* [National Accounts of Iran], Tehran: Central Bank of Iran.
Central Bank of Iran (1984) *Barasi-e Tahavolat-e Eghtesadi-ye Keshvar baad az Enghlab* [Investigation of the Economic Changes after the Revolution], Tehran: Central Bank of Iran.
Central Bank of Iran (1991–99) *Gozaresh Egtesadi va Taraznameh: 1978/79–98/99* [Economic Report and Balance Sheet: 1978/79–98/99], Tehran: Central Bank of Iran.
Centre of Indigenous Studies (1977) *Regional Development project: Selseleh*, Tehran: Ministry of Agriculture
Cernea, M. M. (ed.) (1986) *Putting People First: Sociological Variables in Rural Development*, Oxford: Oxford University Press for the World Bank.
Chambers, R. (1969) *Settlement Schemes in Tropical Africa*, London: Routledge.

Chambers, R. (1974) *Managing Rural Development: Ideas and Experience from East Africa*, Uppsala: The Scandinavian Institute of Africa Studies.
Chambers, R. (1983) *Challenging the Professions: Frontiers for Rural Development*, London: Intermediate Technology Publications.
Chambers, R. (1987) 'Project Selection for Poverty-Focused Rural Development: Simple is Optimal', *World Development*, vol. 6, no. 2, pp. 209–19.
Chambers, R. (1991) 'Participatory Rural Appraisal (PRA): Analysis of Experience', *World Development*, vol. 22, no. 9, pp. 1253–68.
Chambers, R. (1993) 'Method for Analysis of Farmers: the Professional Challenge', *Journal for Farming Systems, Research Extension*, vol. 4, no. 1, pp. 87–101.
Chambers, R. (1994a) 'Participatory Rural Appraisal (PRA): Challenges, Potentials and Paradigm', *World Development*, vol. 22, no. 10, pp. 1437–54.
Chambers, R. (1994b) 'The Origins and Practice of Participatory Rural Appraisal', *World Development*, vol. 22, no. 7, pp. 953–69.
Chenery, C. (1987) 'Political Power and Social Class in the Neo-colonial African States, Review of African Economy', *Journal of Asian Studies*, vol. 45, no. 2.
Chenery, H., Ahluwalia, M. S., Bell, C. L. G., Dalog, J. D. and Jolly, R. (1974) *Redistribution with Growth*: Oxford: Oxford University Press.
Chilcote, R. H. (1984) *Theories of Development and Underdevelopment*, Boulder, CO: Westview.
Clark, J. (1995) 'The State, Popular Participation, and the Voluntary Sector', *World Development*, vol. 23, no. 4, pp. 593–60.
Clayton, E. (1983) *Agriculture, Poverty and Freedom in Developing Countries*, London: Macmillan.
Clements, P. (1993) 'An Approach to Poverty Alleviation for Large International Development Agencies', *World Development*, vol. 21, no. 10, pp. 1633–46.
Clements, P. (1995) 'Poverty-Oriented Cost–Benefit Approach to the Analysis of Development Project', *World Development*, vol. 23, no. 4, pp. 77–92.
Cliffe, L. and Coleman, J. S. (eds) (1977) *Government and Rural Development in East Africa: Essays on Political Penetration*, The Hague: Martinus Nijhoff.
Cohen, J. M. and Uphoff, N. T. (1977) *Rural Development Participation: Concepts and Measures for Projects Design, Implementation and Evaluation*, New York: Cornell University, Rural Development Committee.
Cohen, J. M. and Uphoff, N. T. (1980) 'Participation's Place in Rural Development: Seeking Clarity through Specificity', *World Development*, vol. 8, pp. 213–35.
Coleman, J. S. (1968) 'Modernization: Political Aspects', in D. L. Sills (ed.), *International Encyclopaedia of Social Sciences*, vol. 10, New York: Macmillan.
Consulting Engineers for Development and Regional Planning (1993) *Tarah-e Tabeghe Bandyeh Ruostaha va Taeen-e Khotod-e Strategy-e Toseh va Omran-e Roustaei Marhaleh-e Avval* [Classification Design of Villages and Determination of the Lines of Development Strategy and Rural Development: the First Stage], Tehran: Ministry of Jihad.
Corbridge, S. (1994) 'Post-Marxism and Post-colonialism: The Needs and Rights of Distant Strangers', in D. Booth, *Rethinking Social Development Theory, Research and Practice*, Harlow: Longman.
Coxon, A. P. M. and Jones, C. L. (1975) *Social Mobility*, Harmondsworth: Penguin.
Crush, J. (1995) *Power of Development*, London: Routledge.
Danesh, A. H. (1992) 'Land Reform, State Policy, and Social Change in Iran', *Urban Anthropology and Studies of Cultural System*, vol. 21, no. 2.

Dasgupta, B. (1977) *Agrarian Change and the New Technology in India*, Geneva: United Nations Research Institute for Social Development.
Dasgupta, P. and M. Weale. (1992) 'On Measuring Quality of Life', *World Development*, vol. 20, no. 1, pp. 119–31.
Davis, J., Mack, N. and Kirke, A. (1997) 'New Perspectives on Farm Household Incomes', *Journal of Rural Studies*, vol. 13, no. 1, pp. 57–64.
Dawson, R. E. and Prewitt, K. (1969) *Political Socialization*, Boston, MA: Little, Brown.
Desai, M. (1990) *Poverty and Capability: Towards an Empirically Implementable Measure*, London: Development Economics Research Centre (STICERD), London School of Economics.
De Janvry, A. (1981) *The Agrarian Question and Reformism in Latin America*, Baltimore, MD: The Johns Hopkins University Press.
Denman, D. R. (1978) 'Land Reforms of Shah and People', in G. Lenczowski (ed.), *Iran Under the Pahlavis*, Stanford: Hoover Institution Press.
Denzin, N. K. (1970) *The Research Act in Sociology: A Theoretical Introduction to Sociological Methods*, London: Butterworths.
De Vaus, D. A. (1990) *Survey in Social Research*, London: Unwin Hyman.
Deverger, M. (1967) *The Principle of Political Science* (Persian version by A. Qazi), Tehran: Sherkat Sahami-yeh Ketabhayeh Jibi.
Devitt, P. (1977) 'Notes on Poverty-Oriented Rural Development', *Extension, Planning and the Poor*, London: Overseas Development Institute.
De Vylder, S. (1979) 'Cases and Contradictions in Agricultural Policies', in S. De Vylder and D. Asplund, *Contradictions and Distributions in a rural Economy: the Case of Bangladesh*: Stockholm: Sida.
Diamant, A. (1966) *The Nature of Political Development*, in J. L. Finkle and R. W. Gable (eds), *Political and Social Change*, New York: John Wiley.
Dixon, C. (1990) *Rural Development in the Third World*: London: Routledge.
Dowse, R. E. and Hughes, J. A. (1986) *Political Sociology*, Chichester: John Wiley.
Dube, S. C. (1988) *Modernisation and Development: The Search for Alternative Paradigms*, Avon: UNU.
Dube, S. C. (1992) *Understanding Change*, New Delhi: Vikas.
Duncan, O. D. (1975) 'Metrological Issues in the Analysis of Social Mobility', in A. P. M. Coxon and C. L. Jones, *Social Mobility*, Harmondsworth: Penguin.
Durkheim, E. (1985) *The Division of Labour in Society*, trans. W. D. Halls, London: Macmillan.
Eftekhari, R. (1988) 'Tousehyeh Roustai dar Iran: ba Tavajjoh-e Khas be Amalkart-e Jihad' [With Special Reference to the Implementation Report of Jihad], MA dissertation, Tehran: University of Tarbiyat Moddarres.
Eisenstadt, S. N. (1963) *Modernization: Growth and Diversity*, Bloomington IN: Indiana University Press.
Eisenstadt, S. N. (1966) 'Breakdowns of Modernization', in J. L. Finkle and R. W. Gable (eds), *Political and Social Change*, New York: John Wiley.
Enayat, H. (1982) *Modern Islamic Political Thought*, London: Macmillan.
Ershad, F. (1997) 'Underdevelopment and Internal Brain-Drain: An Outlook on Rural-to-Urban Migration in the Middle East', paper presented to the 1997 British Sociological Association Conference, York, University of York.

FAO (Food and Agriculture Organisation) (1979) 'Review and Analysis of Agrarian Reform and Rural Development in the Developing Countries since mid-1960', mimeograph, World Conference on Agrarian Reform and Rural Development.
FAO (1980) *Production Yearbook: 1979–1980*, Washington, DC: World Bank.
FAO (1990a) *Global Consultation on Agricultural Extension*, Washington, DC: World Bank.
FAO (1990b) *Rural Poverty Alleviation: Strategies and Progress*, Washington, DC: World Bank.
FAO (1992) *Production Yearbook, 1979–92*, Washington, DC: World Bank.
Farazmand, A. (1989) *The State, Bureaucracy, and Revolution in Modern Iran: Agrarian Reform and Regime Politics*, New York: Praeger.
Ferdows, E. (1983) 'The Reconstruction Crusade and Class Conflict in Iran', *MERIP Reports*, vol. 17, no. 4, pp. 11–15.
Ferguson, J. (1990) *The Anti-Politics Machine: 'Development,' Depoliticisation, and Bureaucratic Power in Lesotho*, Cambridge: Cambridge University Press.
Fernandes, W. and Ianton, R. (1981) *Participatory Research and Evaluation*, New Delhi: Indian Social Institute.
Fethres, H. (1995) 'Asar-e Hazinehayeh Doulat bar Shekaf-e Daramadi-e Rousta-Shahri [The Effect of the Governmental Expenditure on the Rural–Urban Income Gap], *Eghtesad-e Keshavarzi va Tosaeh* [Agricultural Economic, and Development] vol. 8, pp. 77–99.
Fisher, Michael M. J. (1980) *Iran: From Religious Dispute to Revolution*, Cambridge, MA: Harvard University Press.
Fitz-Gibbon, C. T. and Morris, L. L. (1987) *How to Analyse Data*, London: Sage.
Frank, A. G. (1969) *Latin America: Underdevelopment or Revolution*, New York: Monthly Review Press.
Frank, A. G. (1977) *Capitalism and Underdevelopment in Latin America: Historical Studies of Chile and Brazil*, New York: Monthly Review Press.
Frank, A. G. (1978) *Dependent Accumulation and Underdevelopment*, London: Macmillan.
Frankel, F. R. (1978) *India's Political Economy 1947–1977: The Gradual Revolution*, Princeton, NJ: Princeton University Press.
Freebairn, D. K. (1995) 'Did the Green Revolution Concentrate Incomes? A Quantitative Study of Research Reports', *World Development*, vol. 23, no. 2, pp. 265–80.
Freire, P. (1972) *Pedagogy of the Oppressed*, Harmondsworth: Penguin.
Freire, P. (1975) *Cultural Action for Freedom*, Harmondsworth: Penguin.
Friedland, W. H. (1969) 'A Sociological Perspective on Modernisation', in C. Moser, D. E. Ashford and T. B. Bent (eds), *Modernisation by Design: Social Change in the Twentieth Century*, Ithaca, NY: Cornell University Press.
Friedmann, J. (1981) 'Urban Bias in Regional Development Policy', in R. P. Misra (ed.), *Humanizing Development: Essays on People, Space and Development in Honour of Masahiko Honjo*, Singapore: Maruzen Asia.
Frouzesh, G. (1987) 'Kodam Toseah baray-e Rousta' (Which Development for Village?), *Mohnameh-e Jihad* [Monthly Jihad], vol. 124, no. 9, pp. 12–19.
Frude, N. (1987) *A Guide to SPSS/PC*, London: Macmillan.
Gaiha, R. (1991) 'Poverty Alleviation Programmes in Rural India: An Assessment', *Development and Change*, vol. 22, no. 1, pp. 117–54.

Bibliography

Galli, R. E. (1981) 'Rural Development and the Contradictions of Capitalist Development', in R. E. Galli (ed.), *The Political Economy of Rural Development: Peasant, International Capital and the State*, Albany, NY: State University of New York.

Galtung, J., O'Brien, B. and Prieswerk, R. (eds) (1980) *Self-Reliance, A Strategy for Development*, London: Bogle L'Ouverture.

Gartell, J. (1981) 'Inequality within Rural Communities in Rural India', *American Sociological Review*, vol. 46 (December).

Ghai, D. P., Khan, A. R., Lee, E. L. and Alfthan, H. T. (1977) *The Basic Needs Approach to Development: Some Issues Regarding Concepts and Methodology*, Geneva: International Labour Organisation.

Ghasimi, M. R. (1992) 'The Iranian Economy after the Revolution: An Economic Appraisal of the Five-Year Plan', *International Journal of Middle East Studies*, vol. 24, no. 4, pp. 599–614.

Gibbons, D. S., De Koninck, R. and Hasan, I. (1980) *Agricultural Modernisation, Poverty and Inequality: The Distributional Impact of the Green Revolution in Regions of Malaysia and Indonesia*, Aldershot: Gower.

Giddens, A. (1993) *Sociology*, Oxford: Basil Blackwell.

Gilbar, Gad G. (1978) 'Persian Agriculture in the late Qujar Period 1960–1906: Some Economic and Social Aspects', *Asian and African Studies*, vol. 11.

Glass, D. V. and Hall, T. R. (1975) 'Social Mobility in Great Britain: A Study of Intergenerational Changes in Status', in A. P. M. Coxon and C. L. Jones, *Social Mobility*, Harmondsworth: Penguin.

Goldsworthy, D. (1988) 'Thinking Politically about Development', *Development and Change*, vol. 19, no. 3, pp. 505–30.

Goulet, D. (1989) 'Participation in Development: New Avenues', *World Development*, vol. 17, no. 2, pp. 165–78.

Gran, G. (1983) *Development by People: Citizen Construction of a Just World*, New York: Praeger.

Grindle, M. S. (1986) *State and Countryside Development Policy and Agrarian Politics in Latin America*, London: Johns Hopkins University Press.

Griffin, K. (1979) *The Political Economy of Agricultural Change: An Essay on the Green Revolution*, London: Macmillan.

Griffin, K. (1981) 'Economic Development in a Changing World', *World Development*, vol. 9, no. 3, pp. 221–6.

Griffin, K. and Khan, A. R. (1982) *Poverty in the Third World: Ugly facts and Fancy Models*, in H. Alavi and T. Shanin (eds), *Poverty and Landlessness in Rural Asia*, Geneva: International Labour Office, Mimeo.

Hagen, E. (1962), *On the Theory of Social Change*, Homewood, IL: Dorsey Press.

Haghayeghi, M. (1990) 'Agrarian Reform Problems in Post-Revolutionary Iran', *Middle Eastern Studies*, vol. 26, no. 1, pp. 35–51.

Haghshenas, J. and Mashahdi, M. (1997) 'Masghan-e Mahromin-e Roustaei' [The Housing of the Rural Oppressed], in The Plan and Budget Organisation, *Majmoehyeh Maghalat-e Gerdhamaei-e Barasiyeh Masaleh-e Fagh va Faghzodaei* [Collected Papers from the Seminar on the Study of Poverty and Poverty Alleviation], vol. 1, Tehran: The Planning and Budget Organisation, pp. 513–26.

Hakimi, A. (1969) *Farm Mechanisation in Iran*, Reading: University of Reading.

Halliday, F. (1979) *Iran, Dictatorship and Development*, Harmondsworth: Penguin.
Halliday, F. (1980) 'Iran's Revolution: The First Year', *MERIP Reports*, vol. 88 (June).
Hamilton, M. and Hirszowicz, M. (1993) *Class and Inequality: Comparative Perspectives*, London: Harvester Wheatsheaf.
Haq, M. (1976) *The Poverty Curtain*, New York: Columbia University Press.
Haq, M. (1978) *The Poverty Curtain*, New York: Oxford University Press.
Haque, W., Menta, N., Rahman, A. and Wignaraja, P. (1975) *Towards a Theory of Rural Development*, Bangkok: Asian Development Institute.
Haralambos, M. and Holborn, M. (1995) *Sociology: Themes and Perspectives*, London: Collins.
Hardary, G. (1951) 'The Agrarian Reform Problems in Iran', *Middle East Journal* vol. 5, no. 2, pp. 181–90.
Hardiman, M. and Midgley, J. (1982) *The Social Dimensions of Development: Social Policy and Planning in the Third World*, Chichester: John Wiley.
Hardjono, J. (1983) 'Rural Development in Indonesia: "The Top-Down" Approach', in D. A. M. Lea and D. P. Chaudri (eds), *Rural Development and the State*, London: Methuen.
Harrison, D. (1988) *The Sociology of Modernisation and Development*, London: Unwin Hyman.
Harriss, J. (ed.) (1982) *Rural Development: Theories of Peasant Economy and Agrarian Change*, London: Hutchinson.
Harriss, J. (1994) 'Between Economism and Post-Modernism: Reflection on Research on Agrarian in India', in D. Booth, *Rethinking Social Development Theory, Research and Practice*, Harlow: Longman.
Hartmann, B. and Boyce, J. (1983) *A Quiet Violence: View from a Bangladesh Village*, London: Zed Press.
Hartwig, M. (1978) 'Capitalism and Aborigines: The Theory of Internal Colonialism and its Rivals', in E. L. Wheelwright and K. Buckley (eds), *Essays in the Political-Economy of Australian Capitalism*, vol. 3, Sydney: An Z Book Company.
Harvey, C. (ed.) (1982) *Rural Employment and Administration in Third World Development: Methods and Alternative Strategies*, London: Macmillan.
Hayami, Y. and Rutten, V. W. (1971) *Agricultural Development: An International Perspective*, Baltimore, MD: Johns Hopkins University Press.
Hechter, M. (1975) *Internal Colonialism: The Celtic Fringe in British National Development, 1536–1966*, Berkeley, CA: University of California Press.
Heck, B. van (1979) *Participation of the Poor in Rural Organizations*, Rome: Food and Agriculture Organization of the UN.
Hegland, M. (1980) 'One Village in the Revolution', *MERIP Reports*, vol. 87 (May), pp. 7–12.
Hettne, B. (1978) *Current Issues in Development Theory*, Swedish Agency for Research Cooperation With Developing Countries, Report R5 1978, Helsingborg: Schmidts Boktryckeri AB.
Hettne, B. (1982) *Development Theory and The Third World*, Swedish Agency for Research Cooperation With Developing Countries, Report R5 1978, Helsingborg: Schmidts Boktryckeri AB.
Hettne, B. (1995) *Development Theory and the Three Worlds*, London: Longman.

Heyer, J., Roberts, D. and Williams, G. (1981) *Rural Development in Tropical Africa*, London: Macmillan.
Hickey, G. C. and Flamming, R. A. (1977) *The Rural Poor Majority in the Phillippines: Their Present and Future Status as Beneficiaries of AID Programs*, Manila: USAID.
Hirashima, S. (1974) 'Interaction between Institutions and Technology in Developing Agriculture: A Case Study of the Disparity in Pakistan Agriculture', PhD dissertation, Cornell University.
Holt, T., Robert, T. and Turner, S. (1970) *The Methodology of Comparative Research*, New York: The Free Press.
Homan, B. (1996) 'Barsiyeh Tahavoulat-e Mahajerathayeh Roustaei-yeh Keshvar az Saleh 1355–1370' [A study of the Developments of Country's Rural Migrations from 1982–1992), *Mohnameh-e Jihad* [Jihad Monthly], vol. 16, nos 184–5, pp. 48–51.
Hooglund, E. (1982) *Land and Revolution in Iran 1960–1980*, Austin, TX: University of Texas Press.
Hournard, B. (1993) 'The Land Question and Islamic Revolution in Iran', *South Asia Bulletin*, vol. 8, nos 1/2, pp. 134–74.
Howe, J. and Richard, P. (1984) *Rural Roads and Poverty Alleviation*, Geneva: International Labour Organisation (ILO).
Howes, M. (1985) *Whose Water? An Investigation of the Consequences of Alternative Approaches to Small Scale Irrigation in Bangladesh*, Dhaka: BIDS.
Huda, A. T. M. S. (1983) *The Small Farmer and the Problem of Access*, Dhaka: Bangladesh Agriculture Council.
Hulme, D. and Turner, M. (1990) *Sociology and Development: Theories, Policies and Practices*, Brighton: Harvester Wheatsheaf.
Humphrey, H. (1963) *Alliance for Progress: A First-Hand Report from Latin America*, pamphlet, Washington, DC: World Bank.
Humphrey, H. (1980) 'Rural Participation in the Revolution', *MERIP Reports* vol. 87 (May), pp. 3–6.
Huntington, S. (1968) *Political Order in Changing Societies*, New Haven, CT: Yale University Press.
Huntington, S. (1976) 'The Change to Change: Modernisation, Development and Politics', in C.E. Black (ed.), *Comparative Modernisation, A Reader*, New York: Free Press.
ILO (1971) *Matching Employment and Expectations: Programme of Action for Ceylon*, Geneva: International Labour Organisation.
ILO (1972) *Employment and Income Policies: Study of Employment in Iran*, Geneva: ILO.
ILO (1976) *Employment, Growth, and Basic Needs*, Geneva: ILO.
ILO (1977) *Poverty and Landlessness in Rural Asia*, Geneva: ILO.
Inkeles, A. and Smith, D. H. (1974) *Becoming Modern*, London: Heinemann.
Issawi, C. (1971) *The Economic History of Iran 1800–1914*, Chicago, IL: University of Chicago Press.
Jazairy, I., Alamgir M. and Panuccio, T. (1992) *The State of World Rural Poverty: An Inquiry into its Causes and Consequences*, London: Intermediate Technology.
Jazani, B. (1982) *Capitalism and Revolution in Iran*, London: Zed Press.
Jenan Sefat, M. S. (1992) 'Barsiyeh Vaziyat-e Hazinehayeh Khanevarhayeh Roustaei' [A Study of the Situation of Rural Household Expenditures], *Mohnameh-e Jihad* [Jihad Monthly], vol. 11, no. 147, pp. 8–18.

Kalantari, I. (1994a) Interview, *Nashriyeh-e Barzgar*, vol. 14, no. 652, pp. 8–10.
Kalantari, I. (1994b) Interview, *Nashriyeh-e Barzgar*, vol. 14, no. 659, pp. 10–11.
Kalantari, I. (1994c) Interview, *Nashriyeh-e Barzgar*, vol. 14, no. 657, pp. 22–3.
Kar, K. (1999) 'Government, People and Other Stakeholders in Rural Infrastructure Development: Reflections from a Few Countries in Asia and Africa', paper presented to the Asian Productivity Organisation seminar on Rural Infrastructure Development, Tehran, 25 October–2 November.
Karami, E. (1993) 'Growth Versus Development Orientation in Iran', *Community Development*, vol. 28, no. 2, pp. 120–8.
Karimi, S. (1986) *Economic Policies and Structural Changes since the Revolution and the Islamic Republic*, Syracuse, NY: Syracuse University Press.
Karshenas, M. (1990) *Oil, State and Industrialisation in Iran*, Cambridge: Cambridge University Press.
Katouzian, H. (1973) 'Land Reform in Iran: A Case Study in the Political Economy of Social Engineering', *Journal of Peasant Studies*, vol. 1, no. 2, pp. 39–220.
Katouzian, H. (1980) *Political Economy of Modern Iran*, Oxford: Oxford University Press.
Katouzian, H. (1995) 'Problems of Political Development in Iran: Democracy, Dictatorship or Arbitrary Government?', *British Journal of Middle Eastern Studies*, vol. 22, nos 1/2, pp. 5–20.
Kazemi, F. (1980) *Poverty and Revolution in Iran*, New York: New York University Press.
Kazemi, F. and E. Abrahamian (1978) 'Non-Revolutionary Peasantry of Modern Iran', *Iranian Studies*, vol. 11, pp. 259–304.
Keddie, N. R. (1960) 'Historical Obstacles to Agrarian Change in Iran', *Claremont Asian Studies*, no. 8 (September).
Keddie, N. R. (1968) 'The Iranian Village Before and After Land Reform', *Journal of Contemporary History*, vol. 3, no. 3, pp. 69–91.
Keddie, N. R. (1972) 'Stratification, Social Control, and Capitalism in Iranian Villages: Before and After Land Reform', in R. Antoun (ed.), *Rural Politics and Social Change in the Middle East*, Bloomington IN: Indiana University Press.
Keddie, N. R. (1981) *Roots of Revolution: An Interpretive History of Modern Iran*, New Haven, CT: Yale University Press.
Kelsall, R. K. and Kelsall, H. M. (1972) *Stratification: An Essay on Class and Inequality*, London: Longman.
Khamsi, R. (1969) 'Land Reform in Iran', *Monthly Review*, vol. 21 (July), pp. 20–8.
Khan, Mehdi H. (1986) *Merori bar Ghozaresh-e Amalkard-e Marakez-e Khadamat-e Roustai Sharestan-e Hashtroud* [A Review on the Implementation Report of the Centres of Services for Rural and Nomadic People of the township of Sarab], Tabriz: the Plan and Budget Organisation of Eastern Azerbaijan.
Khan, M. H. (1989) 'Clientelism, Corporation and Capitalist Development: An Analysis of State Intervention with Special Reference to Bangladesh', PhD thesis, King's College, Cambridge.
Khosravi, K. (1976) *Pazhohshi dar Jameh-e Roustaei-e Iran* [A study on Rural Society in Iran], Tehran: Inteshardt-e Payman.
Korten, D. (1979) *Population and Social Development: A Challenge for Management Schools*, Caracas: Instituto de Estudios Superiores de Administacion (IESA).
Korten, D. C. and Alfonso, F. B. (1983) *Bureaucracy and the Poor*, Makati: Asian Institute of Management.

Korten, F. F. (1982) *Building National Capacity to Develop Water Users' Associations*, World Bank Staff Papers no. 528, Washington DC: World Bank.
Kottak, C. P. (1986) 'When People Don't Come First: Some Sociological Lessons from Completed Projects', in M. M. Cernea (ed.), *Putting People First: Sociological Variables in Rural Development*, Oxford: Oxford University Press for the World Bank.
Krinks, P. (1983) 'Rectifying Inequality or Favouring the few?: Image and Reality', in D. A. M. Lea and D. P. Chaudhri (1983), *Rural Development and the State*, London: Methuen.
Kumar, K. (1987) *Conducting Group Interviews in Developing Countries*, USAID Programme Design and Evaluation Methodology Report no. 13, Washington, DC.
Kumar, K. (1990) *Conducting Mini Surveys in Developing Countries*, USAID Programme Design and Evaluation Methodology Report no. 15, Washington, DC.
Laclau, Ernesto (1979) *Politics and Ideology in Marxist Theory*, London: Verso.
Ladejinsky, W. (1977) 'Economic Situation and Prospects of India', in L. J. Walinsky, *The Selected Papers of Wolf Ladesinsky, Agrarian Reform as Unfinished Business*, Oxford: Oxford University Press.
Lahsaeizadeh, A. (1990) *Tagyare-e Ijtemaei dar Roustaahaye Iran* [Social Change in rural Iran], Shiraz: Entesharat-e-Novin.
Lahsaeizadeh, A. (1993) *Contemporary Rural Iran*, London: Athenaeum.
Lambert, P. J. (1993) *The Distribution and Redistribution of Income: A Mathematical Analysis*, Manchester: Manchester University Press.
Lambton, A. K. S. (1953) *Landlord and Peasant in Persia*, London: Oxford University Press.
Lambton, A. K. S. (1969) *Persia Land Reform, 1962–1966*, Oxford: Clarendon Press.
Land Devolution Committee (1989) Barasiyeh Asarat-e ragozari-e Zamin Der Roustahayeh Garmsar, [Investigation of the effects of Land Devolution in Garmsar's villages], Tehran.
Lea, D. A. M. and Chaudhri, D. P. (1977) *An Introduction to the Sociology of Rural Development*, London: Tavistock.
Lea, D. A. M. and Chaudhri, D. P. (1983) *Rural Development and The State*, London: Methuen.
Lea, D. A. M. and Chaudhri, D. P. (1988) 'Sociological Perspectives on Agrarian Development and State intervention', in A. Hall and J. Midgley, *Development Politics: Sociological Perspectives*, Manchester: Manchester University Press.
Lee, R. M. (1993) *Doing Research on Sensitive Topics*, London: Sage.
Leeson, P. F. and Nixon, F. I. (1988) 'Development Economics and the State', in P. F. Leeson and M. M. Minogue (eds), *Perspectives on Development: Grass-Disciplinary Theory in Development*: Manchester: Manchester University Press.
Leftwich, A. (ed.) (1996) *Democracy and Development: Theory and Practice*, Cambridge: Polity Press.
Lele, U. (1975) *The Design of Rural Development*, Baltimore, MD: Johns Hopkins University Press for the World Bank.
Lerner, D. (1958) 'Modernization: Social Aspects', *The International Encyclopaedia of Social Sciences*, vol. 10., pp. 386–95.

Lerner, D. (1964) *The Passing of Traditional Society*, New York: The Free Press.
Levy, M. S. (1967) 'Social Patterns (Structures) and the Problem of Modernisation', in W. Moore and R. M. Cook (eds), *Reading in Social Change*, Englewood Cliffs, NJ: Prentice-Hall, pp. 189–208.
Lewis, J. P. (ed.) (1988) *Strengthening the Poor: What Have We Learned?* Oxford: Transaction Books.
Lewis, W. A. (1953) *Industrialisation and the Gold Coast*, Accra: Gold Coast Government.
Lewis, W. A. (1955) *The Theory of Economic Growth*, London: George Allen Unwin.
Leys, C. (1975) *Underdevelopment in Kenya: The Political Economy of Neo-colonialism*, London: Heinemann.
Lipton, M. (1977) *Why Poor People Stay Poor: Urban Bias in World Development*, Cambridge, MA: Harvard University Press.
Lipton, M. (1982) 'Strategy for Agriculture Urban Bias and Rural Planning', in J. Harriss (ed.), *Rural Development: Theories of Peasant Economy and Agrarian Change*, London: Hutchinson.
Loeffler, R. (1986) 'Economic Change in a Rural Area since 1979', in N. Keddie and E. Hoogland (eds), *Iranian Revolution and the Islamic Republic*, Syracuse, NY: Syracuse University Press.
Long, N. (1977) *Introduction to the Sociology of Rural Development*, London: Tavistock.
Long, N. (1988) 'Sociological Perspectives on Agrarian Development and State Intervention', in A. Hall and J. Midgley (eds), *Development Policies: Sociological Perspectives*, Manchester: Manchester University Press.
Long, N. and Douwe van der Ploeg, J. (1994) 'Heterogeneity, Actor and Structure: Towards a Reconstition of the Concept of Structure', in D. Booth, *Rethinking Social Development Theory, Research and Practice*, Harlow: Longman.
Luke, T. W. (1990) *Social Theory and Modernity Critique, Dissent, and Revolution*, London: Sage.
Majd, M. G. (1991) 'The Oil Boom and Agricultural Development: A Reconsideration of Agricultural Policy in Iran', *The Journal of Energy and Development*, vol. 15, no. 1, pp. 125–40.
Majd, M. G. (1992) 'On the Relationship Between Land Reform and Rural–Urban Migration in Iran, 1966–1976', *Middle East Journal*, vol. 46, no. 3, pp. 440–56.
Malekaniyan, A. H. (1987) *Pazhouheshi bar Nezam-e Zamindari: Malekiyatha, Nezam-e Bahrebardri, Shivehayeh Toulid-e Keshavarzi-e dar Iran* [A Survey of the Land Ownership System: Ownership, Exploitative System, Modes of Production in Iran], Tehran: Centre for Rural and Agricultural Research, The Ministry of Agriculture.
Mandel, E. (1976) 'Capitalism and Regional Disparity', *South West Economy and Society*, vol. 1.
Mark, N. (1998) 'Beyond Individual Differences: Social Differentiation from First Principles', *American Sociological Review*, vol. 63, pp. 309–30.
Marsden, T. and Murdoch, J. (1998) 'Editorial: The Shifting Nature of Rural Governance and Community Participation', *Journal of Rural Studies*, vol. 14, no. 1, pp. 1–4.

Marx, K. (1964) *Pre-Capitalist Economic Formations*, London: Lawrence & Wishart.
Maslow, A. (1954) *Motivation and Personality*, New York: Harper and Brother.
Mathur, H. M. (ed) (1983) *Reaching the poor in Rural areas: Developmental Issues and Administrative Requirements*, United Nations: Asian and Pacific Development Centre.
May, T. (1997) *Social Research, Issues, Methods and Process*, Buckingham: Open University.
Mayoux, L. (1995) 'Beyond Naivety: Women, Gender Inequality and Participatory Development', *Development and Change*, vol. 26, pp. 235–59.
McCarthy, F. and Feldmen, (1988) 'Process of Impoverishment in Bangladesh: Reconceptualisation of Poverty and Resources', *The Journal of Social Studies*, vol. 39.
McClelland, D. (1961) *The Achieving Society*, Princeton, NJ: van Nostrand.
McLachlan, K. (1968) 'Land Reform in Iran', in *Cambridge History of Iran*, vol. 1, Cambridge: Cambridge University Press.
Means, G. P. (1972) 'Special Rights as a Strategy for Development', *Comparative Politics*, vol. 5 (October).
Mehran, F. (1975) 'Income Distribution in Iran, Statistics of Inequality', Income Distribution Working Paper, Geneva: ILO.
Mehreghan, N. (1996) 'Rosht-e Bakhsh-e Keshavarzi va Touzieh-e Daramad' [The Growth of the Agricultural Sector and Income Distribution], *Ettela'at-e siyasi-Eghtesadi* [Political-Economic Monthly Journal], vol. 7, nos 9/10, pp. 36–43.
Mehta, S. R. (1984) *Rural Development Policies and Programmes: A Sociological Perspective*: New Delhi: Sage Publications India.
Meier, G. (1976) *Leading Issues in Economic Development*, Oxford: Oxford University Press.
Mellor, J. W. (1969) 'Production Economics and the Modernisation of Traditional Agricultures', *Australian Journal of Agricultural Economics*, vol. 13, no. 1.
Merton, R. K., Fisk, M. and Kendall, P. (1965) *The Focused Interview: A Manual of Problems and Procedures*, Glencoe: The Free Press.
Migdal, J. S. (1988) *Strong Societies and Weak States: State–Society Relations and State Capabilities in the Third World*, Princeton, NJ. Princeton University Press.
Miller, S. M. (1975a) 'The Concept and Measurement of Mobility', in A. P. M. Coxon and C. L. Jones, *Social Mobility*, Harmondsworth: Penguin.
Miller, S. M. (1975b) 'Comparative Social Mobility', in A. P. M. Coxon and C. L. Jones, *Social Mobility*, Harmondsworth: Penguin.
Ministry of Agriculture (1979) *Khotot-e Asliyeh Hadafha, Siyastha va Sazeman-e Kesavarzi dar Iran* [Guidelines and Objectives in Iranian Agricultural Policy and Organisation], Tehran.
Ministry of Agriculture (1982) *Quzaresh-e Keshavarzi 1981/2* [Agricultural Report 1981/2], Tehran.
Ministry of Agriculture (1983) *Barasiyeh Mehwar Burdan-e Keshavarziyeh Olawiyyat be Bakhsh-e Keshavarzi* [Investigation of the Pivotal Position of Agriculture or the Priority of Agriculture], Tehran.
Ministry of Agriculture (1983) *Barnamehyeh Panjsaleyeh Tousa-e Keshavarzi* [Five-Year Plan for the Development of Agriculture], vol. 1, Tehran.
Ministry of Agriculture (1985) *Barasiyeh Taavounihayeh Mosha*, [Investigation of the *Mosha* Cooperatives], Tehran.

Ministry of Agriculture (1987a) *Barnameh-e Afzayesh-e Toulid-e Mosulat-e Keshavarzi 1987/8–1996/7* [Plan of Increasing Agrarian Production 1987/8–1996/7] (Self-Sufficiency Plan), Tehran.
Ministry of Agriculture (1987b) *Quzaresh-e Keshavarzi 1987/8* [Agricultural Report 1987/8], Tehran.
Ministry of Corporate and Rural Affairs (1973) *Summary of Statistics Concerning the Three Stages of Land Reform*, Tehran.
Ministry of Energy (1993) *A General view on Iranian Dams: Past, Present and Future*, Tehran.
Ministry of Jihad-e Sazandegi (1980) *Farhang-e Ejtemaei-yeh Dehat va Mazareh* [The Social Culture of Villages and Farms], Tehran.
Ministry of Jihad-e Sazandegi (1983) *Amargiri-e Roustaiyeh Jihad-e Sazandeghi* [Jihad's Rural Census], Tehran.
Ministry of Jihad-e Sazandegi (1992) *Rural Construction*, Tehran: Undersecretary of Rural Construction, Planning and Programming Bureau.
Ministry of Jihad-e Sazandegi (1993) *Eshteqal va Faghr dar Jameh-e Roustaeyh Iran* [Employment and Poverty in Iranian Rural Society], Tehran: Rural Development Department, Ministry of Jihad.
Ministry of the Interior (1960) *Nashriyeh-e Amar-e Gozarsh Kholasheh-e Sarshomaryeh Emomiyeh Keshvar, 1956* [Statistics Report Leaflet: Summary of the National Census, 1956], Tehran.
Ministry of the Interior (1961) *Amarhayeh Melli va Ostaniyeh Nokhustin Sarshomariyeh Iran* [National and Province Statistics of the First Census of Iran], Tehran.
Ministry of the Interior (1962) *Nokhustin Sarshomariyeh Melliyeh Keshavarzi* [First National Census of Agriculture, 1960], Tehran.
Ministry of the Interior (1988) *Tahlili bar Wazehyat-e Shourahayeh Islami-e Rousti* [An Analysis on the States of the Islamic Rural Councils], Tehran.
Mishler, G. (1986) *Research Interviewing Context and Narrative*, London: Harvard University Press.
Misra, R. P. (1985) *Rural Development: Capitalist and Socialist Paths, Volume One, An Overview*, New Delhi: Concept.
Mlay, W. (1985) 'Pitfalls in Rural Development: The Case of Tanzania', in G. Fassil and F. G. Kiros (eds), *Challenging Rural Poverty: Experiences in Institution-Building and Popular Participation for Rural Development in Eastern Africa*, Trenton, NJ: Africa World Press.
Moaddle, M. (1992) *Class, Politics, and Ideology in the Iranian Revolution*: New York, Columbia University Press.
Moaddle, M. (1994) 'Political Conflict in the World Economy: A Cross-National Analysis of Modernisation and World System Theory', *American Sociological Review*, vol. 59, no. 2, pp. 276–303.
Moghadam, F. E. (1988) Nomadic Invasions and the Development of Productive Forces: An Historical Study of Iran (1000–1800), *Science and Society*, vol. 52, no. 4, pp. 389–412.
Moghadam, F. E. (1996) *From Land Reform to Revolution: the Political Economy of Agrarian Relations in Iran*, London: I. B. Tauris.
Mohtadi, H. (1990) 'Rural Inequality and Rural-Push Versus Urban-Pull Migration: The Case of Iran, 1956–1976', *World Development*, vol. 18, pp. 837–45.

Mojtahed, A. and Esfahani H., (1989) 'Agricultural Policy and Performance in Iran: The Post-Revolutionary Experiences', *World Development*, vol. 17, no. 6, pp. 839–60.
Momen, M. (1983) *An Introduction to Shii Islam*, New Haven, CT: Yale University Press.
Moridi, S. (1994) 'Siyasat-e Azadsazi-e Eghtesadi va Keshavarzi-e Iran' [The Economic and Agricultural Liberation Policy of Iran], *Eghtesad-e Keshavarzi va Tosaeh* [Agricultural Economic and Development], special issue.
Morrison, L., Herbert, D. T., Rimmington, M. and Williamson, C. (1979) *The Disintegrating Village: Social Change in Rural Sri Lanka*, Colombo: Lake House Investments.
Mosher, A. M. (1969) *Creating a Progressive Rural Structure*, New York: ADC.
Moser, C. A. and Kalton, G. (1958) *Survey Methods in Social Investigation*, London: Heinemann.
Moore, W. E. (1963) *Social Change*, Englewood Cliffs, NJ: Prentice-Hall.
Murdoch, J. and Abram, S. (1998) 'Defining the Limits of Community Governance', *Journal of Rural Studies*, vol. 14, no. 1, pp. 41–50.
Myrdal, G. (1970) *The Challenge of World Poverty: A World Anti Poverty Programme in Outline*, New York: Pantheon.
Myren, D. T. (1967) 'Integrating the Rural Market into the National Economy of Mexico', *COMERCIO EXTERIOR*, vol. XVII (9 September).
Nabi, I., Hamid, N. and Zahid, S. (1986) *The Agrarian Economy of Pakistan*, Oxford: Oxford University Press.
Najafi, G. A. (1995) 'Sakhtar-e Nezam-e Keshavarzi: Barasi-e Vazeh-e Mojoud va Sharayit-e Azadsazi' [The Structure of the Agricultural System: A study of the existing situation and libration conditions], *Eghtesad-e Keshavarzi va Tosaeh* [Agricultural Economic and development], vol. 8, no. 2, pp. 55–92.
Najmabadi, A. (1987) *Land Reform and Social Change in Iran*, Salt Lake City: University of Utah Press.
Nazir, P. (1991) *Local Development in the Global Economy*, Aldershot: Gower.
Nejelski, P. (1976) *Social Research in Conflict with Law and Ethics*, Cambridge MA: Ballinger.
Nomani, F. (1977) 'Notes on the Economic Obligations of Peasantry in Iran, 300–1600 A. D.', *Iranian Studies*, vol. 5, nos 1–2, pp. 62–83.
Nomani, F. and Rahnema, A. (1992) *Islamic Economic Systems*, London: Zed Books.
Nowshirvani, V. (1981) 'The Beginning of Commercialised Agriculture in Iran', in A. L. Udovitch (ed.), *The Islamic Middle East, 700–1900: Studies in Economic and Social History*, Princeton, NJ: The Darwin Press.
Nurkse, R. (1953) *Problems of Capital Formation in Underdeveloped Countries*, Oxford: Basil Blackwell.
Nurkse, R. (1959) *Patterns of Trade and Development*, Stockholm: Almquist & Wiksell.
Oakley, P. and Marsden, D. (1984) *Approaches to Participation in Rural Development*, Geneva: ILO.
Okazaki, S. (1968) *The Development of Large-Scale Farming in Iran: The Case of the Province of Gorgan*, Tokyo: Institute of Asian Economic Affairs.
Olson, M. Jr (1963) 'Rapid Growth as a Destabilising Force', *Journal of Economic History*, vol. 23, no. 4, pp. 529–52.

Orbridge, S. (1994) 'Post-Marxism and Post-colonialism: The Needs and Rights of Distant Strangers', in D. Booth (ed.), *Rethinking Social Development: Theory, Research and Practice*, Harlow: Longman.
Parkin, F. (1968) *Class, Inequality and Political Order: Middle Class Radicalism*, Manchester: Manchester University Press.
Parsa, M. (1989) *Social Origins of the Iranian Revolution'* London: Rutgers University.
Parsons, T. (1951) *The Social System*, Glencoe, IL: Free Press.
Pearse, A. (1975) *The Latin American Peasant*, London: Frank Cass.
Pearse, A. (1977) 'Technology and Peasant Production: Reflections on a Global Study', *Development and Change*, vol. 8, no. 2, pp. 125–60.
Pearse, A. (1980) *Seeds of Plenty, Seeds of Want: Social and Economic Implications of the Green Revolution*, Oxford: Oxford University Press.
Pearse, A. and Stiefel, M. (1979) *Inquiry into Participation: A Research Approach*, UNRISD Popular Participation Programme.
Perroux, F. (1993) *A New Concept of Development: Basic Fenets*, London, Croom Helm and Paris: UNESCO.
Pesaran, H. (1982) 'The System of Dependent Capitalism in Pre-Revolutionary Iran', *International Journal of Middle East Studies*, vol. 14, pp. 501–22.
Phillips D. L. (1962) *Knowledge from What? Theories and Methods in Social Research*, Chicago: Rand McNally.
Plan and Budget Organisation (1975) *Iran's Fifth Development Plan, Revised 1973–1978: A Summary*, Tehran.
Plan and Budget Organisation (1989–99) *Ghanon-e Bodjeh-e Kol-e Keshvar* [The Budget Law of the Country], Tehran.
Plan and Budget Organisation (1990a) *Chaharchopb-e Nazarieh Toseh: Ostan-e Azarbaijan-e Sharghi* (The Theoretical Framework: Eastern Azarbaijan), Tehran: Department for Spatial Studies, Plan and Budget Organisation.
Plan and Budget Organisation (1990b) *A Summary Version of the First Five-Year Economic, Social and Cultural Development Plan of the Islamic Republic of Iran*, Tehran.
Plan and Budget Organisation of Eastern Azarbaijan (1990–93) *Shakheshay-e Eghtesadi-Ejtemaei va Farhanghiy-e Ostan-e Azarbaijan-e Sharghi: Bar Asa-e Taghsimat-e Jadid* [Socioeconomic and Cultural Indices of Eastern Azarbaijan on the Basis of New Territorial Divisions], Tabriz: Plan and Budget Organisation.
Plan and Budget Organisation of Eastern Azarbaijan (1994) *Amarnameh-e Ostan-e Azarbaijan-e Sharghi* [The Statistic Book of Eastern Azarbaijan], Tabriz: Plan and Budget Organisation.
Plan and Budget Organisation of Eastern Azarbaijan (1995) *Ettalaat-e Eghtesadi-Ejtemaei va Farhanghiy-e Ostan-e Azarbaijan-e Sharghi* [Socioeconomic and Cultural Information on Eastern Azarbaijan], Tabriz: Plan and Budget Organisation.
Plan and Design Department (1998) *Pazhoheshi bar Etebarat-e Roustaei* [A study of Rural Credit], Tehran: Ministry of Jihad.
Poostchi, I. (1986) *Rural Development and the Developing Countries: An Interdisciplinary Introductory Approach*, Oshawa: Alger Press.
Poplin, G. (1979) *A Survey of Theories and Methods of Research*, New York: Schockers Books.
Porter, D. (1995) 'Science from Childhood: The Homesickness of Development Discourse', in J. Crush, *Power of Development*, London: Routledge.

Preston, D. A. (1980) *Environment, Society, and Rural Change in Latin America: The Past, Present, and Future in the Countryside*, New York: John Wiley.
Preston, P. and Simpson-Housley, P. (eds) (1994) *Writing the City: Eden, Babylon and the New Jerusalem*, London: Routledge.
Pretty, J. N. (1995) 'Participatory Learning for Sustainable Agriculture', *World Development*, vol. 23, no. 8, pp. 1247–65.
Prezeworski, A. and Teune, H. (1975) *The Logic of Comparative Social Inquiry*, London: Wiley-Interscience.
Pullum, T. W. (1970) 'What Can Mathematical Models Tell Us about Occupational Mobility', in A. P. M. Coxon and C. L. Jones, *Social Mobility*, Harmondsworth: Penguin.
Pye, L. W. (1966a) 'The Concept of Political Development', in J. L. Finkle and R. W. Gable (eds), *Political and Social Change*, New York: John Wiley.
Pye, L. W. (1966b) *Aspects of Political Development*, Boston, MA: Little, Brown.
Rafipour, F. (1986) *Jamehyeh Riustaei va Niyazhayeh An: Pazhouheshi dar siyo dou Roustayeh bar Ghozidehyeh Ostan-e Yazd* [Rural Society and its Needs: A Survey of Thirty-Two Selected Villages in Yazd Province], Tehran: Sherkat-e Sahami-e Inteshar.
Rafipour, F. (1989) *Sanjesh-e Grayesh-e Roustaeyan Nesbat ba Jahd-e Sazandeghi: Pazhouheshi dar Sa Ostan-e Esfahan, Fars and Khorasan* [Survey of Villagers' Attitudes towards Jihad in the Provinces of Esfahan, Fars and Khorasan], Tehran: Centre for Rural Studies, Ministry of Jihad.
Rahimi, S. and Syeed Razavi, S. H. (1996) 'Negharishi bar jayeghah-e Rousta va Roustaeyan dar Barnamehhayeh Faghzodaei' [A View on the Status of Villages and Villagers in Programmes of The Plan and Budget Organisation], in *Majmoehyeh Maghalat-e Gerdhamaei-e Barasiyeh Masaleh-e fagh va Faghzodaei* [Collected Papers from the Seminar on the Study of Poverty and the Poverty Reduction Problem], vol. 1, Tehran: The Plan and Budget Organisation.
Rahnema, A. (1994) *Pioneers of Islamic Revival*, London: Zed Books.
Rahnema, A. and Nomani, F. (1990) *The Secular Miracle: Religion, Politics and Economic Policy in Iran*, London: Zed Books.
Rajaram, I. (1975) 'Poverty, Inequality, and Economic Growth: Rural Panjab, 1960/61–1970/71', *Journal of Development Studies*, vol. 11, no. 4, pp. 278–900.
Razzaghi, E. (1989) *Egtesad-e Iran* [Iranian Economy], Tehran: Nashr-e Nay.
Razzaghi, E. (1993) 'Sakhtar-e Keshavarzi-e Iran va Tenghnahayeh Aan az Didehghah-e Touseh-e Darounza' [The Iranian Agriculture Structure and its Obstacles from the Perspective of Indigenous Development], *Ettela'at -e siyasi-Eghtesadi* [Political-Economic Monthly Journal], vol. 7, nos 5/6, pp. 70–7.
Redfield, R. (1965) *Peasant Society and Culture*, Chicago, IL: University of Chicago Press.
Richard, H. (1975) 'Land Reform and Agribusiness in Iran', *MERIP Reports*, vol. 43 (December), pp. 3–18.
Richardson S. A., Dohrenwend, B. S. and Klein, D. (1965) *Interviewing Its Forms and Functions*, London: Basic Books.
Robertson, A. F. (1984) *The People and the State*: An *Anthropology of Planned Development*, Cambridge: Cambridge University Press.
Robson, C. (1993) *Real World Research: A Resource for Social Scientists and Practitioner–Researchers*, Oxford: Basil Blackwell.
Rogers, E. (1962) *The Diffusion of Innovations*, Illinois: Free Press.

Rogers, E. (1969) *Modernisation among Peasants: The Impact of Communications*, New York: Holt, Rinehart & Winston.
Rostow, W. W. (1960) *The Stages of Economic Growth: A Non-Communist Manifesto*, Cambridge: Cambridge University Press.
Roxborough, I. (1979) *Theories of Underdevelopment*, London: Macmillan.
Rudra, A. (1984) 'Local Power and Farm Level Decision Making', in M. Desai *et al.* (eds), *Agrarian Power and Agricultural Productivity in South Asia*, New Delhi: Oxford University Press.
Ruttan, V. W. (1984) 'Models of Agricultural Development', in C. K. Eicher and J. M. Staatz (eds), *Agricultural Development in the Third World*, London: Johns Hopkins University Press.
Ruttan, V. W. (1986) 'Access: a Theory of Corruption and Bureaucracy', *Public Administration and Development*, vol. 6.
Ruttan, V. W. and Hayami, Y. (1984) 'Induced Innovation Model of Agricultural Development', in C. K. Eicher and J. M. Staatz (ed.), *Agricultural Development in the Third World*, London: Johns Hopkins University Press.
Sabetghadam, S. (1983) *Merori bar Ghozaresh-e Amalkad-e Marakez-e Kadamat-e Roustai* [A Review of the Implementation Report of the Centres of Services for Rural and Nomadic People], Tehran: Plan and Budget Organisation.
Sa'edlou, H. (1955) 'Nazari beh Masael-e va Moshkelat-e Heghoghi-e Keshavarzi-e Iran' [A View on the Legal Problems and Difficulties of Iranian Agriculture], *Eghtesad-e Keshavarzi va Tosaeh* [Agricultural Economy and Development] vol. 7, pp. 163–79.
Safinazhad, J. (1971) *Boneh*, Tehran: Entesharateh Tous, Chapeh Efsat Heidars.
Sandbrook, R. (1982) *The Politics of Basic Needs: Urban Aspects of Assaulting Poverty in Africa*, London: Heinemann.
SAREC (Swedish Agency for Research Cooperation with Developing Countries) (1979) *Report R5*, Helsingborg: Schmidts Boktryckeri AB.
Sarker, A. E. (1990) 'State Intervention in Rural Development', PhD thesis, University of Liverpool.
Sarma, J. S. (1982) *Agricultural Policy in India: Growth with Equality*, Ottawa: International Development Research Centre.
Schaffer, B. (1980) 'Insiders and Outsiders: Insideness, Incorporation and Bureaucratic Politics', *Development and Change*, vol. 11, no. 2, pp. 65–87.
Schaffer, B. and Huang, W. (1975) 'Distribution and the Theory of Access', *Development and Change*, vol. 6, no. 2.
Schaffer, B. and Lamb G. (1974) 'Exit, Voice and Access', *Social Science Information*, vol. 13, no. 6, pp. 73–90.
Schirazi, A. (1987) 'The Problem of the Land Reform in the Islamic Republic of Iran', *Occasional Papers*, no. 10, Berlin: Free University of Berlin.
Schirazi, A. (1993) *Islamic Policy, The Agrarian Question in Iran*, trans. P. J. Ziess-Lawrence, London: Lynne Rienner.
Schrijvers, J. (1984) 'Blueprint for Undernutrition: an Example from Sri Lanka', *Sociologia Ruralis*, vol. 24.
Schultz, T. W. (1964) *Transforming Traditional Agriculture*, New Haven, CT: Yale University Press.
Scott, J. (1995) *Stratification and Power: Structures of Class, Status and Command*, Cambridge: Polity Press.
Seers, D. (1969) *The Meaning of Development*, IDS, Communication Series, no. 44, University of Sussex.

Seers, D. (1979) *Underdeveloped Europe: Studies in Core–Periphery Relations*, Sussex: Harvester Press.
Sen, A. K. (1977) 'Starvation and Exchange Entitlements: A General Approach and its Application to the Great Bangal Famine', *Cambridge Journal of Economics*, vol. 1, no. 1, pp. 33–59.
Sen, A. K. (1981) 'Public Action and Quality of Life in Developing Countries', *Oxford Bulletin of Economic and Statistics*, vol. 43, pp. 30–53.
Sen, A. K. (1983) 'Development: which way now?', *Economic Journal*, vol. 93, pp. 745–62.
Sen, A. K. and Dreze, J. (1989) *Hunger and Public Action*, Oxford: Clarendon Press.
Sen, A. K., Dreze, J. and Hussain, A. (1995) *The Political Economy of Hunger: Selected Essays*, Oxford: Clarendon Press.
Serkkola, A. and Mann, C. (1985) *The Cultural Dimension of Development*, Helsinki: Finnish National Commission for UNESCO.
Shaditalab, Z. (1994) 'Tadil-e Sakhtar-e Eghtesadi-e va Siyasathayeh Etebari BakhshehKeshavarzi' [The Economic Structural Adjustment and Credit Policies of the Agricultural Sector], *Eghtesad-e Keshavarzi va Tosaeh* [Agricultural Economic and Development], special issue.
Shaji'i, Z. (1965) *Namayanagan-e Majlis-e Shura-e Melli da Bist va yik Dawra-yi Qanunquzari* [Deputies of the National Assembly in Twenty-One Sessions], Tehran: Institute for Social Studies and Research.
Shakoori, A. (1991) 'Mavaneh-e Ejtemaeyeh Tousehyeh Sanat dar Iran: 1850–1907' [Social Obstacles to the Development of Industry in Iran: 1850–1907], MA dissertation, University of Tehran.
Shakoori, A. (1998) 'The Post-Revolutionary Rural Reform Policy in Iran: A Study on the Impact of Rural Development Programmes on Rural People in Selected Villages of Eastern Azerbaijan', DPhil dissertation, University of York.
Shanin, T. (ed.) (1971) *Peasants and Peasant Societies: Selected Readings*, Harmondsworth: Penguin.
Sharman, A. (1977) 'Improving Nutrition in Bukedi District, Uganda', in L. Cliffe, J. S. Coleman and M. R. Doornbos, *Government and Rural Development in East Africa: Essays on Political Penetration*, the Hague: Martinus Njhoff.
Shashani, L. (1985) 'Capitalism, Land Reform, and Agricultural Development: The Case of Iran', PhD thesis, Michigan State University.
Shivji, I. (1976) *Class Struggles in Tanzania*, London: Heinemann.
Shivji, I. (1986) *The State and the Working People in Tanzania*, Dakar: CODESRIA.
Shubert, M. (1971) *Interviewing in Social Work Practice: An Introduction*, New York: Council on Social Work Education.
Siddiqui, K. U. (1983) 'The Political Economy of Rural Poverty in Bangladesh', PhD thesis, University of London.
Silva, A. T. M. (1978) 'Role of Rural Organisations', in R. D. Inayatullah (ed.), *Rural Organisations and Rural Development: Some Asian Experiences*, Kuala Lumpur: APDAC.
Sims, H. (1988) *Political Regimes, Public Policy and Economic Development: Agricultural Performance and Rural Change in Two Punjabs*, New Delhi: Sage.
Sjoberg, G. (1976) 'Ethics, the "Hidden Side" of Bureaucracy, and Social Research', in P. Nejelski, *Social Research in Conflict with Law and Ethics*, Cambridge, MA: Ballinger.

Sjoberg, G., Brymer R. A. and Farris, B. (1966) 'Bureaucracy and the lower class', *Sociology and Social Research*, vol. 50, no. 7, pp. 43–68.
Skocpol, T. (1982) 'Rentier State and Shi' Islam in the Iranian Revolution', *Theory and Society*, vol. 11, no. 3, pp. 265–83.
Skocpol, T. (ed.) (1984) *Vision and Method in Historical Sociology*, New York: Cambridge University Press.
Smelser, N. J. (1964) 'Toward a Theory of Modernization', in A. Etzoni and E. Etzoni (eds), *Social Change*, New York: Basic Books.
Smelser, N. J. (1966) 'Mechanisms of Change and Adjustment to Change', in J. L. Finkle and R. W. Gable (eds), *Political Development and Social Change*, New York: John Wiley.
Smelser, N. J. (1976) *Comparative Methods in the Social Sciences*, London: Prentice-Hall.
Smith, A. (1937) *Inquiry into the Nature and Causes of the Wealth of Nations*, New York: Modern Library.
Smith, B. C. (1988) *Bureaucracy and Political Power*, Sussex: Wheatsheaf.
Smith, D. E. (1970) *Religion and Political Development*, Boston, MA: Little, Brown.
Smith, D. E. (ed.)(1974) *Religion and Political Modernization*: New Haven; CT: Yale University Press.
Smith, S. M., Findeis, J. L., Krabill, D. B. and Nolt, S. M. (1997) 'Nonagricultural Micro-enterprise Development Among the Pennsylvania Amish: A New Phenomenon', *Journal of Rural Studies*, vol. 13, no. 3, pp. 237–51.
Soja, Edward W. (1980) 'The Socio-Spatial Dialectic', *Annals of the Association of American Geographers*, vol. 70, no. 2 (June).
Sorokin, P. A. (1967) *Sociology of Revolution*, New York: Howard Fertig.
Sprinvas, M. N. et al. (1979) *The Field Workers and the Field: Problems and Challenges in Sociology of Investigation*, Oxford: Oxford University Press.
Statistical Centre of Iran (1921–78) *Gozarsh-e Salaneh* [Annual Reports], Tehran.
Statistical Centre of Iran (1956, 1966, 1976, 1986, 1996) *Sar Shomary-e Emomi Nefos va Maskan: Kol-e Keshvar* [National Census of Population and Housing: Total Population of Country], Tehran.
Statistical Centre of Iran (1960) *Kol-e Jameyat-e Keshvar* (Total Population of Country), Tehran.
Statistical Centre of Iran (1960, 1974, 1989) *Agricultural Census*, Tehran.
Statistical Centre of Iran (1967) *Salnama-yi Amari, 1967* [Statistical Yearbook, 1967], Tehran.
Statistical Centre of Iran (1981–99) *Salnama-yi Amari, 1980/81–98/9* [Statistical Yearbook, 1980/81–98/9], Tehran.
Statistical Centre of Iran (1989) *Iran dar Aenehyeh Amar* [Iran in the Mirror of Statistics], Tehran.
Statistical Centre of Iran (1991) *Tarh-e Nemoneh Giryeh Emomyeh Jaryeh Jamyyat* [The Current National Population Sampling Scheme], Tehran.
Stewart, F. (1978) 'Inequality, Technology and Payments Systems', *World Development*, vol. 6, no. 3, pp. 275–93.
Stohr, W. B. and Taylor D. R. F. (eds) (1981) *Development from Above or Below*, New York: John Wiley.
Stravenhagen, R. (1975) *Social Classes in Agrarian Societies*, New York: Anchor Press.

Streeten, P., Burki, S. J., Haq, M. H., Hicks, N., Stewart, F. (1981) *First Things First: Meeting Basic Human Needs in the Developing Countries*, Oxford: Oxford University Press.

Sugar, P. F. (1964) 'Economic and Political Modernization: Turkey', in R. E. Ward and A. Rustow (eds), *Political Modernization in Japan and Turkey*, Princeton, NJ: Princeton University Press.

Sutton, F. X. (1966) 'Analysing Social Systems', in J. L. Finkle and R. W. Gable (eds), *Political Development and Social Change*, New York: John Wiley.

Syeedzonouzi, A. H. (1979) *Marand*, Tehran: Arash.

Tabari, A. (1983) 'Land, Politics, and Capital Accumulation', *MERIP Report*, March–April.

Taylor, D. R. E. (1992) *Development from within and Survival in Rural Africa*, Harlow: Routledge.

Thompson, J. (1995) 'Participatory Approaches in Government Bureaucracies: Facilitating the Process of Institutional Change', *World Development*, vol. 23, no. 9, pp. 1521–54.

Todaro, M. P. (1981) *Economic Development in The Third World*, 2nd edn, London: Longman.

Totonchiyan, G. A. (1986) *Merori bar Ghozaresh-e Amalkad-e Marakez-e Kadamat-e Roustai Sharestan-e Sarab* [A Review of the Implementation Report of The Centres of Services for Rural and Nomadic People of the Township of Sarab], Tabriz: Plan and Budget Organisation of Eastern Azerbaijan.

Trimberger, E. K. (1979) 'World Systems Analysis: The Problem of Unequal Development', *Theory and Society*, vol. 8, pp. 101–26.

Turner, M. and Hulme, D. (1990) *Sociology of Development: Theories, Policies and Practices*, London: Harvester Wheatsheaf.

United Nations (1961) *International Definitions and Measurement of Levels of Living: An Interim Guide*, New York: United Nations.

United Nations (1967) *The Problems and Policies of Economic Development: An Appraisal of Recent Experience*, Part One, New York: United Nations.

United Nations (1975a) *Economic and Social Survey of Asia and the Pacific*, xxvi, 4, Bangkok: Economic Bulletin for Asia and the Pacific.

United Nations (1975b) *Developing Countries and Levels of Development*, New York: United Nations.

University of Tehran (1986) *Barasiyeh Eghtesadi va Egemaei Mosha hayeh Roustaei Dar Garmsar* [The Socioeconomic Investigation of Rural Mosha in Garmsar], Tehran.

UNRISD (1974) *The Social and Economic Implications of Large Scale Introduction of New Varieties of Food Grain*, Geneva: UNRISD.

Uphoff, Norman T., Cohen, John M. and Goldsmith, Arthur A. (1979) *Feasibility and Application of Rural Development Participation*, New York: Committee for International Studies, Cornell University.

Valilier I. (1971) *Comparative Methods in Sociology: Essays on Trends and Applications*, Berkeley: CA: University of California Press.

Vocevoce, T. N. (1999) 'The Rural Infra-structure Development in Fiji', paper presented to the Asian Productivity Organisation Seminar on Rural Infrastructure Development, Tehran, 25 October–2 November.

Von Freyhold, M. (1977) 'The Post-Colonial State and its Tanzanian Version', *Review of African Political Economy*, vol. 8, pp. 75–890.

Waldman, L. K. (1977) 'Types and Measures of Inequality', *Social Science Quarterly*, vol. 58, no. 2, pp. 229–41.
Wallerstein, I. (1964) *The Road to Independence: Ghana and the Ivory Coast*, The Hague: Mouton.
Wallerstein, I. (1987) 'World System Analysis', in A. Giddens and J. H. Turner (eds), *Social Theory*, Stanford, CA: Stanford University Press.
Wallerstein, I. (1988) 'Development, Lodestar or Illusion', *Economic and Political Weekly*, vol. 23, no. 39, pp. 2017–23.
Warick, D. P. and Osherson, S. (eds) (1973) *Comparative Research Methods*, Englewood Ciffs, NJ: Prentice-Hall.
Warner, M. (1997) 'Consensus Participation: An Example for Protected Areas Planning', *Public Administration and Development*, vol. 17, pp. 413–32.
Warren, J. R. and Hauser, R. M. (1977) 'Social Stratification Across Three Generations: New Evidence from the Wisconsin Longitudinal Study', *American Sociological Review*, vol. 62, pp. 561–72.
Warren, R. C. (1978) *The Community in America*, 3rd edn, Chicago, IL: Rand McNally.
Warriner, D. (1969) *Land Reform in Principle and Practice*, Oxford: Clarendon Press.
Wassersfrom, R. (1985) *Grassroots Development in Latin America and the Caribbean: Oral Histories of Change*, New York: Praeger.
Watts, M. (1995) 'A New Deal in Emotions, Theory and Practice and the Crisis of Development', in J. Crush, *Power of Development*, London: Routledge.
Weiner, M. (1966a) *Modernisation, the Dynamic of Growth*, New York: Basic Books.
Weiner, M. (1966b), 'Political Integration and Political Development', in J. L. Finkle and R. W. Gable (eds), *Political Development and Social Change*, New York: John Wiley.
Wester, G. K. (1986) *People's Participation, Local Government and Rural Development, the Case of West Bengals*, India.
Westergaard, K. (1985) *State and Rural Society in Bangladesh*, London: Curzon Press.
White, H. C. (1975) 'Chains of Opportunities', in A. P. M. Coxon and C. L. Jones, *Social Mobility*, Harmondsworth: Penguin.
Wieringa, S. (1994) 'Women's Interests and Empowerment: Gender Planning Reconsidered', *Development and Change*, vol. 25, pp. 829–48.
Wignaraja, P. (1975) *Towards a Theory of Rural Development*, New York: United Nations, Asian Development Institute.
Wignaraja, P. (1991) *Participatory Development: Learning from South Asia*, Oxford: Oxford University Press.
Wijayaratna, C. M. (1999) 'Social Capital and Rural Infra-structure Strengthening: The Active Participation of Local People', paper presented to the Asian Productivity Organisation Seminar on Rural Infrastructure Development, Tehran, 25 October–2 November.
Williams, G. (1982) 'Taking the Part of Peasants', in J. Harriss (ed.), *Rural Development: Theories of Peasant Economy and Agrarian Change*, London: Hutchinson.
Williams, M. and May, T. (1996) *Introduction to the Philosophy of Social Research*, London: UCL Press.
Wittfogel, K. (1957) *Oriental Despotism: A Comparative Study of Total Power*, New Haven, CT: Yale University Press.

Wolf, E. R. (1971) *Peasant Wars of the Twentieth Century*, London: Faber and Faber.
Wood, G. D. (1976) 'The Political Process in Bangladesh: Class Differentiation and Power in Bandakgram: the Minifundist Case', in M. A. Huq (ed.), *Exploitation and the Rural Poor*, Comilla: Bangladesh Academy for Rural Development.
Wood, G. D. (1984) 'State Intervention and Agrarian Class Formation: Dimensions of the Access Problem in the Kosi Development Region of Nebihar, India', *Public Administration and Development*, vol. 4, no. 4.
Wood, G. D. (1985) 'The Politics of Rural Development: Policy Labelling', in G.D. Wood (ed.), *Labelling in Development Policy – Essays in Honour of B. Schaffer*, London: Sage.
Woods, M. (1997) 'Researching Rural Conflicts: Hunting Local Politics and Actor-networks', *Journal of Rural Studies*, vol. 14, no. 3, pp. 321–40.
World Bank (1975a) *The Assault on World Poverty*, Washington, DC: World Bank.
World Bank (1975b) 'Rural Development Sector', policy paper, Washington, DC: World Bank.
World Bank (1978) *World Development, International Bank for Reconstruction and Development*, Washington, DC: World Bank.
World Bank (1979) *World Development Report 1979*, Washington, DC: World Bank.
World Bank (1982) *World Development Report*, New York: Oxford University Press.
World Bank (1991a) *World Development Report 1990: Poverty*, New York: Oxford University Press.
World Bank (1991b) *Iran: Reconstruction and Economic Growth*, vols 1–2, report no. 9072 IRN, Washington, DC: World Bank.
World Bank (1993) *World Development Report (1993) Investing in Health: World Development Indicators*, New York: Oxford University Press.
World Bank (1994) *Islamic Republic of Iran, Services for Agriculture and Rural Development*, vols 1–2, report no. 1196 IRN, Washington, DC: World Bank.
Yeganeh, C. (1986) 'Agrarian Structure Under Adaptation, Reform, and Revolution: The Case of Iran in a Comparative-Historical Perspective' PhD thesis, New York: New School for Social Research.
Zand-e Razavi, S. (1990) 'Barasiyeh Taghyirat-e Sakhtarhayeh Eghtesadi va Ejtemaei dar Jameh-e Roustaei Sistan' [A Study of the Change in Social and Economic Structures in the Rural Society of Sistan], *Ettela'at-e siyasi-Eghtesadi* [Political-Economic Monthly Journal], vol. 7, pp. 67–8.
Zubaida, S. (1988) 'An Islamic State? the Case of Iran', *Middle East Report*, July–August, pp. 3–7.

Index

Abrahamian, E. 40, 42, 46, 61
Absolutist regime 61
Access
 theory of 35, 36, 39
 constellation 37
Adam Smith's *Wealth of Nations* 17
Adamiyat, F. 42
Afshar, H. 2, 3, 55, 56, 59
Agency for International Development 28
Agribusiness 2, 50, 65, 103, 104
Agricultural capital formation 25, 108
Agricultural machinery 49, 56, 74, 100, 117, 118, 127
Agropolitan
 approach 21
 development 21
Ahar (town) 131
Ahluwalia, M. S. 22
Alavi, H. 34, 35
Alfonso, F. B. 27
Amin, G. A. 33
Amin, S. 33
Amirahmadi, E. 61
Amuzegar, J. 115–17, 145
Anglo–Iranian dispute 43
Anoushirvani, A. 94
Anti-Western 61
Ardabil (province) 5, 128
Aresvik, O. 128
Aron, J. 22, 24, 26
Arsanjani, H. 53
Ashraf, A. 3, 4, 46, 55, 58, 64, 66, 67, 68, 69
Authoritarianism 62, 78
Azerbaijan 5, 88, 119, 126, 128, 129, 130, 131, 167, 172
Aziz, S. 25
Azkia, M. 54, 55, 56, 57, 58, 65, 66, 70, 72, 73, 74, 75, 77, 78, 79, 80, 92, 95, 99, 100, 103, 104

Babreh-Olia (village) 133
Babreh-e-Sofla (village) 127, 131, 133
Bafekr, H. 94
Baft (town) 94
Bahrier, S. 53, 99
Baily, F. G. 16
Baluchestan 64
Bandar Abbas (city) 79
Bani-Sader, A. H. 62
Bank
 agricultural 56, 76, 113, 114
 cooperative 56
Bashiriyeh, H. 42, 43, 44, 51, 61
Bazaars (traditional market) 43
Bazargan's resignation 61, 84
Behishti, Ali 67
Behsazi (physical upgrading projects) 5, 88, 127, 151, 155, 157
Bernstein, H. 14
Berry, S. 32
Bertocci, P. J. 35
Bharier, S. 53, 99
Blomstrom, M. 27
Boeke, J. H. 10
Bonab (county district) 173
Boneh (traditional group organisations) 45, 57, 93, 98, 166
Brookfield, H. 21
Budget and Planning Organisation 91, 110
Bujnurd (town) 68
Burkey, S. 27, 134, 142
Byres, T. J. 32, 37

Caliph, political philosophy of 62, 78
Cash crops 13, 47, 49
Caspian Sea 6, 121, 129
Ceasefire with Iraq 62
Central Bank of Iran 100, 102, 105, 109, 111, 114, 123

Centres for Rural and Agricultural
    Development   73
Centres of Services for Rural and
    Nomadic People   5, 70, 73, 75,
    76, 78, 79, 84, 95, 96, 98, 127,
    139, 140, 164, 165, 168
Chahil Nour (mountain)   128
Chambers, R.   23, 26, 29, 134
Chaudhri, D. P.   1, 19, 22, 27, 31
Chenery, H.   19, 20, 22
CIA-backed coup   43
Civil society   51
Clayton, E.   37
Clements, P.   145
Clergy   62, 121
    see also ulama
Clergy–landlord–merchant oligarchy
    42
Cohen, J. M.   142
Coleman, J. S.   13
Committees of Land Development
    66, 68–9, 70, 92
Commodification of land   46
Constitutional Revolution (of Iran)
    42, 43, 45, 47, 51, 60, 164
Cooperatives   4, 56, 57, 92, 93, 95,
    103, 105, 121, 166
Council   9, 58, 66, 67, 68, 72, 73, 74,
    75, 78, 79, 80, 81, 82, 84, 86, 90,
    95, 98, 137, 138, 140, 164, 165
Council of Guardians (of Iran)   67,
    68, 69, 70
Coxon, A. P. M.   144
Critical theory   32, 38

Dam (Pishan)   116
Dam (Saveh)   116
Danesh, A. H.   45, 46, 47, 54, 56
Daran (county district)   173
Dawson, R. E.   140
De Janvry A.   33
Decile distribution
    expenditure   162
    income   159
    wealth   160, 161
Dehyar (village animator)   79
Denman, D. R.   58
Despotic political system   43
Despotic state   46

Development plan
    first   103, 108
    second   26, 72, 106, 112
    third   100, 106
    fourth   100, 106
    fifth   100, 125
    1983   115, 119
Distribution
    benefits of rural programmes   34
    income   20, 158, 159, 170
    living expenditure   161
    wealth   160, 161, 170
Dizaj-Hossein- bayk (village)   127,
    131, 132
Douwe, J.   28
Dowse, R. E.   140
Dube, S. C.   9–10, 17
Duwlat Abad   127, 131, 132

Eastern Harazand (county district)
    173
Eftekhari, R.   72, 76–7, 84
Eisenstadt, S. N.   10, 13
Enayat, H.   44
Esfahan (province)   6
Esfahani, H.   3, 4, 88, 122
Esfahani, Reza   3, 67
Etellaat (daily)   112
Expenditure, inequality   161, 170

Fadayian Marxist   64
FAO   23, 123
Farazmand, A.   5, 6, 46, 90, 91
Farm corporations   4, 56, 72, 75,
    104, 105, 166
Fars (province)   6
Ferdows, E.   6, 82, 84, 85, 91
Ferguson, J.   1, 33
Fesa (city)   94
Fisher, M. J.   44
Flamming, R. A.   28
Foumenat   91
Frank, A. G.   33
Frankel, F. R.   34
Freedom Movement (of Iran)   85
Freire, P.   134, 139
Friedland, W. H.   12, 14
Friedmann, J.   19, 32
Frouzesh, G.   87

Galli, R. E. 27, 37
Galtung, J. 27
Gartell, J. 37
Gazette of the Islamic Republic (journal) 83
GDP 105, 106, 112, 124
Gharajeh-Fazlloah (village) 127, 131, 132
Ghermezi gheshlagh (village) 127, 131, 133
Ghizell-Ozan (river) 128
Gholpayeghani, Ayatollah 67
Ghotour (river) 128
Gibbons, D. S. 30, 32, 37
Giddeins, A. 144, 145
Gilan (province) 50, 91
Gilani, Mohammad 67
GNP 19, 20, 31, 52, 99, 100, 101, 124
Goldsworthy, D. 21
Gorgan (city) 50
Goulet, D. 27, 134, 142
Government *see* Policy (state)
Gran, G. 27
Green Revolution 30
Griffin, K. 1, 19, 21, 22, 24, 25, 27, 30, 31, 32, 36, 37
Grindle, M. S. 31, 32, 37

Hagen, E. 14
Halliday, F. 45, 54, 56, 59
Hamilton, M. 145
Haq, M. 20, 21
Haque, M. 1
Haralambos, M. 144
Harrison, D. 9
Harriss, J. 15, 23, 25, 26, 35
Hasht rude (city) 172
Hayami 1, 31
Hechter, M. 33
Heck, B. van 24, 25
Hettne, B. 27
Heyer, J. 27, 34
Hickey, G. C. 28
Hirashima, S. 22
Hirszowicz, M. 145
Holborn, M. 144
Holistic approach 38
Hooglund, E. 46, 54, 58

Housing and Improvement Bureau (Ministry of Jihad-e Sazandegi) 5, 88
Howes, M. 31–2
Huda, A. T. M. S. 35, 37
Hughes, J. A. 140
Hulme, D. 16
Huntington, S. 33

ILO 1, 19, 22, 23
Improvement and transformation strategies 1
Income
 inequality 158, 159
India's Panchayat Raj co-operative programme 34
Inkeles, A. 14
Institute for Social Studies (the University of Tehran) 5
Institute of Development Studies (the University of Sussex) 20
Iran–Iraq War 62, 70, 86, 89, 143, 144, 166, 167
Iraq 4, 53, 69, 85
Irsi (county district) 173
Issawi, C. 40–1, 47–8, 148

Jazairy, I. *et al.* 19, 22, 31
Jihad-e Sazandegi (Reconstruction crusade) 5, 6, 7, 60, 66, 69, 70, 76, 80, 82, 83, 84, 85, 86, 87, 88, 89, 90, 91, 92, 94, 95, 96, 112, 127, 135, 138, 139, 140, 141, 145, 164, 166, 168, 169
Jiroft (city) 79
Jolfa (town) 173
Jones, C. S. 144

Kalantari, Issa 77
Kalibar (town) 131
Karimi, S. 91
Karshenas, M. 41, 42, 43, 47, 48, 51, 100, 102, 104
Katouzian, H. 41, 42, 43, 46, 47, 50, 51, 52, 54, 58, 100, 102, 103
Kayhan (daily) 106, 107
Kazemi, F. 46
Keddie, N. R. 40, 43, 46, 47, 48, 49, 50

214 Index

Kerman (province) 79
Kadkhoda (village headman) 49, 58, 79
Khaleseh (public land) 45
Khamsi, R. 47, 48
Khan, A. R. 30, 35, 37
Khatami, Mohammad 63
Khomeini, Ayatollah Rohollah 67, 85
Khorasan (province) 6, 64, 71, 81, 90
Khordeh-Maleki (village ownership by two or more individuals) 45
Khosravi, K. 53
Khozistan (province) 50, 68, 81
Khushnishin (villagers without traditional cultivation right) 45, 54, 61
Kishavarz-e Immrouz (weekly) 67
Korten, D. C. 27
Korten, F. F. 28
Koshsarayh (county district) 173
Krinks, P. 37
Kurdistan 64, 68

Ladejinsky, W. 30, 32
Lahsaeizadeh, A. 3, 4, 53, 54, 56, 57, 58, 65, 94
Lamb, G. 35, 36
Lambton, A. K. S. 45, 47, 48, 49, 54
Land Devolution Committee 94
Land redistribution *see* Land reform
Land reform 2, 3, 4, 8, 31, 39, 40, 43, 46, 45, 46, 47–8, 50, 52, 53, 56, 57, 58, 59, 63, 64, 65, 66, 67, 69, 70, 93, 95, 97, 115, 151, 153, 155, 160, 161, 164, 166, 170
Land tenure 47, 106
Lea, D. A. M. 1, 19, 22, 27, 30
Lele, U. 23, 26
Lerner, D. 9, 10, 15
Levy, M. S. 10, 15
Lewis, W. A. 1
Livar-paeen (village) 127, 131, 132
Loeffler, R. 5, 89, 91
Long, N. 1, 10, 15, 21, 25, 28
Lorestan (province) 71
Luke, T. W. 10, 16, 28

Makarim Shirazi Nasir 67
Maktab-e Islam (journal) 67
Maragheh (city) 173
Marand (town) 131, 132, 133, 173
Markazi (province) 81
Marsden, D. 27, 29, 134, 142
Mashad (city) 67
Mathur, H. M. 27
Mazandaran (province) 50, 81
McClelland, D. 14
McLachlan, D. 55
Mehta, S. R. 17
Migdal, J. S. 32
Migration 13, 59, 104, 124
Miller, S. M. 145
Ministry of Agriculture 6, 66, 70, 71, 72, 73, 76, 77, 78, 83, 84, 86, 96, 97, 114, 115, 117, 119, 120, 121
Ministry of Agriculture's Institute for Rural Studies 94
Ministry of Corporate and Rural Affairs 56
Mishkini, Ali 67
Miyaneh (city) 129
Mlay, W. 28
Moaddle, M. 43, 61, 68
Modernisation 2, 7, 9, 10, 11, 12, 13, 14, 15, 16, 18, 21, 25, 28, 31, 32, 33, 37, 38, 40, 44, 51, 95, 164
Moghadam, F. 48, 53, 55, 56
Mohammad Ali Shah 42
Mohammadi Gilani Mohammad 67
Mohtadi, H. 58, 59
Mojtahd 3, 4, 88, 122
Momen, M. 44
Montazeri, Hosseinali 67
Moore, W. E. 9
Morrison, L. 1, 30
Mosha (cooperatives) 5, 8, 60, 92, 93, 94, 95, 98, 135, 164, 166, 167
Moshaver (adviser of mosha) 93
Mosher, A. M. 22
Mossadiq, Mohammad 43, 50
MyrdaL, G. 18, 33

Nabi, I. 31, 32
Najmabadi, A. 59

Nasagh (traditional cultivation right) 45, 55
Nashriyeh-e Barzgar (journal) 111, 112, 115, 116, 118, 119, 197
National Front (of Iran) 85
Nationalism 41, 43, 60
Nazir, P. 31–2, 37
Nojeh Mehr (county district) 173
Nomani, F. 46, 64–5, 67
North Mishab (county district) 173
Nurkse, R. 1

Oakley 27, 29, 134, 142
Oil 42, 51, 52, 53, 100, 105, 106, 107, 108
Okazaki, S. 56
Olson, M. Jr. 145
Omdeh-Maleki (land and villages owned by major landlords) 45

Pahlavi dynasty 2
Parkin, F. 144
Parsa, M. 43, 52, 64
Participation 7, 8, 26, 27, 28, 29, 32, 38, 74, 75, 76, 78, 79, 81, 92, 125, 126, 134, 130, 135, 136, 137, 141, 142, 168, 169, 170
Pearse, A. 27, 31
Peasants' movements 64, 65, 69, 79
Perroux, F. 32
Pesaran, H. 2, 51, 55
Plan and Budget Organisation of Eastern Azerbaijan 129–30, 172, 173
Planning
 bottom–up 29, 73, 84, 95, 169
 centralised 2
 top–down 29, 85, 95
Policy
 agriculture 2, 3, 4, 5, 6, 8, 49, 60, 92, 95, 98, 99, 104, 106, 119, 124, 162, 164, 167, 170
 economic reform 63, 107
 land and water use 8, 60
 liberalisation 125
 modernisation 2, 44, 100
 post-revolution 61, 64, 107
 pre-revolution 95, 124, 164
 pricing 4, 8, 60, 102, 103, 119, 121, 122, 123, 125, 167
 redistribution 34, 35
 rural development 2, 3, 6, 7, 28, 40, 60, 64, 98, 126, 138, 164
 rural reform 31, 69, 126, 154, 170
 state 4, 59, 104
 support 8, 60, 117
Poorer villages 133, 146, 148, 152, 153, 155, 169
Poostchi, I. 26
Post-modernisation 28
Preston, D. A. 16, 30, 32
Pretty, J. N. 28
Prewitt, K. 140
Problem of access (theory) 35
Prosperous villages 137, 138, 140, 146, 152, 153, 156
Provisional government (Bazargan) 61, 78, 85, 97, 166
Pye, L. W. 145

Qajars (dynasty) 44, 49
Qanat (traditional irrigation system) 103, 116
Qazwin (province) 67, 116

Rabbani shirazi Ayatollah 67
Rafipour, F. 6, 90
Rahnema, M. 64, 65, 67, 71
Rajco-cooperative 34
Razzaghi, E. 99, 103, 104, 115
Reza Shah 42, 43, 44, 49, 51, 52
Richard, H. 31, 32, 50
Robertson, A. F. 33
Rogers, E. 15
Rohani 67
Rostow, W. W. 1, 2, 10, 18
Rural programmes
 on income 8, 126, 151, 152, 153, 168, 170
 on wealth, 8, 126, 154, 155, 168, 170
 on well-being 8, 23, 30, 32, 126, 156, 164, 168, 170
Rural reform 2, 69, 153, 128
Ruttan, V. W. 1, 31

Index

Sabalan (mountain) 128
Sabetghadam, S. 75, 76
Sabzevar (town) 94
Saeen (mountain) 128
Safavids (dynasty) 44
Sandbrook, R. 35
Sarab (city) 172
SAREC (World Bank) 23
Sarker, A. E. 34, 35
Sarma, J. S. 30
Sarmosha (director of *mosha*) 93
Saveh (city) 116
Schaffer, B. 35–6
Schirazi, A. 4, 56, 66, 71–2, 74, 76, 78, 82, 84, 85, 92, 94, 100, 102, 103, 107, 113, 115–17, 119, 120, 122, 135, 139
Schultz, T. W. 15
Seers, D. 20
Sen, A. K. 21, 145
Service Centres *see* Centres of Services for Rural and Nomadic People
Seven-Member Committee 115
Shah 40, 43, 50, 51, 52, 53, 58, 64, 66, 70, 93
Shaji'i, Z. 50
Shakoori, A. 41, 126, 136, 148, 150, 157, 158, 159, 161, 175–85
Sharecropping 46, 50, 53, 54, 57
Sharia 63, 69
Shashani, A. 58
Shia 44, 62
Shiite *see* Shia
Shojah (county district) 173
Shoura see council
Sierosem (a kind of soil) 128
Silva, A. T. M. 26
Sims, H. 34
Sistan and Baluchestan (province) 116
Sjoberg, G. 138
Skocpol, T. 52
Smelser, N. J. 12, 13
Smith, A. 17, 36, 37
Smith, B. C. 36
Smith, D. E. 12
Smith, D. H. 14

Social mobility 1, 10, 126, 144, 145, 146, 147, 148, 149, 150, 151, 168, 169, 170
Sorkin, P. A. 144
Statistical Centre of Iran 100, 109, 115, 117, 130, 131
Stravenhagen, R. 27
Sugar, P. F. 10, 11
Sunni 62
Supreme Economic Council 120
Sutton, F. X. 10
Syeedzonouzi, A. H. 131

Tabriz (city) 118, 129
Taylor, D. R. E. 27
Tehran (city) 68, 91, 104, 116
Thomson, J. 29
Todaro, M. P. 20
Totonchyan, G. A. 74, 75
Turner, M. 16
Tuyul (traditional land assignment) 47, 48, 49

Ulama 44, 66, 67, 69, 97, 166
 see also clergy
Ulama's opposition to the state 44
Ulama's opposition to Western influence 43
United Nations 135
United States 67
UNRISD 22
Uphoff, N. T. 28, 142
Urumieh (city) 64
Urumiyeh (lake) 128
USA 17

Vaqf (religious endowments) 44, 45
Velayat-e motlagheh-e faghih (absolute rule of religious leader) 62
Von freyhold, M. 35

Wallerstein, I. 33
Warren, R. S. 16
Wassertrom, R. 30
Wealth distribution 155
Wealth inequality 160, 170
Well-being, inequality 170
Westergaard, K. 35

Western Dizmar (county district) 173
Western Harazand (county district) 173
White Revolution (of Shah)   40, 51, 53
Wignaraja, P.   27, 28, 29, 134
Williams, G.   26, 27, 28
Wolf, E. R.   18
Wood, G. D.   27, 32, 34, 35
World Bank   1, 20, 23, 24, 25, 89, 90, 106, 108, 112, 115, 120, 122, 124

World Bank Development Centre   20

Yazd (province)   6
Yazdi, M.   67
Yeganeh, C.   3, 4, 49, 64, 66
Yekanat (county district)   173

Zali Abbasali   74
Zanjan (city)   81, 128
Zobaida, S.   51
Zonuozagh (county district)   173

DATE DUE

Demco, Inc. 38-293